A **WESTERN HORSEMAN** BOOK

LEGENDS
VOLUME 6

Outstanding Quarter Horse Stallions and Mares

Contributors

Frank Holmes	Glory Ann Kurtz
Patti Campbell	Sally Harrison
Juli S. Thorson	Heidi Nyland
Cheryl Magoteaux	Bev Pechan

Edited by Frank Holmes

Legends

VOLUME 6

Published by
WESTERN HORSEMAN magazine

3850 North Nevada Ave.
Box 7980
Colorado Springs, CO 80933-7980

www.westernhorseman.com

Design, Typography, and Production
Western Horseman
Fort Worth, TX

Cover painting by
Suanne Wamsley

Printing
Branch Smith
Fort Worth, TX

Manufactured in the United States of America.

2nd Printing: August 2007

ISBN 978-0-911647-73-0

INTRODUCTION

WESTERN HORSEMAN—"World's Leading Horse Magazine Since 1936"—has also been involved in equine book publishing since 1959. Those who ran the magazine at that time recognized a need for practical "how-to" books on horse topics that focused mainly on health care and training.

This was done as a service to readers, because there just weren't many equine books available in those days. Our earliest books contained serialized material that had appeared previously in the magazine, and was simply put together between covers for easy reader reference. The popular soft-bound little books sold for $1 each. We added to our line of *Western Horseman* books through the years to the point where staff members were investing a lot of time and effort into them. Then as now, we prided ourselves on providing practical how-to information in an attractive book at an affordable price.

Our thinking on popular book topics expanded, however, after the March 1990 issue of *Western Horseman* magazine completely sold out. In that issue we paid special tribute to the American Quarter Horse Association in honor of its 50th anniversary. Included were brief profiles of legendary Quarter Horse stallions. Readers told us they were definitely interested in stories about great horses that helped make the Quarter Horse breed what it is today.

Pat Close, editor at the time, proposed a new book titled *Legends*, featuring outstanding Quarter Horse stallions and mares. Despite the success of that March issue, this topic was a departure from what we'd always done in the book department and, therefore, was met with a little resistance from some staff members. Undaunted, Pat persuaded us to publish a *Legends* book, which we did in 1993.

We printed 10,000 copies of the book initially, and that first printing quickly sold out and was reprinted. It's been reprinted continuously ever since. And *Legends* was followed by *Legends, Volume*(s) *2, 3, 4* and *5*. This is the most popular book series we've ever published, and we're now happy to present *Legends, Volume 6*.

In terms of the disciplines it covers, *Legends, Volume 6* is the most versatile edition in the series. It covers such early-day personalities as Paul A, Croton Oil, Okie Leo, Flit Bar and Billietta. It further covers the great father-son team of Coy's Bonanza and Major Bonanza.

For cutting-horse fans, the book is a mother-lode, with chapters on seven legendary stallions. Included are two of Doc Bar's top sons, Doc Quixote and Doc's Prescription. The influential Jewel's Leo Bar ("Freckles") is profiled, along with two of his top sons, Colonel Freckles and Freckles Playboy. Finally, the two famous full brothers, Peppy San and Mr San Peppy are profiled.

For reining-horse fans, there's Great Pine; for halter horse followers, there's Conclusive; and for pleasure-horse followers there are The Invester, Speedy Glow and Dynamic Deluxe. Finally, for barrel racers, there are stories on Flit Bar, one of that industry's most influential sires, and *Caseys Charm*, one of its most-accomplished producers.

The eight authors of this book, all well-respected for their experience and expertise in equine journalism, include Patricia Campbell, Sally Harrison, Frank Holmes, Glory Ann Kurtz, Cheryl Magoteaux, Heidi Nyland, Bev Pechan and Juli Thorson.

Suanne Wamsley painted the cover for this book, depicting Conclusive, The Invester and Freckles Playboy.

Special thanks, as always, to the many photographers who helped record history with their portraits of all the horses included in this volume. The photographers' names appear next to the photos they took. Access to many of these great photos comes from the *American Quarter Horse Journal*, official publication of the American Quarter Horse Association in Amarillo, Texas.

AQHA does a wonderful job of serving the breed and all its members. The association has all pedigrees, performance summaries, and sire and dam production records of registered Quarter Horses available to those with internet access. Visit their web site at *www.aqha.com.*

Each time we produce another volume of the Legends series, we find readers who want to purchase the entire collection. We're always happy to oblige.

Randy Witte
Publisher
Western Horseman

CONTENTS

1 PAUL A

He was one of the breed's first AQHA Champions.

Frank Holmes

PAUL A, A 1948 BLACK STALLION by Star Deck and out of Little Dixie Beach, was one of the breed's first American Quarter Horse Association Champions and founder of a prominent line of early-day halter champions.

Paul A, one of the breed's first AQHA Champions, was also an influential early-day sire.

G. E. Nicholson of Tulsa, Okla., was the horse's breeder and initially registered him with AQHA as N R Paul A. The prefix initials for "Nicholson Ranch" were subsequently dropped.

Nicholson, who at one time owned Bert (see *Legends 1*), was a top Quarter Horse breeder. In building his program he drew heavily from the livestock of such earlier Sooner State horsemen as S. Coke Blake, "Uncle" John Dawson and Ronald Mason.

Star Deck, Paul A's sire, was a 1940 bay stallion by Oklahoma Star P-6 and out of Jane Hunt. Owned in succession by Nicholson; Perry McGlone of Dearborn, Mo.; and Ray and Edna Guthrie of Prineville, Ore.; Star Deck sired six AQHA Champions — Paul A, Dixie Siemon, Guthrie Bob, Guthrie Lantie, Husky Deck and Ima Dandy.

Jane Hunt, Star Deck's dam, was a 1933 bay mare by Button and out of Blake's Queen. In addition to Star Deck, she also produced N R Chipper, a champion halter mare and multiple AQHA Champion producer.

As well-bred as Paul A was on the top side of his pedigree, he was equally as well bred on the bottom.

His dam, Little Dixie Beach, was a 1943 brown mare by Tommy Clegg and out of Dixie Beach. In addition to Paul A, she also produced two notable full brothers — Dixie's Paul, a 1951 bay stallion who once sold for $25,000; and Dixie's Roper, a 1954 bay stallion who earned a performance Register of Merit with points in reining, roping and cutting.

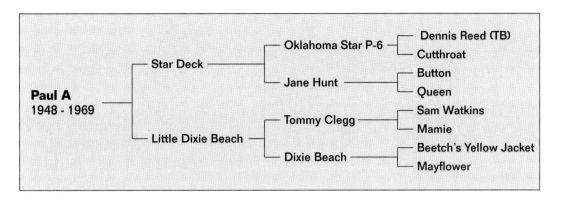

			Dennis Reed (TB)
		Oklahoma Star P-6	
	Star Deck		Cutthroat
			Button
		Jane Hunt	
Paul A			Queen
1948 - 1969			Sam Watkins
		Tommy Clegg	
	Little Dixie Beach		Mamie
			Beetch's Yellow Jacket
		Dixie Beach	
			Mayflower

Breeding Champions to Champions

Paul A, the first and foremost representative of the Star Deck-Little Dixie Beach cross, was shown sparingly at halter during his first two years.

He reportedly earned his first grand championship while still at his dam's side. His first documented win occurred at the 1950 Tulsa State Fair, Tulsa, Okla., where he placed first in the 2-year-old stallion class.

Halter and Performance Record:
Performance Register of Merit; AQHA Champion.

Progeny Record:

Foal Crops: 8
Foals Registered: 223
AQHA Champions: 11
Halter Point-Earners: 57
Halter Points Earned: 1,104

Superior Halter Awards: 6
Performance Point-Earners: 34
Performance Points Earned: 344
Performance Registers of Merit: 21

Star Deck, a 1940 bay stallion by Oklahoma Star P-6 and out of Jane Hunt, was a grand champion halter horse and the sire of six AQHA Champions.

Little Dixie Beach, Paul A's dam, was also a champion show horse. Here she is—with Paul A at her side—after winning the mare and foal class at the 1948 Enid, Okla, show.

Here's a rare shot of Paul as a yearling.

In February 1951, Robert Q. Sutherland acquired Paul A. He made him a top show horse and one of the breed's premier halter sires. Sutherland's R. S. Bar Ranch on the outskirts of Kansas City, Mo., was home to some of the breed's best-bred Quarter Horses throughout the late 1940s and '50s.

Sutherland was a natural-born promoter. The author of *The Quarter Horse as I See Him* — one of the first books ever written on the breed — Sutherland built his program around the philosophy and motto: "We breed champions to champions to get champions."

In Paul A, he reasoned that he had just the horse to head his program. First, though, he had to make him a champion.

First AQHA Champions

The year 1951 marked Paul A's debut under the R. S. Bar banner, and it was highly successful. Conditioned and shown by resident trainer George Garrett, the 3-year-old

Paulalika, a 1953 black mare by Paul A and out of Mitzie Doane, was an AQHA Champion and Superior halter horse. She is shown here with owner Robert Q. Sutherland of Kansas City, Mo., after winning the yearling filly class at the 1954 Pikes Peak Quarter Horse Show in Colorado Springs, Colorado.

stallion won grand championships at such shows as the Kansas State Fair, Hutchinson, Kan.; Tulsa State Fair, Tulsa, Okla.; AK-SAR-BEN, Omaha, Neb.; American Royal, Kansas City, Mo.; and Chicago International, Chicago.

In January 1952, competing as an aged stallion and reportedly conditioned only on prairie hay and oats, Paul A was named the grand champion stallion of the National Western Stock Show, Denver, Colo; and the champion aged stallion at the Southwestern Livestock Exposition, Fort Worth, Texas.

In February, Paul A went global.

John Ballweg of Stillwell, Kan., the R. S. Bar trainer from mid-1954 through 1966, recalled the incident.

"As the story was told to me," he said, "Bob received a special invitation from the Cuban government to exhibit Paul A at their premier livestock show called the Exposition Nacional de Ganaderia, held in Havana.

"Cuba was overhauling its livestock industry at the time and had been importing Santa Gertrudis cattle and Old Sorrel-bred Quarter Horses from the King Ranch of Texas," Ballweg continued. "I think they'd bought stock from other breeders, as well.

"George Garrett hauled Paul A to Florida and put him on a plane to Cuba. The King Ranch shipped some cattle on the same flight. I guess they couldn't get some of those big Santa Gertrudis bulls to walk up the ramp into the plane. So George saddled Paul A and pulled every one of them into the cargo bay.

"Paul A wasn't the greatest athlete," he continued. "But I'll say this for him — he was a stout little sucker."

After being named grand champion stallion at the Cuban show, Paul A returned to the United States to stand grand at the Houston Fat Stock Show. He finished the year with similar victories at Neosho, Mo., and Prescott, Ariz.

In addition to being shown at halter, Paul A was also campaigned in cutting. Shown sparingly during his 3- and 4-year-old years in AQHA competition at Claremore, Okla.; Charlotte, Mich;

Columbus, Ohio; and Neosho, Mo., he earned eight points. He collected $251.59 in National Cutting Horse Association contests.

The year 1952 was significant for Paul A for yet another reason. In August, by action of the AQHA executive committee, three stallions, two mares and two geldings were recognized as the breed's first seven AQHA Champions.

Paul A was on the list, as was J B King, a 1948 bay stallion by Harmon Baker's Star and out of Lady Coolidge. Because Lady Coolidge was a full sister to Dixie Beach, Paul A's maternal granddam, this proved the power of that particular mare line.

Rounding out the hallmark list were Babe Mac C, a 1946 King Ranch-bred stallion by Macanudo and out of a mare by Babe Grande; Pondora, a 1946 dun mare by Pondie and out of Ellen H; Little Egypt, a 1949 chestnut mare by Texas Dandy and out of Jezabel; Star Jack Jr, a 1948 bay gelding by Scroggin's Little Star and out of Miss Lary S; and Snipper W, a 1946 Waggoner Ranch-bred dun gelding by Pretty Buck and out of Snipette.

By the time the official announcements, with accompanying full-page photos of each horse, were printed in the October 1952 issue of *The Quarter Horse Journal*, an eighth horse — Poco Tivio, a 1949 bay stallion by Poco Bueno and out of Sheilwin — was added to the list.

Get-of-Sire Star

Back at the R. S. Bar Ranch, the winds of change were blowing.

No doubt spurred on by the fame that Paul A had garnered as one of the breed's most visible show horses, Sutherland decided the time was ripe to sell him. He sold the stallion in the fall 1952 to Gordon Wheeler of Riverside, Calif., for a reported $30,000.

By this time, Sutherland had begun showing Paul A's get. Exhibited first at halter and later in performance events, they took the Quarter Horse world by storm. Sutherland, realizing that he'd made a mistake in selling their sire, promptly bought him back.

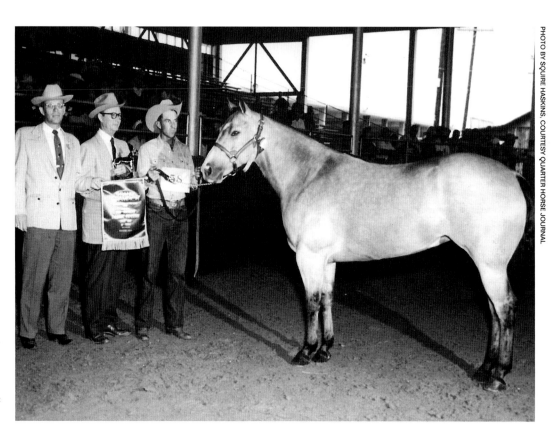

Miss Paulite, a 1953 dun mare by Paul A and out of Tangerine W, earned 84 points and a Superior at halter. While owned by B.F. Phillips of Frisco, Texas, she was exhibited by Matlock Rose to earn honors as the grand champion mare at the 1956 State Fair of Texas, Dallas, Tex.

PHOTO BY SQUIRE HASKINS, COURTESY QUARTER HORSE JOURNAL

PHOTO BY ORREN MIXER, COURTESY QUARTER HORSE JOURNAL

Paulyana, a 1953 brown mare by Paul A and out of Westmoreland, was yet another R.S. Bar Ranch-bred Superior halter horse.

COURTESY QUARTER HORSE JOURNAL

Here's Paul Easter, a 1956 dun stallion by Paul A and out of Sutherland's Lady. He sold to Fritz and Helen Watkins of Wasco, Wash., and went on to become an AQHA Champion and a top broodmare sire.

Star Spangled, a 1958 brown mare by Paul A and out of AQHA High Point Halter Horse Barbara Star, serves as a classic example of Robert Sutherland's philosophy of "breeding champions to champions to get champions." Like so many of her half-brothers and sisters, the well-balanced show mare was an AQHA Champion and Superior halter horse.

Paulyola, a 1960 bay mare by Paul A and out of Miss Crayola, earned 57 halter points and 12 performance points en route to earning her AQHA Champion and Superior halter horse awards.

As the R. S. Bar Ranch resident trainer, Ballweg trained and showed the bulk of Paul A horses.

"Bob Sutherland was primarily a bloodline man," Ballweg contended. "He firmly believed that blood would tell, and that's how he approached the breeding end of the business. He bought a lot of horses in Texas, sight unseen, based on their bloodlines. Sometimes that worked out and sometimes it didn't. But, in the process, he wound up with some great producing mares.

"At one time he owned Tangerine W and Westmoreland, two of the greatest daughters of Bert. He also had such well-known halter mares as Pretty Pam, the 1954 Honor Roll Halter Horse; Barbara Star, the 1956 Honor Roll Halter Horse; Suits Me H, who stood grand at the Southwestern Livestock Exposition in Fort Worth, Texas, and Ballerina's Dunny, who stood grand at the American Royal in Kansas City, Mo.

"Bred to Paul A, these mares began producing excellent halter-type foals for that day and age. And they were like peas in a pod — mostly coal black; pretty-headed and heavily muscled. We won a ton of halter championships with them."

Paulika, a 1953 black mare out of Mitzi Doane, was one of the first Paul A horses Ballweg showed.

He exhibited her to win the Oklahoma Yearling Halter Futurity, and she went on to earn the blue ribbon at such prestigious shows as the San Antonio Livestock Exposition, San Antonio, Tex.; National Western Stock Show, Houston Fat Stock Show, American Royal, and the Missouri, Illinois and Iowa State Fairs.

By the time her show career was over, Paulika earned 165 points and a Superior at halter, 10 cutting points, and an AQHA Championship.

Over the next dozen years, Ballweg fed, trained, shod and exhibited numerous other Paul A get to show-ring glory. Among them were AQHA Champions and/or Superior halter horses, such as Miss Paulette, Miss Paulite, Paula Nite,

PHOTO BY COLBY, COURTESY QUARTER HORSE JOURNAL

Pauline Petite, a 1960 bay mare by Paul A and out of Lady Red Smith, was the last of her famous sire's get to earn an AQHA Championship.

Paulyana, Paul Easter, Nino Paul, Paul Lewis, Paularine, Paulalynda and Star Spangled.

In fact, of the 11 AQHA Champions sired by Paul A, Ballweg trained and exhibited 10.

As tough as they were in halter competition, there was yet another event in which the Paul A horses were even tougher to beat — get-of-sire.

"Paul A was truly a consistent sire," Ballweg explained. "Whenever and wherever we showed in the get-of-sire class — and we showed against the likes of the Poco Buenos, the King Ranch horses and the Wiescamp horses — we were the ones to beat.

"We won the Southwestern Livestock Exposition in Fort Worth — which at the time was the biggest show in the nation — in 1955, 1956, 1957 and 1958. We did the same at the Houston Fat Stock Show in 1956 and 1957; and the American Royal and AK-SAR-BEN shows in 1954 and 1955. In addition, we won at too many state fairs to remember.

"Like I said, we were always the ones to beat."

For the record, Paul A's progeny competed in 54 get-of-sire classes, and recorded 48 firsts, five seconds and one third.

Entered in 54 get-of-sire classes, Paul A recorded 48 wins. The consistent sire's winning entry at the 1955 Fort Worth Livestock Show was comprised of Paulalika, held by John Ballweg; Paulyana, held by Connie Wills; and Miss Paulette, held by Daisy Ballweg.

Historic Sales

In May 1957, Sutherland held the Dividend-Dissolution Sale, a watershed for both the R. S. Bar Ranch and the Quarter Horse breed.

With Colorado legend Hank Wiescamp serving as auctioneer, and 1,500 people from 17 states in attendance, the sale set a record high average per head of $3,401. With gross revenues of $149,625, it was also the first Quarter Horse sale to eclipse the $100,000 mark.

In addition, Paulyana, a 1953 brown mare by Paul A and out of Westmoreland, set a record high for a Quarter Horse mare sold at public auction, drawing a final bid of $10,400 from J. P. Davidson of Albuquerque, N. M.

As monumental as the event was, Sutherland was not through making headlines. One short year later, he stunned the Quarter Horse world by dispersing his entire band of horses at private treaty.

The price tag for the unprecedented sale was never publicly known, but given the number and quality of the animals involved, the buzz was that it was probably the largest transaction of its kind in history.

Edgar Brown III of Houston, the buyer, acquired 55 head for his Pinehurst Ranch.

In addition to Paul A, the acquisition included such great stallions as Power Command, a John Ballweg-made AQHA Champion who went on to sire King Fritz; and Beau Chance by Skipper W.

Among the broodmares to change hands were four daughters of Bert; two daughters of King, including My Mona Lisa; a full sister to Poco Bueno; three daughters of Scooter S; a full sister to Paul A; and daughters of San Siemon, Tommy Clegg and Oklahoma Star Jr.

The entire R. S. Bar show string was included in the offering, as well as all the ranch's replacement yearlings and weanlings.

Pinehurst became Paul A's final home. Although he was a fixture there for more than a decade and sired a number of top halter and cutting horses, he never again became the object of the intense promotion he'd enjoyed under Sutherland's ownership.

In 1959, Pinehurst Ranch held a production sale of its own. In it, Paul A's progeny set yet another world's record, averaging $6,000.

Eventually, Sutherland got back into the Quarter Horse breeding and exhibiting business. Standing such stallions as Capital Gain and Net Profit — AQHA Champions by Custus Rastus (TB) and out of Miss Revenue — he continued to feature Paul A blood in his broodmare band for years.

And, just as he'd done as a paternal sire, Paul A proved to be a superior broodmare sire.

AQHA records reveal that his daughters produced six AQHA Champions and the earners of four Superiors at halter and two Superiors in performance. Oddly enough, although he was never known as a speed sire, Paul A sired daughters that produced 16 Register-of-Merit racehorses earning $75,309.

Paul A died in Houston in 1969, at 21.

One of the last and greatest of the true "bulldog" Quarter Horses, he teamed with Sutherland and Ballweg to write a colorful chapter in the breed's history.

COURTESY WESTERN HORSEMAN

The May 1957 RS Bar Ranch "Dividend-Dissolution" Sale was a record-setting affair. Here are the watershed event's four principals—seller R.Q. Sutherland; Sale-topper Paulyana; purchaser J.D. Davidson of Albuquerque, N.M.; and auctioneer Hank Wiescamp.

2 CROTON OIL

He was bred specifically to be Leo's replacement.

Frank Holmes

ORGANIZED QUARTER HORSE racing was born — courtesy of the American Quarter Racing Association (AQRA) — in southern Arizona in the early 1940s. During the next decade, it spread like wildfire throughout New Mexico, Colorado, Texas and California. Although several great families of speed-bred horses contributed to the industry's birth and phenomenal early growth, few matched the Leo line's accomplishments.

Leo (*Legends 1*), a 1940 sorrel stallion by Joe Reed II and out of Little Fanny, was among the breed's top sprinters in the early to mid-1940s. Purchased by Bud Warren of Perry, Okla., in 1947 and bred to a select band of Zantanon- and King-P-234-bred mares, Leo quickly made a name for himself as a sire. By the mid-1950s, with world champion runners such as Leota W, Mona Leta, Miss Meyers and Palleo Pete to his credit, Leo was generally acknowledged as a top source for speed.

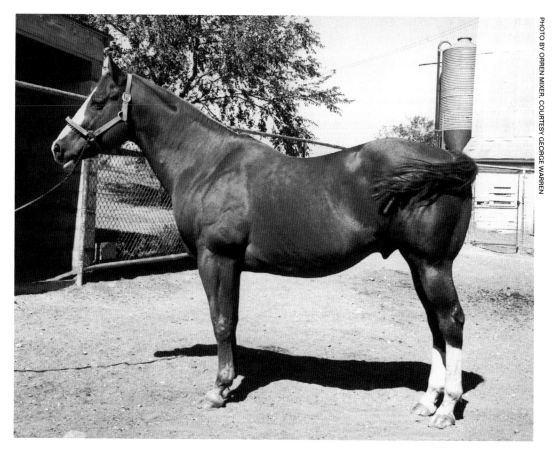

Croton Oil was bred to be a race horse, but made his biggest contributions to the breed as a show horse sire.

PHOTO BY ORREN MIXER, COURTESY GEORGE WARREN

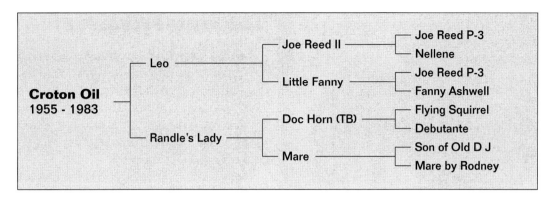

Croton Oil
1955 - 1983

- Leo
  - Joe Reed II
    - Joe Reed P-3
    - Nellene
  - Little Fanny
    - Joe Reed P-3
    - Fanny Ashwell
- Randle's Lady
  - Doc Horn (TB)
    - Flying Squirrel
    - Debutante
  - Mare
    - Son of Old D J
    - Mare by Rodney

Replacement Needed

For Bud Warren and the short-horse racing fraternity, one problem concerning the future AQHA Hall-of-Fame stallion had to be circumvented. Simply put, Leo was getting old and his replacement had to be found.

A successful dairyman before he became a Quarter Horse man, Bud Warren had a true livestock breeder's "forward-thinking" mentality. In the early 1950s he searched for just the right mare for raising a suitable junior stallion.

He found what he was looking for by delving into the famous sire's past. Only two horses had defeated Leo on the straightaway tracks. Rosalita, a 1938 sorrel mare by Doc Horn (TB) and out of a mare by a son of Old D. J., was one of them.

Bred by Tobias Cominer of Welsh, La., Rosalita was later owned by Helen Michaelis of Eagle Pass, Texas. Raced during the early to mid-1940s in Texas and Arizona, Rosalita was one of the few horses considered able to push the vaunted Shue Fly to her full limits. The AQRA recognized Rosalita in 1944 as a "Celebrated American Quarter Running Horse." That honor, accorded to but 18 of the 130 horses competing at AQRA-sanctioned race meets that year, resulted from the blaze-faced sorrel mare's top times in events ranging from 220 to 440 yards.

After her retirement from racing, Rosalita sold to V. S. Randle of Richmond, Texas, and registered with the American Quarter Horse Association as Randle's Lady.

In 1952, Bud Warren became owner of the then-14-year-old mare. Purchased, as

Halter and Performance Record:
Race Register of Merit.

Progeny Record:

Foal Crops: 16	Performance Point-Earners: 46
Foals Registered: 373	Performance Points Earned: 822.5
AQHA Champions: 13	Performance Registers of Merit: 30
Youth Champions: 3	Superior Performance Awards: 2
Halter Point-Earners: 70	Race Starters: 154
Halter Points Earned: 1,915	Race Money Earned: $100,269
Superior Halter Awards: 10	Race Registers of Merit: 63
Leading Race Money-Earner: Miss Croton Oil ($29,406)	

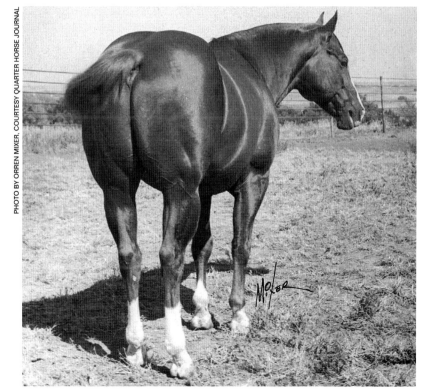

PHOTO BY ORREN MIXER, COURTESY QUARTER HORSE JOURNAL

Leo, Croton Oil's AQHA Hall of Fame sire, has influenced the breed at every aspect and at every level.

PHOTO BY REGGIE RUSSELL, COURTESY QUARTER HORSE JOURNAL

Randle's Lady, Croton Oil's dam, was a celebrated early-day racehorse.

COURTESY QUARTER HORSE JOURNAL

Captain Croton, shown here as a yearling, was one of the first of the Croton Oils to enjoy success as a show horse.

The Heir Apparent

In 1955, Randle's Lady presented Warren with the stud colt he wanted. Warren named the blaze-faced sorrel with two hind stockings Croton Oil—after the yellowish-brown cathartic medicine of the same name—and immediately designated him as Leo's heir apparent.

If Warren hoped his junior stallion would prove as competitive on the racetrack as his famous sire, the Oklahoma horseman, no doubt, was disappointed in the horse's abbreviated straightaway career.

From five starts, Croton Oil could muster only one second-place finish and $770 in earnings. In May 1958, as a 3-year-old, he earned his racing Register of Merit with a AA rating, which was updated later to a speed index of 85.

Still Warren was confident that his well-bred stallion, who reminded him of Leo more than any colt he'd raised, would become a successful sire. With that in mind, he promptly retired him to the breeding shed.

Croton Oil was relatively easy to get along with. "I was in my early teens when Dad first started using Croton Oil as a stallion," George Warren of Perry, Okla., said. "I remember him as being a little taller and rangier than Leo — he stood 15.1 and weighed 1,150 pounds. He was a nice-headed, speckle-faced horse with a tremendous hind leg.

"In those years, I helped with the feeding and breeding," George continued. "Leo and Jet Deck were the easiest stallions to be around; they were like big dogs. Croton Oil wasn't as laid back and friendly as those two — he could get a little 'stud-ornery' at times. But he was easy to bluff, so he never presented any real problems."

A Different Direction

Croton Oil's first Warren-bred foals hit the ground in 1959. From the very onset, two things were apparent.

First, they couldn't compete on the racetracks with the best of the Three Bars (TB)

noted earlier, for the express purpose of raising a replacement stallion for Leo, "Lady" responded by having four consecutive fillies. Although two of the fillies died, the remaining two — Rosa Leo and South Pacific — achieved fame on the racetrack, in the broodmare band or both.

PHOTO BY ALFRED JANSSEN III, COURTESY QUARTER HORSE JOURNAL

Rinski, a 1960 sorrel stallion by Croton Oil and out of Sorrel Sue, was AA-rated on the tracks. Retired from race competition and re-trained as a show horse, he was an AQHA Champion.

and Top Deck (TB) get. The half-Thoroughbreds were simply a notch or two speedier.

Second — and this was the factor that ultimately determined the direction the overall Croton Oil line eventually took — from a conformation standpoint, the Croton Oils were model Quarter Horses, and, consequently, ideally suited for the show ring.

That they ultimately headed away from the track and toward the halter arena came as no surprise to a man who knew the Warren horses intimately.

"Beginning in the late 1940s," famed artist Orren Mixer said, "I spent a lot of time at Bud and Reba's. I first photographed and painted Leo, and then did the same with Sugar Bars, Croton Oil and Jet Deck. I remember Croton Oil as a good-looking horse, but not necessarily the running type. To me, he was all horse; a stout, cowboy's kind of horse; the kind you'd like to get on and ride. I know that Bud wanted

him to be a great speed sire, but it just didn't work out that way. His get became halter horses instead."

Captain Croton, a 1960 sorrel stallion out of Sally's D M by Del Monte, and Rinski, a 1960 sorrel stallion out of Sorrel Sue by King P-234, were two of the first Croton Oil get to make their mark as show horses. Both earned their AQHA Championships in 1967.

They were followed, in short order, by such AQHA Champions and/or Superior halter horses as Miss Sun Oil, Montleon, Oil Play, Doc Croton, Croton All, Speed Shift, Croton Oil Bill, Wallaby, Oil Loot, Envoy, Leo's Egonos, Noble George, Rare Croton Oil and Alice Croton.

Of these, Wallaby, Miss Sun Oil and Oil Loot acquitted themselves the best.

Wallaby, a 1964 sorrel stallion out of Niner by Sugar Bars, was the 1967 AQHA High-Point Halter Stallion. Exhibited 131 times at halter, he racked up an amazing record of 123 firsts and 90 grand championships. He was a

Superior halter horse, an AQHA Champion and earned 340 halter and 19 western pleasure points.

Oil Loot, a 1965 sorrel stallion out of Real Sugar by Sugar Bars, and Miss Sun Oil, a 1961 sorrel mare out of Dawson's Dee by Dawson's Star, were also Superior horses — he with 210 points, and she with 173.

Fleet of Foot

And, just because they couldn't fully take the measure of racehorses the ilk of Pokey Bar, Jet Deck, Goetta Bar and Go Josie Go, didn't mean the Croton Oils weren't swift.

From Croton Oil's first foal crop came the likes of Salad Oil and Strip Runner. Salad Oil, a 1959 sorrel mare out of Lena Horn by Dock, became a AAA-rated AQHA Champion. Strip Runner, a 1959 sorrel mare out of 89'er by King P-234, earned a speed index of 95 and notched four wins and two seconds from 11 starts.

Overall, Miss Croton Oil and Croton's Jill were their sire's top race performers. Miss Croton Oil, a 1961 sorrel mare out of How Cute by Clint Higgins, achieved a speed index of 100, was a two-time stakes winner and earned $29,406 in addition to an AQHA Championship and a Superior racing award.

Croton's Jill, a 1965 sorrel mare out of Whizet by Furry's Winet, also achieved a speed index of 100, was a stakes winner and earned $13,262.

Among Croton Oil's other top racehorse get — all with speed indexes of 90 or higher — were Sissie Croton, Chaparral Croton, Mike Stead, Oil's Jane, Sport Coat, Three In

Wallaby, a 1964 sorrel stallion by Croton Oil and out of Niner, was the 1967 AQHA High-Point Halter Stallion.

One Oil, Crotie Bo, Dono Rosa Leo, Ninerette, Red Croton, Croton's Pay Day, Kid Croton, Miss Oil Strike, Smart Talkin, Smart Living and Freckles D Chase.

By the mid-1960s Croton Oil had firmly established himself as a better-than-average sire of conformation, working ability and speed.

Along Came Jet Deck

Still, his breeder and owner Bud Warren was first and foremost a racehorse man. In 1964, the astute Oklahoman first leased and then purchased one-half interest in a Top Deck- and Three Bars-bred world champion runner by the name of Jet Deck.

Within a few short years, Jet Deck zoomed to the top of virtually all of the racehorse leading-sire lists. His ascent, as good as it was for both the Quarter Horse racing industry in general and the Warren breeding program in particular, basically put Croton Oil out of a job.

The stallion's last three foal crops in 1972, 1973 and 1974 averaged less than 10 each. And from them would come only one Register of Merit racehorse.

Three Sons

But the Croton Oil story was far from over. It was now the second generation's turn.

To begin with, three Croton Oil sons — Wallaby, Rinski and Montleon — went on to noteworthy careers as sires.

Shelton Ranch of Kerrville, Texas acquired Wallaby, the 1967 AQHA High-Point Halter Stallion, to stand at stud alongside world champion halter stallion Skipa Star and AQHA Superhorse Leonard Milligan.

Wallaby sired a total of 230 foals and 86 performers. Seven of his get earned AQHA Championships, five were Superior halter horses, and four earned Superior performance awards. In open, amateur and youth competition they amassed 26 Registers of Merit and 3,362 points.

PHOTO BY DAROL DICKINSON, COURTESY QUARTER HORSE JOURNAL

Miss Sun Oil, a 1961 sorrel mare by Croton Oil and out of Dawson's Dee, was a Superior halter horse and the earner of 173 halter points.

PHOTO BY DAROL DICKINSON, COURTESY QUARTER HORSE JOURNAL

Montleon, an AQHA Champion son of Croton Oil, was a top sire in his own right.

Doc Croton, a 1962 sorrel stallion by Croton Oil and out of Gold Digger W, also earned an AQHA Championship.

Rinski, one of Croton Oil's most versatile sons, was an AQHA Champion, a Superior halter horse, earned Registers of Merit in performance and racing, and was a National Cutting Horse Association money-earner.

Retired to stud, he sired 169 foals and 34 performers. Among the latter were three AQHA Champions and one Superior halter horse.

Montleon, also an AQHA Champion and a Superior halter horse, sired 305 foals, of which 49 were performers and two were Superior halter horses. More importantly, Montleon served as the cornerstone herd sire for Howard Dahlof's breeding program in Walnut, Iowa. Beginning with Montleon and a small, select band of mares, Dahlof became the leading breeder of halter-class winners in 1988, 1989, 1990 and 1991.

An Appaloosa Influence

Croton Oil even managed to exert a positive influence on the Appaloosa halter industry. In the mid-1960s, the Appaloosa breed enjoyed a robust economy, and numbers were up in every aspect of the industry including halter. In 1965 and 1966, Croton All, the AQHA Champion Croton Oil son, was bred to a grand-champion Appaloosa halter mare named Snowcap's Startoo.

In 1966, "Startoo" foaled a bay, blanket-hipped filly named Snowcap's Lady Pitt. The following spring, Startoo foaled a chestnut snowflake-pattern colt named Johnny Snowcap. The full siblings became two of the breed's top halter horses during the late 1960s and early 1970s.

In 1968, at the huge 21st National Appaloosa Show in Oklahoma City, Okla., "Lady Pitt" was reserve champion mare and champion 2-year-old filly. At the 22nd National in Baton Rouge, La., she was named grand champion mare and champion 3-year-old mare.

Johnny Snowcap fared even better. At the 22nd National, he won grand champion stallion and champion 2-year-old stallion, and at the 23rd National in Huron, S. D., he was named grand champion stallion and champion 3-year-old stallion. At the 24th National in Las Vegas, Nev., he was favored to become the only three-time national grand champion stallion in the breed's history. Unfortunately, fate intervened and he died of colic at the show.

Represented by her two Croton Oil-bred offspring, Snowcap's Startoo earned honors as national champion produce-of-dam winner in both 1969 and 1970.

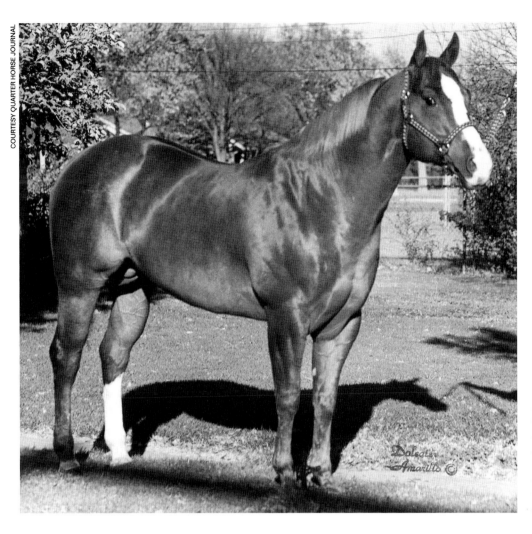

Envoy, a 1966 sorrel stallion by Croton Oil and out of Niner, amassed 84 halter points and 27 performance points on his way to earning an AQHA Championship and Superior halter award.

Salad Oil, shown here as a weanling, went on to earn a AAA rating on the track and an AQHA Championship in the show ring.

Miss Croton Oil, a 1961 sorrel mare by Croton Oil and out of How Cute, achieved a speed index of 100, was a two-time stakes winner and earned a Superior in racing. One of her sire's most versatile get, the talented mare was also an AQHA Champion.

Snowcap's Lady Pitt, a 1966 chestnut mare by Croton All (QH) and out of Snowcap's Startoo, was the Grand Champion Mare and Champion 3-Year-Old Mare at the 22nd National Appaloosa Show, Baton Rouge, La. The blanket-hipped mare was owned by Cliff Welling of Des Moines, Iowa, and shown by Billy Landers.

The Distaff Side

The Croton Oil line wasn't solely male-oriented, though. The distaff side made its contributions as well.

With the added benefit of the elite Bud Warren broodmare band backing up the bottom side of their pedigrees, and bred to such legendary stallions as Sugar Bars, Jet Deck and Jet Charger, Croton Oil daughters proved to be superior producers.

As racing matrons, 157 Croton Oil mares produced 362 performers. Of these, 190 were winners, 176 earned race Registers of Merit, and 10 earned Superior race awards. Their total race earnings were $951,047.

Croton Oil daughters produced 153 show performers. Among their number were 12 AQHA Champions, 10 Superior halter- and 10 Superior performance-award winners. In open, amateur and youth competition, they amassed 5,753.5 points.

The maternal grandsons and grand-daughters of Croton also fared well as cutting horses and earned $205,156 in NCHA-sanctioned events.

The Blind Gentleman

Although Croton Oil's last foal crop hit the ground in 1974, the stallion wasn't reported dead by his last owner — T. M. Jones of Cordell, Okla. — until almost a decade later.

In a letter to AQHA dated October 21, 1983, Jones wrote:

"Please find enclosed the registration certificate of Croton Oil. He died October 18, 1983, from apparent natural causes. Bud Warren gave us this famous son of Leo in May of 1983. We were hoping we might get a few mares in foal to him, but failed.

"It was a real pleasure to care for him in the past few months. He was completely blind, but could find his feed and water easy. He could even find his way through two gates to go to the yard and parking lot to graze at times. There were vehicles and trailers in the area, but Croton Oil never ran into any of them and could find his way any place he wanted to go.

"Visitors and friends were amazed by watching the actions of this blind horse. He was so intelligent he could care for himself as well as any horse. I am very pleased to have been associated with him because he broadened my knowledge of good Quarter Horses and what they can do."

As a racehorse and speed sire, Croton Oil might not have been just what Bud Warren wanted. Still, as an all-around sire of conformation and working ability, he made a positive and long-lasting impact on the breed.

And did his Daddy proud in the process.

PHOTO BY JOHNNY JOHNSTON, COURTESY WESTERN HORSEMAN

Johnny Snowcap, a 1967 chestnut full brother to "Lady Pitt," was the Grand Champion Stallion and Champion 3-Year-Old Stallion at the 23rd National Appaloosa Show, Huron, S.D. The snowflake-patterned stallion was owned by Russo Farms, Naperville, Ill., and shown by Tommy Manion.

3

OKIE LEO

One man took a look at Okie Leo and saw much more in him than just the potential to go fast.

Patti Campbell

Although bred to be a racehorse, Okie Leo made his reputation as an arena performer.

PHOTO BY ORREN MIXER

OKIE LEO WAS SUPPOSED TO BE A RUNNER.

After all, the 1956 sorrel stallion was sired by Leo, one of the breed's premiere racehorse sires. What's more, he was out of Sorrel Sue by King P-234. With such top sprinters as Squaw H, Hank H and Booger H to his credit, King was also known as a horse capable of begetting speed.

But one man took a look at Okie Leo as a young horse, saw much more in him than just the potential to go fast, and changed the course of history. That man was Dick Robey of Edmond, Okla.

"Okie Leo was bred by Bud Warren of Perry, Oklahoma," Robey said. "When he was a yearling, he was purchased by Mr. E.L. "Les" Gosselin of Edmond. Gosselin was the 'G' in the TG&Y stores, and he had built one of the finest horse farms in Oklahoma.

"Gosselin was the kind of man the Quarter Horse breed needed," he continued. "On the breeding side, he had gone out and bought horses like Go Man Go, the three-time Champion Quarter Running Horse.

"On the racing end, he had acquired such well-bred race prospects like Okie Leo; Flit Bar, a 1956 stallion by Sugar Bars and out of Flit; and Joe Blair, a 1956 stallion by Vandy and out of Josie's Bar.

"He was determined to get in the racing business in a big way."

Gosselin's initial plans for his trio of race-bred colts called for them to be placed in training and pointed toward the 1959 inaugural running of the All-American Futurity in Ruidoso, New Mexico.

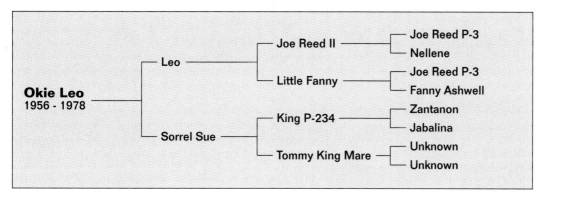

Okie Leo
1956 - 1978

- Leo
  - Joe Reed II
    - Joe Reed P-3
    - Nellene
  - Little Fanny
    - Joe Reed P-3
    - Fanny Ashwell
- Sorrel Sue
  - King P-234
    - Zantanon
    - Jabalina
  - Tommy King Mare
    - Unknown
    - Unknown

Flit Bar and Joe Blair apparently took to the training well, but Okie Leo seemed to have other plans. Instead of learning to break from the gates and breeze down the straightaway, he concentrated instead on bucking his exercise boys off. Gosselin was determined though and, in the summer of 1959, shipped all three youngsters to Ruidoso, N.M., for advanced training.

Misfortune beset the effort, however, and two of the three prospects suffered career-ending injuries.

Halter and Performance Record:
Performance Register of Merit; AQHA Champion; Superior Reining.

Progeny Record:
Foal Crops: 21	Performance Point-Earners: 202
Foals Registered: 531	Performance Points Earned: 4,203.5
AQHA Champions: 4	Performance Register of Merits: 78
Halter Point-Earners: 37	Superior Performance Awards: 11
Halter Points Earned: 363	World Champions: 4
Superior Halter Awards: 1	High-Point Winners: 1

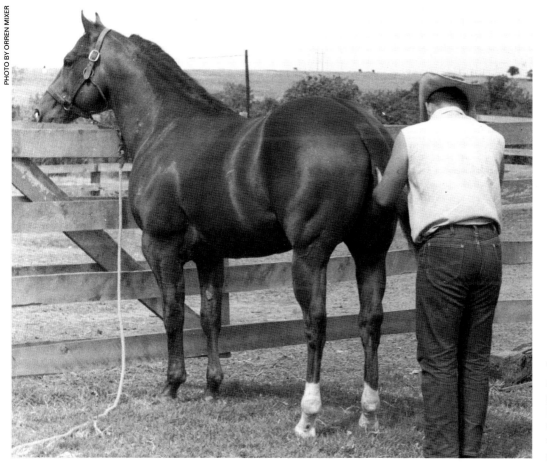

PHOTO BY ORREN MIXER

This three-quarter rear shot of "Okie" being groomed by owner Dick Robey shows off the compact stallion's well-defined forearm and gaskin muscling.

In addition to being an AQHA Champion, Okie Leo was also a Superior reining horse. Here, renowned western artist Orren Mixer's 10-year-old son John takes his first ride on the well-dispositioned stallion.

This shot of John Mixer, Okie Leo and Dick Robey was taken inside the Mixer art studio after John had won an early 1960s youth reining title in Dallas, Texas.

"Gosselin's trainer crippled both Flit Bar and Joe Blair," Robey said. "He probably would have crippled Okie Leo too, but the colt kept bucking his riders off so they never were able to train on him hard enough to hurt him."

By the fall of 1959, Okie Leo's owner had become disenchanted with the racing industry and was ready to sell out.

"Gosselin didn't know anything about the horse business," Robey said. "Consequently, a lot of people took advantage of him. Everybody wanted some of his money. He finally had enough of it and sold out."

A New Beginning

But one man's final chapter in the horse business gave birth to another man's first.

"I was working in the veterinarian's office in Edmond," Robey recalled. "Bob Gosselin — Les' son — came in one day and announced that he'd just sold Flit Bar. So I asked him about Okie Leo.

PHOTO BY ORREN MIXER

Although his best performance event was reining, Okie Leo was also a talented cutting horse. As these two action shots show, the King P-234 grandson was capable of bold and decisive moves.

PHOTO BY ORREN MIXER

"Bob priced him to me for $2,000. I didn't have a dime, but I said I'd consider taking him if he'd give me some time to pay him out. He agreed, and we shook hands on it."

Unbeknownst to Robey, though, there was one minor detail that still had to be worked out.

"When Les Gosselin found out what his son had done," Robey said, "he called me up. It seems he'd already sold Okie Leo for $5,000 to a banker from McCloud, Oklahoma.

PHOTO BY ORREN MIXER

Either with or without a bridle, Dick Robey and "Okie" routinely put in long hours in the practice pen.

"The banker was hedging on the deal though. He told Gosselin that he'd thought it over, and he only wanted to give $3,000 for the colt. That made Gosselin a little mad, so he called the whole thing off. Then he told me he'd take the lesser price from me.

"I decided if you couldn't make money off of a Leo-bred stallion that was out of a King mare, you've got no business being in horses at all. So I bought him."

Still not knowing exactly how he was going to pay for Okie Leo, Robey took him home and began to prepare him for a reining career. Although the colt was virtually unbroken, he seemed to have gotten over his aversion to being ridden, and his training progressed at an encouraging clip. Then the stallion's education was side-tracked for nearly two years due to an injury in which he cut a tendon in his right hind leg. As soon as it healed, the training regimen was resumed.

Ahead of His Time

"I probably ran a hundred reining patterns on Okie Leo before I ever took him to a horse show," Robey said. "And you know, we should never have been able to do good with him because he should've been sour. But he wasn't."

"His first official outing was in August of 1960. It was a free horse show in Mountain View, Oklahoma. It was on a Wednesday and we thought there wouldn't be anybody there.

"But since it was free, every farmer and rancher in the country turned out. There were 400 head of horses that day. We won the reining, and just continued on from there."

By the end of the 1960 show season, Okie Leo had earned a Register of Merit in reining and the first of what would be two back-to-back state reining championships. In 1962, he qualified for an AQHA Championship and a Superior reining award.

In addition to his prowess in reining, the versatile stallion proved that he had other talents as well. Robey's wife, Helen, showed the stallion in western pleasure and both Robey and a "catch rider" showed him in cutting.

"In 1966, we were at a show in Shawnee, Oklahoma," Robey said. "Ed Bottom, the well-known cutting horse trainer, was a friend of mine.

"Ed came up to me at the show and said, 'Dick, you always promised me I could show this horse.'

"Now, Dick had never been on Okie Leo in his life, but I said, 'Be my guest.'

"And then he got on the horse and went out there and beat Patty Conger, the 1965 world champion cutting horse!"

Later that year, 9-year-old Okie Leo competed in his final AQHA performance class. His lifetime show record includes 108 total points: 20 halter; 16 cutting; 15.5 western pleasure; and 57 reining.

Even today, Robey remains modest about his success with Okie Leo.

"Everything we asked the horse to do, he did," he said. "I had never put the finish on a reining horse, but I had always trained my own horses and had been able to put a decent handle on them. When I started trying to fine-tune Okie Leo, he was way ahead of me. That's why I never, ever told anybody that I made him. On the contrary, he made me."

According to Robey, many great trainers of the day, including Matlock Rose and Don Wilcox, saw Okie Leo's dynamic potential and offered to train the stallion.

"Everybody wanted to train 'Okie,'" said Robey. "But we didn't have the money and we weren't about to let him out of our sight."

Standing Success

The Robeys were deeply attached to Okie Leo, and the stallion made money for the family as a show horse and as a sire. Robey bred Okie Leo to his own mares as soon as the stallion's tendon healed.

"We bred him the whole time we showed him," said Robey. "We used to breed him four times a day. I'd get up in the morning and breed him and then go to the horse show, come home and breed him again that night. We never had any trouble with him."

Leonard Milligan, a 1974 bay stallion by Okie Leo and out of Farafield Star, was the 1980 Open World Show Superhorse.

Kim's Pica Pride, a 1974 chestnut stallion by Okie Leo and out of Kim's Pica, was a two-time AQHA world champion.

PHOTO BY ANDY, COURTESY QUARTER HORSE JOURNAL

Okie Chex, a 1980 chestnut mare by Kim's Pica Pride and out of Miss Billy Chex, was the winner of the 1983 Canadian Reined Cowhorse Association's Snaffle Bit Futurity.

COURTESY QUARTER HORSE JOURNAL

Okie Leah, a 1972 sorrel mare by Okie Leo and out of Britton Flicker, was another of her sire's talented performers. Reining horse icon Bob Loomis of Marietta, Okla., is up in this nice action shot.

During his first show season, Okie Leo won the reining in 10 out of the 12 shows he entered, earning 16 points. In the other two shows, the stallion placed second. Breeders interested in raising performance horses soon found their way to the Robeys' farm.

When Okie Leo's first foals were old enough to compete, they made it apparent that the apples didn't fall far from the tree.

"Training an Okie Leo horse was just like breathing air," Robey exclaimed. "It was the easiest thing in the world. I showed a 2-year-old we'd raised named Bumble Bee Leo at the Tulsa Fair. It was the 14th saddling I had on the colt, and I beat all the good horses in the open reining! Back then the reining was for all ages and I was on a 2-year-old!

"I hate to tell you this, but it's the truth — I never claimed to be a horse trainer. I just had the best bloomin' horses in the country."

Over the course of the next two decades, the Dick Robey - Okie Leo partnership proceeded to churn out champion after champion. Heading the list of the prepotent stallion's most-accomplished get would have to be his four AQHA World Champions — Kim's Pica Pride, Miss Arkie Okie, Leonard Milligan and Smoke Um Okie.

Kim's Pica Pride, a 1974 chestnut stallion out of Kim's Pica, was the 1977 World Champion Jr. Calf Roping Horse, and the 1984 World Champion Sr. Working Cowhorse; and Miss Arkie Okie, a 1975 chestnut mare out of Mini Bar Blaze, was the 1981 World Champion Sr. Working Cowhorse.

Leonard Milligan, a 1974 bay stallion out of Farafield Star, was the 1978 World Champion Working Cowhorse, and the 1980 World Show Superhorse, World Champion Sr. Heeling Horse, and World Champion Sr. Calf Roping Horse.

Smoke Um Okie, a 1976 bay gelding out of Farafield Star, was the 1985 World Champion Sr. Reining Horse; and the 1986 World Show Superhorse, World Champion Sr. Heeling Horse, and World Champion Sr. Calf Roping Horse.

Okies Last Step, a 1979 chestnut stallion by Okie Leo and out of Mrs Band Step, was a member of his famous sire's last foal crop. The Register of Merit performer's pipe-smoking owner Kim Bass of Cashion, Okla., seems to be enjoying the ride in this cutting shot.

In addition to his world champion headliners, Okie Leo sired a host of top open and youth competitors. Among them were:

· Okie Chloe — 1961 sorrel mare out of Bobbie Cargill — AQHA Champion.

· Okie Flyer — 1961 brown gelding out of Irene 70 — 1970 and 1974 High-Point Youth Barrel Racing; AQHA Champion.

· Okleo Skeet — 1965 sorrel stallion out of Staples' Babe — 1973 High-Point Pole Bending Stallion.

· Okie's Teddy Bear — 1971 sorrel stallion out of Eternal Dee Gee — 1976 High-Point Jr. Calf Roping; 1976 High-Point Calf Roping Stallion; Superior calf roping.

· Up Front Okie — 1973 sorrel gelding out of McCue's Bee — 1982 and 1984 High-Point Working Cow Horse Gelding; 1983 Reserve World Champion Sr. Working Cow Horse; AQHA Versatility Award; Superior Working Cow Horse.

Still other Okie Leos proved the versatility of their sire by earning Superiors in halter, barrel racing, calf roping, steer roping and working cowhorse.

"Okie Leo horses made more trainers than trainers made Okie Leo horses," stated Robey.

Many of those famous horses were out of Robey's own mares, including the two World Show Superhorses.

To compensate for a limited advertising budget, the Robeys came up with a unique way to market their foals.

"We sold Okie Leo horses to good trainers, say for $500," said Robey. "They could sell them, but they had to promise me they would train the horses. And they did. It made several of them. Okie Leo horses won a bunch.

"The versatility horse that they're raising today — we've been raising that horse for 50 years," he added. "And we've still got them.

The Okie Leo story was always a family affair. Here, Dick Robey and "Okie" engage in a little "rock climbing," while Helen Robey and Okie Chloe strike a more traditional pose. As the sign above the barn door clearly indicates, both Okie Leo and the legendary Harlan called the Robey Ranch home.

"People would ask, 'What kind of mares cross on him?', and I'd say, 'Well, they need to be alive.'"

Personality Plus

Okie Leo's athleticism, talent and proficiency as a sire would be enough to make most any horse a legend, but it was perhaps the stallion's idiosyncrasies and loving disposition that made him a one-of-a-kind.

"His disposition couldn't have been any better," explained Robey. "He was a big, gentle horse that anybody could get along with. You could put your child on him and he'd take better care of that child than you would.

"When we took him to a horse show, Okie didn't act like a stallion," he said. "But you couldn't breed him artificially, and he

was not a teasing horse. If you wanted the mares bred and they were ready, then he'd breed them. But, as far as he was concerned, teasing was somebody else's job."

During the time the Robeys were building a new barn, they kept Okie Leo in a two-strand slick wire pen. He never tried to escape, even when they drove the mares by him.

But once the barn was built and Okie Leo had a new, fortified stall, the stallion liked nothing better than to fiddle with the latches and occasionally escape.

"Of course, if he got out, he wouldn't go anywhere," laughed Robey. "He was just a pleasure to have around."

In 1970, Robey transferred ownership of Okie Leo to a friend, Bruce Stultz, as security on a personal loan. However, Stultz maintains that he never took possession of the stallion and that Dick Robey resumed ownership of the stallion shortly before his death.

Through the years, Okie Leo spent only one night away from the Robey farm. The sleepover took place at Orren Mixer's ranch when the artist was painting the stallion's portrait.

"He took Okie Leo into the studio with him," said Robey. "And you know the picture of the ideal Quarter Horse that Mixer painted for AQHA? If you look closely, the star and rear white socks came from Okie Leo."

Okie Leo died of a heart attack in 1978. He remained on the AQHA Leading Sires of Performance Class Winners list until 1985. At that time, he was the only stallion that had been on that list for 13 consecutive years.

"We buried him in front of the barn that he built," said Robey. "That's where he belonged, right there under his big maple tree."

PHOTO BY ORREN MIXER

Okie Leo was as well-known for his stellar disposition as he was for his athletic prowess. Young John Mixer seems to be completely at ease with the AQHA Champion stallion in tow.

FLIT BAR

Bred to be a racehorse, he founded one of the first great barrel racing lines.

Cheryl Magoteaux

IN 1959, FLIT BAR became the fulfillment of a promise to Rebecca Tyler Lockhart. Nearly half a decade later, the blood of Flit Bar was still fulfilling the promise of his heritage.

When a horse is fast enough to run a barrel pattern in world class time, he's said to be able to "stop the clock." Flit Bar's get would stop the clock in the barrel racing world and their presence there would be measured in dollars, championships and dreams.

Flit Bar was born in 1956 to an aristocracy of accomplishment. His sire was Sugar Bars, the prominent racehorse. In those days, the extent of Sugar Bars' impact on the Quarter Horse industry was still untold, but his foals were soon rewriting history. In his breeding career, Sugar Bars would produce 867 foals, with 139 Race ROMs, 240 money earners, nine stakes winners and two Superior racehorses with earnings of $378,557. His 266 arena performers earned 7,080 performance points,

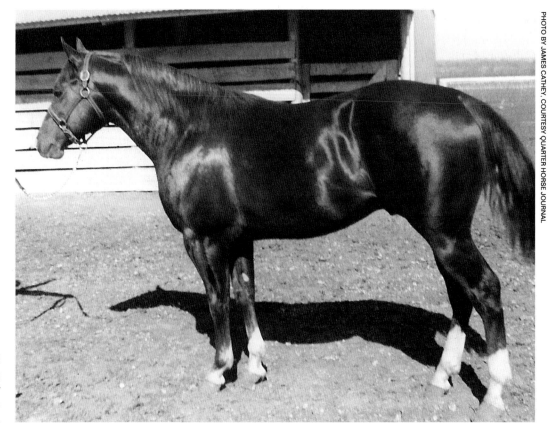

Although he possessed balance and show-ring conformation, Flit Bar made his mark on the breed solely as a sire.

PHOTO BY JAMES CATHEY, COURTESY QUARTER HORSE JOURNAL

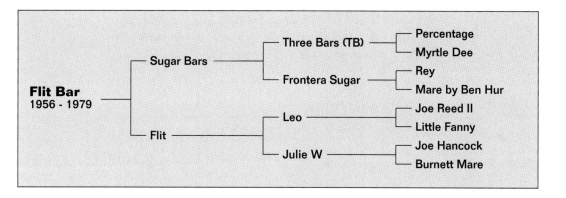

Flit Bar
1956 - 1979

- Sugar Bars
  - Three Bars (TB)
    - Percentage
    - Myrtle Dee
  - Frontera Sugar
    - Rey
    - Mare by Ben Hur
- Flit
  - Leo
    - Joe Reed II
    - Little Fanny
  - Julie W
    - Joe Hancock
    - Burnett Mare

2,816 halter points, 114 ROMs and 36 AQHA Championships.

Flit Bar's dam, Flit, was a legendary producer. By Leo and out of Julie W by Joe Hancock, she was a pretty bay 14.3-hand mare. In 1949, she was match-raced with a tough sprinting mare, Black Polly. Flit won the race, carrying not only her jockey, but also her first foal and future world champion cutting horse, Kings Pistol. Flit set a track record of 13.8 in the 250-yard race, and that record held until it was broken by her full sister Juleo.

Flit Bar was Flit's sixth foal, bred by Bud Warren of the Warren Ranch of Perry, Okla. Warren would be inducted into the American Quarter Horse Association Hall of Fame, along with three of the stallions he owned and stood—Leo, Jet Deck and Sugar Bars.

So when the handsome chestnut yearling was sold to E.L. Gosselin of Edmond, Okla., as a race prospect, he brought a hefty price and was headed toward the track. Once there, Flit Bar had a disappointing race career, due, it is thought, to a starting gate injury he sustained early in his 2-year-old year. In any case, as a 2-year old he was quick out of the gate, but couldn't sustain the speed. He started three races but didn't place, turning in a less-than-expected speed index of 65.

He was sold late in his 2-year-old year to A.T. Ferree of Skiatook, Okla. Ferree, who regularly bought and sold horses, showed him the next spring to George Tyler, who purchased him for $1,750.

"That was a lot less than had originally been given for him," commented Rebecca

Halter and Performance Record:
None

Progeny Record:

Foal Crops: 20	Performance Points Earned: 1,200
Foals Registered: 335	Performance Registers of Merit: 30
AQHA Champions: 5	Superior Performance Awards: 5
Halter Point-Earners: 21	Race Starters: 32
Halter Points Earned: 441	Race Money Earned: $7,533
Superior Halter Awards: 3	Race Registers of Merit: 6
Performance Point-Earners: 21	
Leading Race Money-Earner: Webster 65 ($2,274)	

COURTESY WESTERN HORSEMAN

Sugar Bars, Flit Bar's sire, was a AAA-rated speedster and an AQHA Hall of Fame sire. The legendary stallion is shown here, after being named reserve champion stallion at a 1956 Enid, Okla., show.

Flit, Flit Bar's dam, was likewise a winning racehorse and renowned producer. Here she is in 1957 with Bar Flit at her side.

Hall of Fame horsewoman Rebecca Lockhart is the woman behind Flit Bar's rise to prominence as a sire. In addition to being a top Quarter Horse breeder, the Ryan, Okla., native founded the American Paint Horse Association. Here she is with Cherokee Maiden after winning grand champion mare honors at the 1962 Southwestern Exposition and Fat Stock Show in Fort Worth.

Tyler Lockhart. She added, with the wisdom that's long been borne out, "But with horses, it's not what you give for them. It's what they're worth!"

Later in life, Rebecca would help create the American Paint Horse Association, earning well-deserved recognition and Hall of Fame status. But in 1959, she was a young wife, and Flit Bar was the horse she had been looking for. When she married George Tyler, she had 10 mares but no stallion and he had promised her he'd get her a good horse to go with her mares.

A few years later, she still hadn't found one she really wanted, but when George Tyler bought Flit Bar, Rebecca saw potential. "He was gorgeous. He had a little head and long hip."

The stallion was well worth a wedding bargain. "He was smart, pretty and quick! I was raised down here in Hancock country; I knew Leos were good and I thought the Sugar Bars would be good."

"George," she said. "You promised me when we got married you'd get me a stud. Now we've got a daughter 4 years old!"

"I couldn't find one," he replied.

"You have now. I want Flit Bar."

Rebecca actually already had a stallion that she had paid $3,500 for, but she liked Flit Bar much better. "I gave George that horse and he resold him the next week and I kept Flit Bar."

Four decades later, she laughed as she remembered, "George bought him and I claimed him."

And when informed that the venerable stallion would be included in the *Legends* book, she added, "That's good. He is a legend."

But at the time, Rebecca was looking less for a legend than for a horse that could produce quality babies. "I wanted looks, proven cow horse performance bloodlines and some speed. I didn't want a racehorse; I wanted to raise horses that could do everything."

Flit Bar's career as a stallion was set and she opted to begin breeding right away. He was never campaigned on the show horse trail. "We never showed him—

PHOTO BY HAROLD ISRAEL, COURTESY QUARTER HORSE JOURNAL

Like his Hall of Fame sire, Flit Bar was endowed with a beautiful head and large, intelligent-looking eyes.

never won anything—we didn't have a reason to."

Neither did they ride him. "We didn't buy him to ride. We had a lot of other horses."

The first year he stood at stud, he sired 29 foals, 11 of which would perform, including Carcy Bueno, an NCHA money earner; and Flit Bar Maid, winner of five races.

The next foal crop, in 1961, included Scar Bar; an AQHA Champion; Bar Roll, an Open Superior barrel horse; and Bar Bubbles, a reserve world champion senior calf roping horse.

In 1962, he produced Fancy Flit Bar, a flashy palomino filly which won the yearling halter class at the Denver Stock Show, San Antonio and the Houston Livestock Show, and was an AQHA Champion. Also born in 1962 was Flashy Flit Bar, an AQHA Champion and Superior calf roping horse.

Rebecca unequivocally stated, "Flit Bar was my favorite Quarter Horse of all time."

She meant that both for his accomplishments and for his personality. Flit Bar had a wonderful disposition and was intelligent and an easy keeper, at least after the first year. She remembered, "He got fever-foundered the first year we got him. We stood him in water and he got over it."

Simply, she believed in him with all her heart, and her advertisements reflected that. "I ran an ad on him in which I had an artist draw a picture of a tree with a bunch of coons in it."

The caption of the ad that ran in the Quarter Horse Journal in the spring of 1959 contained Rebecca's heartfelt words. "It's hard to get all your coons in one tree. I looked a long time before I found a horse with all the qualities I wanted. Flit Bar has speed, cow sense and good disposition."

Flit Bar was turning out to be a solid sire with winners in diverse events. Flit Bardot

Flashy Flit Bar, a 1962 sorrel stallion by Flit Bar and out of Vi Irving, was an AQHA Champion and a Superior calf roping horse.

PHOTO BY ORREN MIXER, COURTESY QUARTER HORSE JOURNAL

Manzanito, a 1965 sorrel gelding by Flit Bar and out of Maxine Dublin, was also an AQHA Champion and a Superior halter horse.

was a Superior reining horse, and Manzanito was an AQHA Champion and Superior halter horse.

Flit Bar's sire record would have made him remembered as a "heads above the rest" sire, but it was out of the AQHA annals and into the barrel horse world that Flit Bar would acquire icon status.

Flit Bar's emergence as a barrel horse sire was serendipitous. Rebecca remembers, "Those barrel racers got hold of these horses and did so well with them. It was just kind of luck."

The luck came, largely, because the right horses got into the right hands, early on.

Kenneth Springer, the preeminent barrel racing photographer, has been shooting barrel horses since 1970, and he remembers clearly the beginning of the buzz about the Flit Bars in the barrel racing world.

"Karen Walls, from central Texas, started the craze with Shadow Bar," he said. "She bought the 4-year-old gelding in 1966. A year later, while attending Tarleton State College in Stephenville, she became the National Intercollegiate Rodeo Association Southwestern Region Runner-up and was fourth in the national standings. The next year,

Flit Bardot, a 1967 sorrel mare by Flit Bar and out of Spark's Suzy Que, was a Superior reining horse.

she won her region, and was runner-up to the national title.

"She hauled Shadow Bar to the tough West Texas Barrel Racing and Texas Barrel Racing Association (TBRA) events and everyone began to notice him. In 1971 and 1972, they were in the standings of both associations.

"Shadow Bar was a little horse with a gorgeous style. He worked so low in the rear and had such rate that everyone talked about him."

Flit Rose—another great Flit Bar performer—emerged about the same time. Nicknamed "Elmer," the gelding set a track record as a 2-year-old in 1964, and was purchased by C.J. and Sadie Shellenberger of

Gainesville, Tex., as a 5-year-old. Sadie made the TBRA Top 20 on Elmer and then sold him to her niece, Vickie Adams, who made the TBRA Finals two years in a row on him.

Joining the Girls Rodeo Association (now the Women's Pro Rodeo Association) in 1972, Adams won some of the larger rodeos, including Lafayette, La., before retiring Elmer.

Vickie was more familiar than anyone with the Flit Bars. She and her mother, Loraine Shea, lived near the Tylers, and she rode horses for Rebecca. She remembers Flit Bar.

"He was so handsome," she said. "He looked almost just like Sugar Bars. He had a big, kind eye and was easy to handle. He passes that down to his foals. All the studs by him have been easy to handle."

Adams' early exposure to Flit Bar set her focus in the horse world and she would go on to be one of the most prominent individuals to ride, promote and breed Flit Bar horses for the barrel racing world.

Seeing Shadow Bar and Flit Rose spurred Jim and Blevins Gibbs of Valley Mills, Tex., to search for a Flit Bar horse of their own.

In 1970 they went to the source—Rebecca Tyler. The goal was to buy a horse for daughter Jimmie to college rodeo on.

"We had seen several of those horses doing well," Jimmie recalled, "so we went looking for one that was old enough to go ahead and get going. Rebecca had one 5-year-old—Mac's Flit Bar that was broke enough and handled fairly nice."

As Jimmie was trying the sorrel gelding, her mom was looking around at the other horses on the place. A pretty little bay stood saddled in one of the lots.

"Mom fell in love with that little gelding," Jimmie said. "I didn't want an unbroken 3-year-old. My dad and I were trying to get the 5-year-old bought."

Jimmie remembers that she and her father finally asked Rebecca what she'd take for the two horses – mostly to pacify her mom. Rebecca had been asking $1,100 for the older horse and said she'd take $1,500 for both. "The colt only cost us $400 so we went ahead and bought him, too."

That colt's name was Robin Flit Bar but he was better known to the rodeo world as "Billy." He would carry Jimmie into rodeo's history books.

Jimmie and Billy swept their college region for four years and won the NIRA All-Around title in 1974. When she joined the GRA in 1974, she was runner-up for Rookie of the Year. The next year, she won her first world championship, and for the next two years, won more money than any other barrel racer in the Girls Rodeo Association.

Looking back, Jimmie remembers, "The Flit Bars were such athletes. Some had more speed than others but they all worked off their back ends and had such natural rate.

People would see a horse running and recognize it was a Flit Bar."

More and more people were realizing that there was something about the Flit Bar breeding.

The Flit Bars' recognizable low-in-the-rear style of turning a barrel became a trademark, and a woman who never ran barrels herself suddenly had "the" sire for barrel racers.

"My daughter, Robin, liked to run barrels," Rebecca Lockhart recalled. "But her daddy didn't think much about barrel racing. He discouraged the kids from running barrels."

Rebecca's main interest was in raising and breeding but she did have some rodeo ties. She was raised in southern Oklahoma, near

PHOTO BY SPRINGER, COURTESY JIMMIE GIBBS MUNROE

Robin Flit Bar, a 1967 bay gelding by Flit Bar and Robin Hood Price, was one of the first Flit Bars to excel on the pro rodeo circuit. More commonly known as "Billy," the hard-knocking runner carried owner Jimmie Gibbs Munroe, Valley Mills, Tex., to numerous pro rodeo wins.

43

Flit Rose, a 1962 sorrel gelding by Flit Bar and out of Rose Clifton, was an early Flit Bar standout. Nicknamed "Elmer," he carried Vickie Adams, Gainesville, Tex., to an "in the money" run at a 1973 Bridgeport, Tex., rodeo.

Here's Wabena Bar Flit, a 1972 bay mare by Flit Bar and out of Bar X Wabena. The hard-knocking runner, nicknamed "Koochie," took Vickie Adams to the 1977 National Finals Rodeo.

Ryan, and her family exemplified the ranching lifestyle. "My uncles were ranchers. Dad and Granddad were bankers." One of her uncles, Foreman Faulkner, became a world champion steer roper.

So it was exciting when the rodeo world took notice. That happened with increasing regularity, as when Sally Preston bought a "just started" 3-year-old gelding in 1972, Alamosa Flit Bar, nicknamed "Tyler," and went on to win the barrel race at the Fort Worth Stock Show and Rodeo.

Sally also rode Petska's Flit Bar (a younger brother to Billy) owned by Jimmie Gibbs to a third-place finish in the 1976 Texas Barrel Racing Association Futurity against over 100 entries. Second place at that event went to Wabena Bar Flit, nicknamed "Koochie," owned by Vickie Adams and ridden by Celie Whitcomb (Ray).

In 1977, Vickie qualified for the National Finals Rodeo on the bay mare, which became the first 5-year-old to qualify for the NFR.

But with the years of success had come changes to Flit Bar and the Tylers. When the Tylers divorced in the early '70s, George bought Flit Bar from Rebecca and brought him back to Gainesville.

He gave the horse to his daughter, Robin, and in 1974, they sent him to Junior Hudspeth to stand at his ranch in Era, Texas, just south of Gainesville. Extremely arthritic, Flit Bar was a high-maintenance horse. Hudspeth remembered, "George Tyler told me to just take him and keep him until he died and that's what I did."

With Flit Bar on the ranch, Hudspeth had more requests for breeding than he could handle. Rebecca noted, "The barrel racers wouldn't let him alone. Flit Bar could only breed a limited number of horses as he got older, so when people would call, Junior would just turn them down."

One notable turndown came when Vickie Adams called for a breeding. She and her friend, Celie Ray, had made an agreement to breed Slash J Harletta. The mare was a legend herself. She qualified for the NFR in 1971 and produced Ray's other great gelding, I Got

Bar Ours, a 1977 sorrel stallion by Flit Bar and out of Pleasure's Ours, carried Lisa Davis to the NFR.

Here's Ima Etta Too – a 1979 palomino mare by Flit Bar and out of Slash J Harletta – and Celie Whitcomb Ray making a run during the 1983 North Texas Fall Futurity.

Fire Water Flit, a 1978 palomino stallion by Flit Bar and out of Slash J Harletta, founded a barrel racing dynasty. The colorful stallion is shown here with owner Vickie Adams, Gainesville, Tex.

Bugs. Vickie wanted a stallion and Celie wanted a mare.

Rebecca said, "They called to get a breeding and Junior turned them down, so they called me and we had to get Robin to call Junior and tell him he needed to breed their horse!"

The first baby from that bargain was Fire Water Flit, and the second, born in 1979 and part of Flit Bar's last foal crop, was Ima Etta Too

At the Champion of Champions Barrel Futurity and Derby in 1984, Ima Etta Too and Ray won the Futurity. Adams and Fire Water Flit won both goes and the finals to win the Derby.

Hudspeth stood Flit Bar until he was put down in 1979 and the stallion was buried on his farm. He also did his part to perpetuate the Flit Bar legacy by standing one of his notable sons, Flit Bar Beggar.

Lana Merrick rode Scotti Flit Bar, a son of Flit Bar Beggar that Hudspeth raised, to a reserve finish at the Champion of Champions Derby. The good bay won the Fall Lazy E Derby and other derbies in 1986, and went on to qualify for the NFR in 1987 and 1989.

Flit Bar Beggar also sired American Paint Horse Association Reserve World Champion Flit Bar Rambo, who won the San Antonio Barrel Futurity in 1989.

Other Flit Bar sons gained prominence as breeders, too.

Vickie Adams' Fire Water Flit, Flit Bar's most successful siring son, has produced foals that had earned just shy of $1.8 million through 2003. They included Too Much Firewater and Florida Flit, both of whom won more than $100,000, and 2001 AQHA Women's Pro Rodeo Association Horse of the Year and three-time NFR Qualifier, Firewater Fiesta, who won more than $300,000.

Flash N Bar Light, Firewater Fanny, Firewater Bugs, Jigger Of Firewater, Ima Flitty Baby, Fiery Zara and Firewater Surprise each won more than $40,000.

Other outstanding Fire Water Flit get were World Champion Paint Horse, Paint Me Firewater; World Champion Buckskin, Miss Kitty Firewater; AQHA Superior Heading Horse and *Quarter Horse News* Challenge Champion Rowdy Flit; and 2000 and 2003 WPRA Great Lakes Horse of the Year, Circuit Champion and Finals Champion Firewater Fanny.

Dr Nick Bar was born as part of Flit Bar's last foal crop in 1979. He ran the fastest qualifying time at the Fort Smith Futurity as a

3-year-old, and then carried his owner, Fallon Taylor, to the National Finals Rodeo.

He sired Willy Nick Bar, the 1997 World Champion Barrel Futurity Horse and 1998 AQHA World Champion Junior Barrel Horse and earner of more than $100,000.

Dr Nick Bar also sired Christie Nick Bar, Futurity winner and earner of more than $40,000; and Casey Flit Bar, earner of more than $80,000.

Born in 1979, Flit Bars Top Man, owned by Jack and Janie Proffer of Calera, Okla., was the 1987 AQHA World Champion, Youth World Champion and a Superior barrel horse. Before he was gelded, he sired some notable foals, including the flashy Paint, Bold Bars Top Man that Charmayne James rode to the NFR. He was also the sire of Kachina Flit, the 1995 American Buckskin World Champion Amateur Barrel Champion.

Flashy Flit Bar sired Flashy Motor, the 1978 AQHA Junior Barrel Racing World Championship.

The list seems endless, as Flit Bar's battery of get and grand-get helped create the breeding industry for the barrel racing world. Their impact will continue through countless generations.

"Horses are like stars," concluded Kenneth Springer. "Reba McEntire might never have gotten started without Red Steagall. Those Flit Bars might never have been recognized for their talent if not for Karen and Vickie and Jimmie and Celie and some of the others. They recognized the star quality in these horses."

That star quality shone back on them and others who rode Flit Bars, making careers, reaching lifelong goals and fulfilling dreams for generations to come.

PHOTO BY JENNINGS

Firewater Fiesta, a 1994 gray mare by Fire Water Flit and out of Mighty Mindy, has carried owner Kelly Ann Yates, Pueblo, Colo., to more than $500,000 in earnings. In addition, "Fiesta" was the 2000 and 2001 AQHA/WPRA barrel horse of the year.

5 BILLIETTA

As both a performer and producer, she was one of the breed's most colorful characters.

Frank Holmes

PHOTO BY DAROL DICKINSON, COURTESY QUARTER HORSE JOURNAL

Billietta, shown here with Stanley Glover, was a great athlete known for her honest attitude and heart.

BILLIETTA—ONE OF THE BREED'S most enduring characters — achieved fame as both a performer and a producer.

American Quarter Horse Association records list Billietta as a 1958 dun mare by Smutty Bill and out of Frogetta; bred and owned by Guy Hunt of Lincoln, Nebraska. These records are inaccurate on two accounts.

To begin, Billietta was not a dun; she was a golden palomino with a snow white mane and tail. Secondly, although Guy Hunt did register Billietta with the AQHA, he was not her breeder.

That honor belongs to C. G. and Milo Whitcomb of Sterling, Colorado, for it was the Whitcombs — who also bred and raced the legendary Tonto Bars Hank — who made the cross that produced the talented mare.

The Whitcomb Quarter Horse program dates back to the mid-1940s. From the onset, it was designed to produce "Quarter Horses that work, show and win."

"Dad and I were big believers in the all-around halter and performance horse," Milo Whitcomb says, "and that was the type of horse we tried to breed.

"C.F. White of Grand Island, Nebraska, was a contemporary of ours. His main stallion during the mid- to late 1950s was Smutty Bill. We competed against C.F. and his horses, and we liked Smutty Bill enough to breed several mares to him."

In 1957, the Whitcombs hauled a 5-year-old sorrel mare named Frogetta to the court of Smutty Bill. The following spring, Frogetta foaled a bald-faced, stocking-legged palomino filly that was named Billietta.

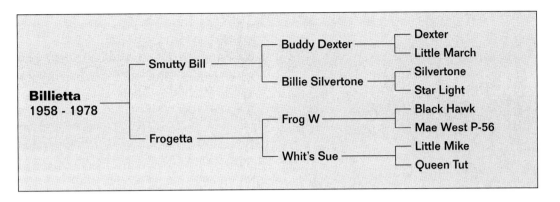

Billietta
1958 - 1978

- Smutty Bill
  - Buddy Dexter
    - Dexter
    - Little March
  - Billie Silvertone
    - Silvertone
    - Star Light
- Frogetta
  - Frog W
    - Black Hawk
    - Mae West P-56
  - Whit's Sue
    - Little Mike
    - Queen Tut

Bred to be Good

If ever a foal had a genetic license to be a top-notch performer, it was Billietta.

Smutty Bill, her sire, was a 1953 R.L. Underwood-bred dun stallion by Buddy Dexter and out of Billie Silvertone. One of the breed's early AQHA Champions, he was the embodiment of what the Underwood program was all about.

Buddy Dexter, Smutty Bill's sire, was a top halter horse, and one of the few horses to defeat Poco Bueno in the show ring. Billie Silvertone, Smutty Bill's dam, was also a top halter horse. Among her many wins was the grand champion mare award at the 1945 Southwestern Exposition and Fat Stock Show in Fort Worth, Texas.

In addition to Smutty Bill, the Buddy Dexter/Billie Silvertone cross resulted in two other noteworthy performers.

Buddy Bill, a 1954 sorrel stallion, was an NFR-caliber calf roping horse. Cutter Bill, a 1955 palomino stallion, was the 1959 AQHA Honor Roll Junior Cutting Horse, and the 1962 NCHA World Champion Cutting Horse and World Champion Cutting Stallion.

The top side of Billietta's pedigree, then, was laden with top performers.

So, too, was the bottom side.

Frogetta, Billietta's dam, was a 1952 sorrel mare by Frog W. and out of Whit's Sue.

Frog W., a 1946 Jack Casement-bred sorrel stallion by Black Hawk and out of Mae West P-56, was the Whitcomb program's cornerstone sire.

"Frog W. was probably our first great performer," Milo Whitcomb says. "We raced him as a 2-year-old and he won 11

Halter and Performance Record:
Performance Register of Merit; AQHA Champion; Superior Reining; Superior Youth Reining; Superior Youth Showmanship.

Progeny Record:

Foals Registered: 5	Performance Point-Earners: 5
AQHA Champions: 1	Performance Points Earned: 229
Halter Point-Earners: 2	Performance Registers of Merit: 2
Halter Points Earned: 20	Superior Performance Awards: 1

races. Then he went on to be a grand champion at halter, a top reining horse, and an NCHA Certificate of Achievement cutting horse."

Frogetta, although unshown, was a full sister to two AQHA Champions — Whitcomb's Frogette and Frog's Croaker.

So, on both sides of her pedigree, Billietta was bred to be good.

COURTESY QUARTER HORSE JOURNAL

Smutty Bill, Billietta's sire, was an AQHA Champion and a multiple AQHA Champion sire.

PHOTO BY JAMES CATHEY, COURTESY WESTERN HORSEMAN

Much of Billietta's early training was handled by 11-year-old Celie Whitcomb of Sterling, Colorado. The talented young horsewoman, who went on to achieve great success as a professional barrel racer, is shown here at age seven on Whitcomb's Frogette.

Partnering Up

In the fall of 1959, Milo Whitcomb was approached with the offer to buy part of his well-bred palomino filly.

"Guy Hunt was an acquaintance of mine from Lincoln, Nebraska," he says. "He had a horse-crazy daughter named Dallas, who had been the 1957 Miss Rodeo America. Guy wanted Billietta to be groomed as Dallas' show mount, but he didn't have the knowledge or experience to do it.

"So he asked to buy a half-interest in the filly. I was to grow her up, break, train and show her a little, and then send her back to Nebraska for Dallas to go on with."

The partnership deal was struck, and Billietta was allowed to remain at the Whitcomb Ranch and grow up naturally through the spring of her 2-year-old year. At that time, she was started under saddle.

"I put the first few rides on Billietta," Milo says, "and she never did give me any trouble. She was intelligent and talented, and she wanted to please you. I just had to show her something one time. Once she understood what it was I wanted, she just

went ahead and did it. And, once she learned something, she never forgot it."

As much as he liked Billietta and enjoyed riding her, Milo was quick to turn her over to someone else to train.

"Our daughter Celie was just eleven at the time," he says. "But she was a great little rider, with the lightest hands imaginable. So, after I had put a half-dozen or so saddles on Billietta, I turned her over to Celie to ride.

"They got along right from the very beginning, and it was Celie who really got the filly going."

With a barn full of outside horses to train and show, Milo Whitcomb did not feel the need to push Billietta. As a 2-, 3- and 4-year-old, she was only shown a handful of times.

AQHA records reveal that, between June of 1960 and January of 1963, she recorded two wins at halter and two wins in western pleasure. Her most prestigious victory came on June 10, 1962, when judge Walter Merrick placed her first in a class of 22 junior western pleasure horses.

By the fall of 1962, 13-year-old Celie Whitcomb and 4-year-old Billietta were a winning combination. In addition to AQHA competition, the two were also consistent winners in open and 4-H competition. It came as quite a shock to the teenager, then, when the decision was made to sell Billietta.

"We never really wanted to part with Billietta," Milo Whitcomb says. "But, we were partners on her, and Guy Hunt wanted to sell his half interest back to us. We agreed that the mare was worth $5,000. But, we had so many horses of our own at the time, that we just couldn't justify giving $2,500 to own all of Billietta. So we sold her to M.L. "Dutch" Watters of Cheraw, Colorado, for $5,000."

That Celie Whitcomb was upset over the sale of her favorite mount was understandable. In an attempt to pacify his daughter, Milo Whitcomb told her that she could have the pick of any of the ranch's coming 2-year-old fillies.

The horse that Celie wound up choosing was Slash J Harletta, a 1961 palomino mare by Harlan and out of Frog's Annette. "Harletta," of course, would go on to become an AQHA Champion, an NFR barrel racing qualifier and one of the most renowned barrel racing producers of all-time.

For Billietta, though, it was on to a new home and an increased presence in the show ring. With Stanley Glover as her new trainer and open rider; and Joyce Watters as her new youth exhibitor, the bald-faced palomino began racking up the wins in earnest.

"The first time I ever saw Billietta," Stanley Glover of Pueblo, Colorado, recalls, "Celie won an AQHA junior reining on her. Celie was 12, and the mare was three.

"I went to work for Dutch Watters in the spring of 1962. Dutch was a rancher. He was big in cattle and bigger in turkeys. He owned Hug Bars — a top Three Bars (TB) son — and he had leased Sir Chance and a bunch of mares from Warren Shoemaker of Watrous, New Mexico.

"Dutch told me he was looking for a mare for his daughter Joyce to show, and I told him about Billietta. So, in the fall of 1962, we went and bought her. I hauled Billietta and Joyce for a couple of years, and we both won a lot on the mare. I can't remember all that we won, but I do recall that we won the senior reining at the 1964 Colorado State Fair in Pueblo and the open western riding at the 1964 New Mexico State Fair in Albuquerque."

In the fall of 1964, Stanley Glover decided to leave the Watters Ranch and open his own training facility at Castle Rock, Colorado. In need of a top mount to show potential customers what he could do, he arranged to lease Billietta from Watters.

"By this time," he says, "Joyce had lost some of her interest in showing. I called Dutch and told him I need a horse to show. I asked if I could haul Billietta and he said, 'Sure; she's just standing around here.'

"So I went and got her and took dead aim on the 1964 winter stock show circuit."

At the National Western Stock Show in Denver, Colorado, Billietta and Glover could manage no more than a 5th in

PHOTO BY DAROL DICKINSON, COURTESY QUARTER HORSE JOURNAL

After being sold as a 4-year-old to Dutch Watters of Cheraw, Colo., Billietta was shown to her AQHA Championship by Stanley Glover.

senior reining.

At the Southwestern Exposition and Fat Stock Show in Fort Worth, Texas, it was a different story.

"At Fort Worth," Glover says, "I showed Billietta in both Palomino and Quarter Horse competition. She was the grand champion palomino mare there and placed second in the senior reining to Lanham Riley and Sword Play.

In those days, they held a $500 palomino reining stakes. They brought back the top three finishers in the junior and senior reining and let 'em run at each other. We won it."

After changing hands in 1966 for the third and final time, Billietta was shown in open competition by Jack Kyle of Santa Rosa, New Mexico. The flashy mare's trademark roan shoulder patch is apparent in this halter shot.

In addition to halter, Kyle also campaigned Billietta in reining, calf roping, heeling, western pleasure and western riding.

Half-way through the 1964 stock show season, Dutch Watters and Warren Shoemaker ended their multiple-year horse leasing arrangement. In the final accounting, Warren got Billietta, an Oldsmobile station wagon and a two-horse, in-line trailer. Luckily for Stanley Glover, it was business as usual as far as Billietta was concerned.

"Warren called me up one day," Glover says, "and told me he was Billietta's new owner. He asked me if I wanted to keep showing her, and I told him I did.

"So then he sold me the station wagon and horse trailer. It was the same rig I'd hauled the mare in when I was working for Dutch. And we just kept going down the road."

In February of 1964, Glover showed Billietta at El Paso, Texas, with great success.

"Billietta won both the senior reining and the western riding at El Paso," he says. "Prior to the show, I had only roped 20 calves off the mare. But it didn't matter to her. She knew what I expected of her, and she just went out and did it.

"We won those two classes at El Paso; placed in several more; and I came away with enough prize money to buy a 4-year-old son of Parker's Trouble named Againu. He went on to be an AQHA Champion and my main herd sire."

Glover continued showing Billietta for Warren Shoemaker in 1964 and 1965. In 1965, the talented mare attained her AQHA Championship.

Then, at the 1965 New Mexico State Fair, the pair had what was arguably their greatest outing.

"We won 11 trophies at Albuquerque," Glover says. "Billietta was the High-Point Quarter Horse; the High-Point Palomino Horse; and the High-Point New Mexico-owned Horse.

"Howard Linger, the AQHA Executive Secretary, was in attendance there. Near the end of the show, I was warming Billietta up in the arena. Mr. Linger called me over to his box and said, 'I've been watching your little palomino mare for several days now. She hasn't made one mistake.

Although a proven champion in open competition, Billietta's primary lot in life was to serve as Jackie Kyle's youth mount. Here is the duo after a show ring victory at the 1967 New Mexico State Fair in Albuquerque. Lee Ross Hammond, president of the New Mexico Quarter Horse Association, presents the trophy.

The team of Billietta and Jackie Kyle was a tough one to beat, in both the youth and open divisions. This classic reining shot, taken during the late 1960s, features the type of sliding stop that was en vogue at the time. Even though Jackie lost her right stirrup early on in the pattern, her ranch training and natural "deep seat" kept her in control throughout the run.

One of the top youth pairs of their day, Billietta and Jackie earned a Superior in youth showmanship.

Skip A Barb, Jack Kyle's AQHA Champion son of Skipper's King and Barbara Star, was the sire of Billietta's first four foals.

I was due to go home two days ago, but I told my wife I had to stay to see if your mare ever messed up. To this point, she just hasn't.'

"I guess that pretty much sums up how I remember Billietta," Glover continues. "She was probably the greatest all-around horse I ever rode. She was so honest; there was no larceny in her whatsoever."

By this time, Billietta was one of the Rocky Mountain region's best-known competitors. As fate would have it, she was destined to change hands once again. This time, however, would be the last.

"Warren called me up in the spring of 1966," Glover says, "and asked me, 'Do you need Billietta to show this year?'

"'A person can always use a mare like Billietta,' I said. 'Why?'

"'Because Jack Kyle's daughter Jackie needs a better horse to show, and I want to make him a deal on Billietta,' he said.

"'Go ahead then,' I said.

"So Jackie Kyle wound up with Billietta, and then those two just went out and smoked 'em."

Changing Places

Like Stanley Glover, Jack Kyle of Yukon, Oklahoma, can remember the first time he laid eyes on Billietta.

"I was at a horse show in Sterling, Colorado, in 1960," the AQHA Hall of Fame horseman recalls. "The Whitcombs had Billietta there and showed her in the 2-year-old-mare class. I had a customer that was looking for a palomino mare, so I went up to Milo and asked if the mare was for sale. The answer was no.

"Once I've seen a good horse though, I never forget it. The next time I saw Billietta was three years later. This time, it was at Walsenburg, Colorado, and Joyce Watters had her in open senior reining there. They won it. But the mare still wasn't for sale."

Several years later, a long-standing friendship and some family ties would come into play to make Billietta available.

"Warren Shoemaker was my wife's uncle," Jack Kyle says, "and it was him who really got me my start as a horse trainer. Throughout the 1950s, he gave me some truly great horses to show; horses like Nugget McCue S, Sailor Cue, Shoemaker's Dude and Show Boy S.

"Training and showing horses of that caliber helped me make a name for myself and resulted in more and better horses to show.

"Warren Shoemaker was a good man. And, not just to me and my family. He was the kind of a man who wanted everyone to succeed, and would generally go out of his way to lend a helping hand.

"In a lifetime of association with Warren though, I can honestly say that the best thing he ever did for me was to sell me Billietta."

The story of how Jack Kyle, and ultimately his daughter Jackie, came to acquire Billietta remains as a living testimony to the type of man that Warren Shoemaker was.

"It was in April of 1966," Jack Kyle recalls. "Warren came to me at a horse show and said, 'Jack, your daughter needs a better horse to ride.'

PHOTO BY KAY, COURTESY JACK KYLE

Billietta Two, a 1972 palomino mare by Skip A Barb and out of Billietta was a winning performance horse and a world champion producer.

"'I know she does,' I said.

"'I'm going to sell you Billietta,' he said.

"'I can't afford her,' I replied.

"'I'll make it so you can,' he said.

"'What'll it take?' I asked.

"'$6,000,' he said, "and I'll let you pay her out. Give me $1,000 down, and the rest whenever you can.'

"'Warren, I'm no closer to owning the mare now than I ever was. I don't have $1,000 to give you.

"'You do now,' he said.

"Then he reached in his pocket, pulled out ten $100 bills and handed them to me.

"'Now, give 'em back,' he said, 'and we've got ourselves a deal.'

"And that's how we came to own Billietta."

PHOTO BY KAY, COURTESY JACK KYLE

Billietta's Jewel, a 1973 sorrel full sister to Billietta Two, was the 1977 AQHA World Champion Junior Heeling Horse and a top producer.

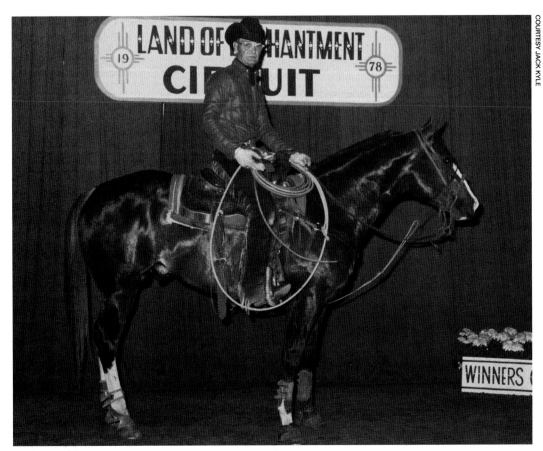

COURTESY JACK KYLE

Skip N Stage, the Kyle Ranch's junior stallion, was the sire of Billietta's fifth and final foal.

Home at Last

Like Celie Whitcomb, who was 12 years her senior, Jackie Kyle had been raised around top-notch horseflesh. Unlike Celie, Jackie's earliest experiences were of a more practical nature

"I was ranch-raised," she says, "and it was a great upbringing. We ran up to 3,500 head of cattle and 100 head of horses on our ranch near Santa Rosa, New Mexico.

"Our horses, whether they were in the show string or not, had to earn their keep. There were no 'box stall babies' or prima donnas back then."

Jackie learned to ride almost before she could walk. A big, black grade gelding with only one speed served as her "break-in" horse. He was replaced in due time with a more capable mount.

"When I was around seven," she recalls, "dad bought me a little grulla gelding named Pay Day. He came off the Navajo reservation, and he was an awesome horse.

"I roped off him, reined off him, and ran barrels and poles off him. I also got bucked and rubbed off him more times than you can imagine. But he taught me how to ride."

By 1966, Jackie Kyle was nine years old and a seasoned hand. Due, in part, to the good will of her great-uncle Warren Shoemaker, she woke up one day and found herself in the possession of one of the country's top show horses. It was a life-altering experience and one that she remembers with deep emotion.

"I was just a little, pig-tailed girl when I got Billietta," she says. "Uncle Warren did ask us $6,000 for Billietta, and that was a lot of money back then. But she was the investment of a lifetime, and she would have been cheap at ten times that price."

Over the course of the next four years, there were no doubt any number of AQHA competitors — both adult and youth — who would wholeheartedly agree with Jackie's assessment of her bald-faced mare.

Whenever and wherever the Kyle trio of Jack, Jackie and Billietta showed up, they were the team to beat.

Jack showed Billietta in the open division — at halter and in reining, calf roping, heeling, western pleasure and western riding. With him in the saddle, Billietta earned a Superior in reining in 1968.

Jackie also showed the mare in the open division, and competed on her in youth — at halter and in showmanship, reining, breakaway roping, western pleasure and western riding. With her in the saddle, Billietta earned Superiors in youth reining and youth showmanship in 1970.

Typical of the type of performance that Billietta could be counted on to turn in was her showing at the 1966 Colorado State Fair. Shown at halter, she was named as the reserve champion mare. Shown in performance, she won the calf roping and western riding, placed second in the senior reining, and fifth in the senior western pleasure.

In June of 1970, Jackie Kyle — then all of 13 years old — showed Billietta at the big Santa Fe, New Mexico AQHA show. Competing in the open division, the duo took first in a class of 10 senior reining horses, first in a class of nine western riding horses, and third in a class of 15 senior western pleasure horses.

At Billietta's last show — the 1970 New Mexico State Fair — the 12-year-old campaigner placed first in a class of 17 western riding horses, and third in a class of 24 senior reining horses.

Billietta's final show tally was one that anyone would be proud to own.

She was an AQHA Champion; a Superior Open and Youth Reining horse; and a Superior Youth Showmanship horse.

In open competition, she had 62 wins and earned 143.5 points in halter, reining, calf roping, western pleasure, working cow horse, heeling and western riding.

In youth competition, she earned nine all-around championships and tallied 49 wins and 135.5 points in halter, showmanship, reining, breakaway roping and western riding.

After the end of the 1970 show season, the decision was made to pull Billietta's shoes off and give her a crack at motherhood.

Sweet And Innocent, a 1978 palomino mare by Skip N Stage and out of Billietta, lived up to her birthright as a top all-around performer.

A Top Producer

Skip A Barb was chosen as the sire of Billietta's first foal. A Hank Wiescamp-bred 1960 sorrel stallion by Skipper's King and out of Barbara Star, he had been purchased by Jack Kyle as a 2-year-old and shown just enough to earn his AQHA Championship. Although still a young horse, he was rapidly developing into a top ranch and show horse sire.

Billietta was bred to Skip A Barb for the first time in 1971. The cross resulted in:

Billietta Two — 1972 palomino mare — open and youth performance point earner. She was also the dam of six performers including Stage Idol — 1982 AQHA Amateur World Champion Reining Horse.

Encouraged by the quality of Billietta Two, her dam was re-bred to Skip A Barb three more times. The crosses resulted in:

Billiettas Jewel — 1973 sorrel mare — 1977 AQHA World Champion Junior Heeling Horse, 1977 AQHA High-Point Steer Roping Horse, AQHA Champion, Superior

Steer Roping Horse. She was also the dam of nine performers including Billy Dun It, NRHA earner of $37,943.

Bill's Skipper — 1974 palomino gelding — open performance point earner.

Smoother Than Silk — 1976 palomino mare — no show or production record.

In 1977, Billietta was bred to Skip'N Stage for what would be her fifth and final foal.

Just as Smutty Bill was a classic example of the R.L. Underwood Quarter Horse program, so was Skip'N Stage the epitome of the Jack Kyle program. A 1974 sorrel stallion by Skip A Barb and out of Flying Stage, Skip N Stage was the 1978 AQHA High-Point Working Cow Horse and Reserve High-Point Steer Roping Horse. An AQHA Champion, he also earned Superiors in heading and heeling.

In addition, at the 1978 AQHA World Show, he finished in a tie for third-place in the inaugural Superhorse competition.

By the fall of 1978 though, Billietta was gone and the Kyles had successfully raised and weaned her last, orphaned, foal.

"Billietta had just turned 20 years old," Jackie Kyle Krshka says. "It was a Sunday night in May and Dad and I had just returned from a horse show. We heard some commotion in the 360-acre pasture by the house.

"We found Billietta on the trail leading to the water trough. She looked like she dropped dead of a heart attack. Sweet And Innocent — her palomino filly by Skip'N Stage — was only about 4 weeks old. It took awhile to find her and, when we did, one of her legs was badly cut up. We put her in a stall, stitched her up, and raised her on a bottle. From that point on, she was part of the family. She trusted us, and she wound up being one of the best."

It was decided at an early age to school Sweet And Innocent for the one show prize that had eluded her sire, and the one that her dam had never even had the chance to vie for — the AQHA Superhorse award.

Trained solely by the Kyle clan, Sweet And Innocent qualified for the 1982 World Show in five events — halter, junior western riding, junior working cowhorse, junior calf roping and junior reining.

She responded by winning the coveted Superhorse title over Reprise Bar, owned by Matlock and Carol Rose; and Whims Niner Baby, owned by E.B. Gee. In addition, and with Tom Krshka in the saddle, she was named as the World Champion Junior Calf Roping Horse.

The event marked the end of Sweet And Innocent's show career. It was a fitting climax to, not only her personal endeavors, but those of her dam as well.

"Great horses, like great men, have great mothers."

This was the motto that AQHA founding father and past president R.L. Underwood had painted on his stallion barn.

Billietta took the Underwood adage, and did it one better.

She was both a great horse and a great mother.

PHOTO BY HAROLD CAMPTON, COURTESY JACK KYLE

Harold Campton

En route to earning the 1982 AQHA World Show Superhorse award, Sweet And Innocent was trained and ridden by Jackie Kyle Krshka, Tom Krshka and Jack Kyle.

6 COY'S BONANZA

After getting his first glimpse at the colt, Bill Coy knew he'd struck a bonanza.

Frank Holmes

PHOTO BY ORREN MIXER, COURTESY BILL MOOMEY

Coy's Bonanza, the 1963 AQHA High-Point Halter Stallion, possessed a "look of eagles" that translated into a dominant show and breeding career.

IT WAS ALMOST A GIVEN – COY'S BONANZA would be a champion show horse and sire. The deck was stacked that heavily in his favor.

He was bred by one of the Rocky Mountain region's great early-day horsemen, and he had impeccable breeding – on both the top and bottom of his pedigree. He was also owned and managed for the better part of his life by one of the top Quarter Horse breeders and promoters of all time.

With all that firepower behind him, how could he have been anything other than a huge hit?

The Coy Legacy

Any in-depth study of Coy's Bonanza must start with his breeder, Bill Coy.

Coy was born into a western Nebraska ranching family in 1922, and spent much of his life as a rancher, rodeo cowboy and horse trainer in the Torrington, Wyo., area. He succumbed to cancer in 1974.

In 1946, at age 24, Coy was one of eight horsemen to found the Rocky Mountain Quarter Horse Association (RMQHA). Several years later, he initiated a ranch- and show-breeding program with the help of several older horsemen.

"When Dad was in his late 20s and early 30s," Joe Coy of Cody, Wyo., recollected, "Jack Casement of Westplains, Colo., and Charley and Elmer Hepler of Carlsbad, N. M., kind of took him under their wing.

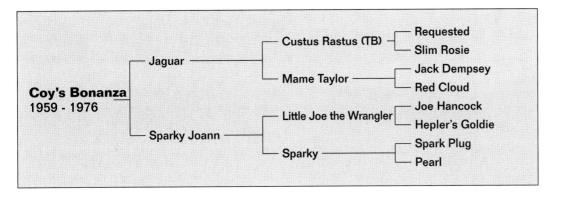

Coy's Bonanza
1959 - 1976

- Jaguar
  - Custus Rastus (TB)
    - Requested
    - Slim Rosie
  - Mame Taylor
    - Jack Dempsey
    - Red Cloud
- Sparky Joann
  - Little Joe the Wrangler
    - Joe Hancock
    - Hepler's Goldie
  - Sparky
    - Spark Plug
    - Pearl

"In the early 1940s, Jack sold Dad some good Red Dog-bred horses. A couple of years later, the two men partnered on a gelding named Black Gnat. Dad trained and showed him, and won the RMQHA all-around performance championship with him in 1948, 1949 and 1950.

"Beginning in the mid-1940s, the Hepler brothers sold Dad some of their best stock. Among them were Little Joe The Wrangler, a top son of Joe Hancock; Sparky, an older foundation broodmare; and Jackie McCue and Little Jackie, two of Sparky's best daughters.

"Those Casement and Hepler horses were the foundation of Dad's breeding program and did a lot to help him and establish Quarter Horses in the area," Joe Coy continued.

Sparky P-748, the cornerstone mare of the Bill Coy program, was a 1936 bay mare by Spark Plug and out of Pearl by Jim Trammel. Bred by J. Frank Norfleet of Hale Center, Texas, she was a three-quarter sister to the famed race mare Panzarita P-747. Sparky and her descendants played a pivotal role in establishing Quarter Horses in the Rocky Mountain region.

Coy trained and rode Little Jackie and Sparky Joann — two Sparky daughters — to championships in the 1954 and 1957 RMQHA Working Stake. Held each summer during the Laramie Jubilee Days in Laramie, Wyo., this grueling event pitted 4-year-old Quarter Horses against each other in five events — calf roping, steer roping, reining, cutting and barrel racing.

In addition, Spade Ace — a Sparky son — and Viv and Little Meow — two Sparky

Halter and Performance Record:
Race Register of Merit; 1963 AQHA High Point Halter Stallion; Superior Halter (154 points); Performance Register of Merit; AQHA Champion.

Progeny Record:

Foal Crops: 16	Performance Point-Earners: 117
Foals Registered: 228	Performance Points Earned: 4,248
AQHA Champions: 26	Performance Registers of Merit: 73
Youth Champions: 5	Superior Performance Awards: 24
Halter Point-Earners: 112	Race Starters: 5
Halter Points Earned: 4,633	Race Money Earned: $2,825
Superior Halter Awards: 23	Race Registers of Merit: 2
Leading Race Money-Earner: Candy Bonanza ($2,012)	

granddaughters — all earned multiple honors at halter, racing and performance.

Of all Sparky's descendants, though, Sparky Joann probably did the most to ensure the perpetuation of Bill Coy's legacy as a top horseman and breeder.

"Joann" wasn't heavily shown. In addition to her big win in the RMQHA Working Stake, the only other high point of her abbreviated show career came at the 1957 Wyoming State Fair in Douglas. There, she was named the reserve grand champion mare (behind Little Meow), placed first in hackamore reining and was part of Little Joe The Wrangler's winning get-of-sire entry and Sparky's winning produce-of-dam entry.

The Douglas show marked the end of Joann's show career, and she was retired to the broodmare band.

For the sire of his champion mare's first foal, Bill Coy chose Jaguar, a 1952 bay stallion by Custus Rastus (TB) and out of

PHOTO BY FRANK FRASCA, COURTESY QUARTER HORSE JOURNAL

Jaguar, "Bonanza's" sire, was a AAA-rated racehorse and an AQHA Champion show horse. Shown here at age 20, he retains the conformation and class that made him one of the more popular sires of his era.

Mame Taylor (see Legends 5). Owned by Ed Honnen of Aurora, Colo., Jaguar was AAA-rated on the tracks, an AQHA Champion and one of the breed's brightest young sires.

Coy hauled Sparky Joann to Honnen's Quincy Farms and the court of Jaguar in the spring of 1958. Back home in Torrington the following spring, she foaled a blaze-faced sorrel colt.

Birth of a Bonanza

After getting his first glimpse of the foal, Coy reportedly ran back to the house and told his wife, Charlene, that he'd "struck a bonanza." The name stuck, and the promising youngster was registered with the AQHA as Coy's Bonanza.

Just like his dam, Coy's Bonanza was lightly shown at first. In fact, his only outing while under the ownership of Bill Coy came in August 1960, at the Wyoming State Fair. There, he placed first in a class of 17 yearling stallions.

The following January, he was consigned to the RMQHA Quarter Horse Sale held in conjunction with the National Western Stock Show and Rodeo. Although not one of the high-sellers, the typey yearling elicited a final bid of $3,950 from Ed Coppola of Des Moines, Iowa.

Coppola initially turned his new acquisition over to Dean and Myrna Landers of Des Moines to be fitted and shown at halter. Exhibited at 20 shows as a 2-year-old, Coy's Bonanza tallied seven grand championships, 10 reserves, 13 firsts and four seconds.

As a 3-year-old, the race-bred stallion was sent to L. R. "Pat" Thompson of Sterling, Colo., to be conditioned for the track. After qualifying for his Register of Merit, the young stallion shin-bucked and was taken off the track to recuperate. In the meantime, Coppola decided to place him back under the care of the Landerses and have him hauled for AQHA high-point halter honors.

The year 1963 was hectic. Between March 16 and December 7, Coy's Bonanza was hauled to 53 shows, amassing 40 grand championships, 13 reserves, 44 firsts and five seconds.

Among his more prestigious victories were grand championships at the American Royal in Kansas City, Kan.; the Illinois State Fair in Springfield; the Nebraska State Fair in Lincoln; and the Arkansas State Fair in Springdale. He also was named reserve champion at the Texas State Fair in Dallas and the Chicago International Livestock Show.

By year-end, he'd earned 110 halter points and that was good enough to secure the 1963 AQHA High-Point Halter Stallion title.

For the first three months of 1964, Bonanza rested. He returned to the show ring in April to post a grand at Albert Lea, Minn., and a reserve at Austin, Minn. In August, he earned a grand at Boone, Iowa.

Coy's Bonanza attracted attention from the time he entered the sale ring at Denver, especially from a man who now stood poised to enter his life and influence it in a positive and permanent way. That man's name was Bill Moomey.

A Man for all Seasons

Moomey—a talented high school and college athlete from York, Neb.—graduated from the University of Nebraska in 1950 with a degree in art history and philosophy. Immediately thereafter, he moved to the Rocky Mountain region to pursue an advanced degree from the University of Colorado at Boulder.

In 1951, he joined the university's staff as an art and industrial design instructor. Two years later, he accepted a position as director of the Denver Art Academy. While with the academy, he organized and became the first president of the Denver Art Directors Club and the International Design Conference in Aspen, Colo.

In 1955, Moomey left the Denver Art Academy to form BMF Studios, a commercial art and motion picture studio. He began producing all of the Coors Brewery Company's advertising and continued doing so until 1961, when he accepted an advertising job with the Joseph Schlitz Brewing Company and moved from Golden, Colo., to Milwaukee, Wis.

Dating back to his high school and college days, Moomey also had been an avid outdoorsman and horse lover. While in Colorado, he combined the two interests by becoming a collegiate rodeo competitor, a state-licensed big-game guide and pack outfitter, and a Quarter Horse breeder.

In pursuit of his rodeo and Quarter Horse endeavors, his path crossed Bill Coy's path.

"As far as the rodeos went," Moomey said, "I was primarily a bareback bronc rider. Coy was a few years older than me, and a better-than-average calf roper and bulldogger. I became acquainted with him at places like Cheyenne and Laramie, and

PHOTO BY JAMES CATHEY, FROM WESTERN HORSEMAN PHOTO ARCHIVES.

Sparky Joann, the dam of Coy's Bonanza, was one of the Rocky Mountain region's top early-day performers. The good-looking mare is shown here with owner/trainer Bill Coy of Torrington, Wyo., at the 1957 Wyoming State Fair in Douglas.

it didn't take me long to realize that he had some pretty good horses.

"I was at Denver the day Bill sold Coy to Eddie Coppola. I liked the colt as well as any horse I'd ever seen, but I wasn't in the position to buy him. I didn't forget about him though."

"Eddie boarded his horses at Landerses' place near Des Moines," Moomey continued. "In the summer of 1964, I called Dean and told him I was interested in buying Coy's Bonanza. He put the deal together for me, and we finalized it in the late fall."

After acquiring Coy's Bonanza, Moomey showed him twice at halter. In November 1964, the big sorrel placed second in a class of 21 aged stallions at the Chicago International Livestock Show.

The following January, he placed second in a class of 22 aged stallions and was named reserve champion stallion at the National Western Stock Show.

With a total of 154 halter points to his credit, Coy's Bonanza was retired from that event and prepared for a performance career.

"Coy's Bonanza was a great athlete," Moomey stated. "Because he was such a dominant halter horse, he was never given a full opportunity to show what he could do under saddle.

"He was bred to run and perform and I wanted him to be an AQHA Champion. With that goal in mind, I sent him to Keith Moon of Rochester, Minn., for reining, western pleasure and western riding training. Keith also started Coy in calf roping, but we never showed him in that event. I could rope a little, though, and I caught enough calves off him to know that he would've made a great rope horse if we'd gone on with him," Moomey concluded.

Shown primarily by Moon, Coy's Bonanza earned his performance Register

In his last appearance in the halter ring, Coy's Bonanza earned honors as the reserve champion stallion at the 1965 National Western Stock Show in Denver, Colo.

of Merit in 1966, and his AQHA Champion status in 1967.

Sandwiched between the two awards was a return trip to the racetrack.

On the Track Again

"In the spring of 1967," Moomey said, "I decided to put Coy back in race training. He was really too old to put on the track, but I knew he'd never really gotten a chance to show how fast he was capable of running the first time around. So I gave him another crack at it.

D. Wayne Lukas, now a famous Thoroughbred trainer, was a high school basketball coach in a small town near Eau Claire, Wis., at the time. He was just beginning to get interested in racehorses, and I sent Coy to him to train.

"We took him to Centennial racetrack in Denver first," Moomey continued. "It proved too hard to get him into any races there, so we headed south to Will Rogers Downs at Claremore, Okla.

"We entered Coy in a 350-yard race there on April 4, 1967, and he won it in the AAA time of :18.13 seconds. That was all I had set out to accomplish with him in the first place, so I retired him."

Having now proved himself as a halter, performance and racehorse, the only challenge left for Coy's Bonanza was to prove his prepotency as a stallion and reproduce himself.

Toward that end, the big sorrel stallion had the good fortune of being owned by Moomey - an extremely savvy horse breeder and marketer.

"When I first got interested in Quarter Horses," Moomey explained, "the King P-234 horses were all the rage. Almost everyone I talked to said, 'If you get in the business, you've got to have a King-bred horse.'

"That any one horse could be that popular made quite an impression on me. Then it occurred to me that there were King-bred horses on virtually every street corner. There were too many of them, and some of them weren't out of the best mares.

After acquiring Coy's Bonanza in the fall of 1964, Bill Moomey of Waukesha, Wisconsin, developed the talented stallion into a AAA AQHA Champion and leading sire.

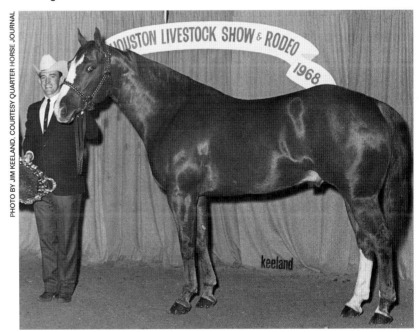

Frosty Bonanza, a 1963 sorrel gelding by Coy's Bonanza and out of Poco Lady Frost, earned 418 halter points. He is shown here after being named as the grand champion gelding at the 1968 Houston Livestock Show & Rodeo. That's well-known NCHA exhibitor Tommy Manion at "Frosty's" head.

Frosty's Brother, a 1968 sorrel stallion, was a full brother to Frosty Bonanza. One of the breed's brightest halter stars, his life was cut short as the result of a freak trailer accident.

"How much better would it have been, I reasoned, if Jess Hankins — King's owner — had limited and controlled both the quality of the mares that King was bred to and the market for the foals that resulted?

"When I bought Coy, I decided from the very beginning that he wouldn't stand to outside mares. He'd be bred only to the best mares that I could lay my hands on. Furthermore, if people wanted to get their hands on his foals, they'd have to come to me first.

"I took a lot of heat for that at first. People thought I was arrogant and too controlling. In the end, though, it worked out like I hoped and most of the criticism died down," he said.

Prior to being purchased by Moomey, Coy's Bonanza had been bred to only a handful of mares. His first foal crop — numbering six — was born in 1962. From it would come Bonanza's Liz, the first of the big stallion's get to become an AQHA Champion.

First Star

Frosty Bonanza, a 1963 sorrel gelding out of Poco Lady Frost, was an Iowa-bred member of Coy's second foal crop. Purchased by Moomey as a yearling, he was promptly developed into Coy's first halter superstar.

"Joe Lindholm of Des Moines bred 'Frosty,'" Moomey said. "I first saw him when I was negotiating to buy Coy. After I got Coy home, I wanted to get my hands on a young show prospect by him. So I went back and bought Frosty.

"He was a stallion when I bought him and one of the best-looking colts you could ever imagine. He was sure good enough to be considered a stud prospect, and I took a lot of heat when I gelded him. But I reasoned that, if he was good enough to show and win as a stallion, he could show and win even more as a gelding.

"And, he did exactly what I wanted him to do. More than any of Coy's early foals, Frosty was the one who put us on the map."

COURTESY QUARTER HORSE JOURNAL

Wrangler Bonanza, a 1967 sorrel stallion by Coy's Bonanza and out of Miss Edsel, was one of the first Moomey-bred Bonanzas to earn an AQHA Championship.

COURTESY QUARTER HORSE JOURNAL

Miss Coysbonanza, a 1967 sorrel mare by Bonanza and out of Warbonnet Fuzzy, was shown by owner Margie Haines of Morrison, Ill., to her AQHA Championship.

PHOTO BY TOM ESLER, COURTESY QUARTER HORSE JOURNAL

Ricky Bonanza, a 1967 sorrel stallion by Coy's Bonanza and out of Rickie Ashwood, was shown by Bill Edmundson of Stewart, Minn., to the 1970 AQHA High-Point Halter Stallion title. "Ricky" was the first of four Bill Moomey-bred sons of Bonanza to earn high-point halter horse awards.

PHOTO BY TOM ESLER, COURTESY QUARTER HORSE JOURNAL

Beau Bonanza, a 1967 stallion out of Dawson Beauty, was the second Coy's Bonanza son to be named an AQHA High-Point Halter Stallion. After achieving that honor in 1971, "Beau" went on to earn additional fame as an AQHA Champion and top sire.

Shown by Moomey, Frosty Bonanza earned 418 halter points, 95 western pleasure points and earned Superiors in both events. He stood grand at virtually every major show in the country, including the National Western Stock Show in Denver, the Southwestern Livestock Show at Fort Worth, the Houston Livestock Show & Rodeo, the Chicago International Livestock Show, and the American Royal at Kansas City, Kan.

Flush with the success of his first Coy's Bonanza show horse, Moomey decided that it would be advantageous to acquire some full siblings to Frosty. With that in mind, he went back to Iowa to purchase Poco Lady Frost.

"I bought 'Lady' from Joe Lindholm in 1966," he said. "When I tracked her down, she was standing in a muddy feedlot. I don't think Joe thought too much of her and, to tell you the truth, she wasn't all that good-looking. But I had the proof of what she could produce, so I bought her."

Bred back to Coy's Bonanza in 1967, Poco Lady Frost foaled a sorrel colt in 1968. Named Frosty's Brother, he was sold to Miles Cooperman of Chicago as a yearling and was turned over to Bill Edmundson to show at halter.

During the first eight months of the year, the pair dominated the AQHA stallion halter scene. "Brother" collected 51 grands, 31 reserves and 158 halter points. Then, in August, he was killed as the result of a freak trailer accident and the breed lost one of its brightest young show-ring stars.

But there were more than enough Coy's Bonanza foals now on the ground to pick up the slack.

Moomey-Bred Bonanzas

The years 1965, 1966 and 1967 marked the arrival of the first of the Moomey-bred Coy's Bonanzas. Those first two crops would produce a host of AQHA Champions and Superior halter and performance horses, including Wells Missie, Pixy's Bonanza,

Roca's Bonanza, Senorita Bonanza, Wrangler Bonanza and Miss Coysbonanza.

From the 1967 crop would also come Ricky Bonanza — Moomey's first home-bred AQHA high-point halter stallion.

Moomey kept the sorrel stallion out of Rickie Ashwood and turned him over to Bill Edmundson to show. In 1970, "Ricky" accumulated 78 grands, 20 reserves and 98 firsts. The 1970 AQHA High-Point Halter Stallion, he earned a total of 370 halter points.

Ricky Bonanza was the first of four Moomey-bred sons of Coy's Bonanza to earn high-point halter honors.

Beau Bonanza, a 1969 sorrel stallion out of Dawson Beauty, was the 1971 AQHA High-Point Halter Stallion; War Leo Bonanza, a 1968 sorrel stallion out of War Leo's Penny, was the 1972 High-Point Halter Stallion; and Mister Bonanza, a 1974 sorrel stallion out of Show Mist, was the 1976 High-Point Halter Stallion.

Throughout the 1970s, Coy's Bonanza's get dominated the industry's halter classes. They earned 23 Superiors in the event, and amassed 4,633 points.

But they were not, by any stretch of the imagination, "one-trick ponies." They were versatile performance horses, as well.

More Than Just a Pretty Face

"From the very beginning," Moomey said, "Coy and his foals were tagged as halter horses. And they were that. They were big, pretty weanlings and yearlings that just cried to be shown and people couldn't wait to get them into the halter ring. But, Coy and his foals were kind, willing horses with plenty of natural athleticism.

"Coy himself was very easy to get along with, and virtually unflappable.

"Just to give you an example, one year I led the big circus parade in Milwaukee, Wis., with him. In the staging area, there were all sorts of distractions; everything from clowns and motor scooters to elephants, lions and tigers. Nothing bothered Coy.

"I also took him to the first All

Although known primarily as halter horses, the Coy's Bonanzas were also talented arena performers. War Leo Bonanza, a 1968 sorrel stallion out of War Leo's Penny, was the 1972 AQHA High-Point Halter Stallion and the 1972 AQHA High-Point Hunter Under Saddle Horse.

American Quarter Horse Congress in Columbus, Ohio. I had him on Stallion Alley there and he was a big draw.

"People wanted to see him outside the stall, so I'd go in and get him. I wouldn't put a halter on him; I'd just lead him out with a twine around his throatlatch. I'd set him up and he'd just stand there like a statue. The crowd would press in all around him, but he still just stood there. He didn't mind the commotion at all.

"If I had it to do all over again," he continued, "I would've stressed that disposition and trainability. I would've put more of Coy's foals in performance training myself, and encouraged the people who bought them to do the same."

PHOTO BY TOM ESLER, COURTESY BILL MOOMEY

Entered in get-of-sire competition, Coy's Bonanza took home the blue at the largest and most prestigious shows in the nation. This mid-1970s entry is made up of Moomey's Bonanza, held by Bill Edmundson; Pixy's Bonanza, held by Bill Moomey; and Ricky Bonanza, held by Tommy Manion.

Encouraged or not, the owners of Coy's Bonanza-bred horses did eventually realize that the horses were athletes. More and more of the family were pointed toward performance careers. They responded by earning 24 Superiors, 71 Registers of Merit and 4,248 points.

Leading the way as members of the Coy's Bonanza performance set were such horses as Major Bonanza, Mi Bonanza, War Leo Bonanza, and Coy's War Leo.

Major Bonanza, a 1972 sorrel stallion out of Manana's Rosa, evolved into one of the Northwest's greatest all-around working horses and sires. (He's profiled in the following chapter.)

Mi Bonanza, a 1974 bay mare out of The Siren Song, was the 1978 AQHA Reserve World Champion Junior Heeling Horse and the 1978 AQHA High-Point Steer Roping Mare. She was also an AQHA Champion and a Superior Steer Roping Horse.

As noted earlier, War Leo Bonanza was the 1972 AQHA High-Point Halter Stallion. That same year, he was also named as the AQHA High-Point Hunter Under Saddle Stallion and the AQHA High-Point Jr. Hunter Under Saddle Horse.

The Look of Eagles

As the late 1970s arrived, Moomey and Coy's Bonanza sat perched at a crossroads.

Coy's Bonanza was one of the best-known and highest-regarded Quarter Horse stallions in the nation. His foals were in demand, and were a threat to win at halter and in performance anywhere they were shown.

By this time, Moomey had a junior stallion in place that he considered a replacement. A decision regarding Coy's future role had to be made.

"In the mid-1970s," Moomey said, "I got my hands on one of the greatest all-around mares I ever owned. Her name was Spice O'Lee and, in addition to being a Superior halter horse, she had 62 performance points in reining, western pleasure, western riding and hunter under saddle.

"I bred 'Spice' to Coy twice. In 1976, she had a filly named Spice O Bonanza. The following year, she had colt named Big Daddy Bonanza. The colt was a classic — a blaze-faced sorrel with that big 'Bonanza' hip and stifle. By the end of the year, I knew he was going to be the horse that I went on with. I decided to turn loose of Coy," he explained.

In early 1976, Moomey sold Coy's Bonanza to Western World Farms, a Kansas City, Mo., syndicate headed by Hank Christopherson. Plans were set in motion to open up the then-19-year-old living legend's book to outside mares. Before the onset of the breeding season, however, the popular stallion died.

"There wasn't a thing wrong with Coy when I delivered him to Missouri," Moomey stressed. "He was in great shape then, and probably was right up until the very end. The way it was told to me, there was no real pain or suffering associated with his death. One minute he was standing there, and the next he dropped dead of an aneurysm.

"I've second-guessed myself a lot about my decision to sell Coy. He was such a dominating presence that I didn't think anyone would take Big Daddy seriously as long as

Coy was physically around. And the Kansas City syndicate really wanted him; they made it pretty hard for me to say no.

"If I had it all to do over, I'd probably just turn Coy out in a nice lot and let him live out his life. When you get right down to it, though, he never really left. He was never transferred from my name, and he never sired another colt. I was spared the discomfort of witnessing his death, and I'm grateful for that.

"Coy's Bonanza was a great horse," he continued. "More than any horse I've ever been connected with, he had a presence, a look of eagles.

"Years ago, I made a promotional film for AQHA. Near the end, I spliced some footage of Coy galloping free in a lush, hilly pasture. At the very end, Coy froze. He stood so still that most viewers thought I'd frozen the last frame.

"Then, after several seconds that seemed to last for an eternity, he blinked. At that point, most of the people who ever viewed the film in my presence would let out a gasp.

"Coy's Bonanza was that kind of horse. He'd take your breath away."

COURTESY QUARTER HORSE JOURNAL

Here's one of the last photos ever taken of Coy's Bonanza. Even at age 19, the big sorrel stallion possessed a heart-stopping presence that was uniquely his own.

7 MAJOR BONANZA

Good-looking and talented, he changed the look of the contemporary performance horse.

Juli S. Thorson

A pretty horse himself, Major Bonanza has been credited with "prettying up" the contemporary performance horse.

MAJOR BONANZA'S STORY could begin with the words "once upon a time," for it has elements of a fairy tale — the kind with a happy ending.

At 12 hours old, the 1972 chestnut was purchased sight unseen by Andy and Carol Rees, a starry-eyed young couple who owned (or co-owned) him for the rest of his life. Sired by a stallion best known for achievements in the halter arena, he excelled not just in halter but also two totally disparate performance events — working cow horse and western pleasure.

He also put now-renowned trainer Bob Avila on the path to superstardom. He ranked as a leading sire for almost a decade, with 271 performing foals and winners of 15 AQHA open, youth or amateur world championships to his credit.

"'Major' was the real thing," states Christy Avila, Bob's former spouse and the person who showed the horse in western and English pleasure during most of his show career. "He really could go out and impress the hell out of you. Everywhere he went, he caused a stir. He was gorgeous as a halter horse and equally gorgeous when he worked a cow — which nobody could believe, since he was by a stallion that wasn't cow-horse-bred.

"He made a statement with everything he did," Christy continues. "There was no gray area — you either liked him or you didn't. He had to fight to be accepted in any world he went in. He wasn't a big horse, for instance, barely 15 hands, but he was Superior at halter and sired a lot of halter

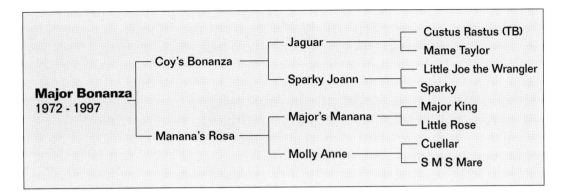

Major Bonanza
1972 - 1997

- Coy's Bonanza
  - Jaguar
    - Custus Rastus (TB)
    - Mame Taylor
  - Sparky Joann
    - Little Joe the Wrangler
    - Sparky
- Manana's Rosa
  - Major's Manana
    - Major King
    - Little Rose
  - Molly Anne
    - Cuellar
    - S M S Mare

champions. He wasn't bred with cattle events in mind, but he could eat your lunch if you showed against him in working cow horse. He didn't always draw the most elite of mares, but he sired horses that could do everything.

"He made a lot of people eat their words."

Not an Ugly Duckling

Major Bonanza, bred to be pretty, correct and versatile, lived up to that legacy and passed it on.

His sire, Coy's Bonanza (featured in Chapter 6), earned a Superior rating at halter and was the 1963 AQHA High-Point Halter Stallion. In addition, he was AAA on the track and an AQHA Champion. Major Bonanza's dam, Manana's Rosa, also earned a Superior at halter and was an AQHA Champion.

By the time the Reeses came into the picture in the early 1970s, as 25-year-olds living in Langley, B.C., Coy's Bonanza had achieved considerable fame, primarily as a halter sire. He was owned by Bill Moomey of Waukesha, Wis., and as Andy tells it, Moomey was one sharp cookie when it came to sales and quality control.

"Bill didn't stand Coy's Bonanza to outside mares at that time," he explains. "He had his own band of broodmares, and the only way you could get a Coy's Bonanza baby was to buy one out of one of those mares. Basically, you had to put in an order with a deposit and be on a waiting list. When a mare had a foal

Halter and Performance Record:
Performance Register of Merit; Superior Halter (86 points); AQHA Champion; 1977 High-Point Working Cow Horse Stallion; Superior Western Pleasure.

Progeny Record:

Foal Crops: 24	Performance Point-Earners: 304
Foals Registered: 786	Performance Points Earned: 8,108.5
AQHA Champions: 10	Performance Registers of Merit: 143
Youth Champions: 1	Superior Performance Awards: 41
Halter Point-Earners: 96	World Champions: 11
Halter Points Earned: 1,206	High Point Winners: 1
Superior Halter Awards: 7	

PHOTO BY DAROL DICKINSON

Coy's Bonanza, Major's sire, was the 1963 AQHA High-Point Halter Stallion.

Sparky Joann, Major's paternal granddam, was a top arena performer. She is shown here with owner/trainer Bill Coy after winning the 1957 Rocky Mountain Quarter Horse Association's All-Around Stake at Laramie, Wyoming. That's rodeo great Shoat Webster presenting Coy with the trophy saddle.

that matched your order, you'd get a phone call telling you to make up your mind, yes or no, right then and there.

"Carol and I had this big dream of owning and standing our own stallion, and that's how we ended up with Major. He was 12 hours old when we got the call from Bill, saying that Manana's Rosa had had a stud colt. I didn't actually see him in person until he was about 6 weeks old. I was prejudiced, of course, but I thought he was the prettiest colt on Bill's place."

Carol had to wait until the colt was weaned at 5 months and shipped to Canada before she could lay eyes on him. Her first impression was that he was proud, arrogant and very cocky.

"He was the kind of baby who'd go right up to you and tell you how good he was," she recalls. "He knew he was great."

Judges agreed. The Reeses began showing their prize at halter soon after taking possession of him and he was a winner from the start. He claimed numerous futurity

titles and grand championships on his way to joining his sire and dam as a Superior halter horse. He bred his first mares at 2 while continuing to be one of the horses to beat on the Pacific Northwest Quarter Horse circuit.

By the time Major Bonanza was 3, Andy had started him under saddle and shown him in a few western pleasure classes. That's when the Reeses and their horse hooked up with Bob Avila, who in 1975 was an up-and-coming trainer based in Yamhill, Ore.

"Andy approached me about training Major for cutting, which was his favorite event," Bob remembers. "I was pretty skeptical, to tell you the truth, because the Coy's Bonanzas weren't known to be cutters, but I agreed to take the horse home and try him. I got him after his 3-year-old breeding season and spent that fall and the following winter finishing getting him broke and seeing what he could do."

As it turned out, Major Bonanza could do a lot. The Avilas showed him in all-

PHOTO BY JAMES CATHEY. COURTESY QUARTER HORSE JOURNAL

Major Bonanza was also cow-bred on the bottom side of his pedigree. Major King, his maternal great-grandsire, was one of the breed's top early day cutting horses.

around competition, earning his performance Register of Merit and finishing his halter Superior in 1976. In 1977, he earned his AQHA Champion title, placed sixth at the World Show in working cow horse, and was the nation's high-point working cow horse stallion. The next year, he repeated his top-10 World Show finish in working cow horse and became a Superior western pleasure horse to boot.

"He was incredible to ride, just a great individual," says Bob. "He could do some wild stuff, right up there with the best athletes. When he got beat at halter, it was usually because of his size — but after judges saw what he could do as a performance horse, he won even more at halter than he did earlier. They came to appreciate what he could do."

Still, the horse's aptitude for working cattle surprised everyone, including Bob.

"No one could believe a halter horse could work the way he did, and at first, I wasn't sure I could believe it, either," he says. "But Major had so much ability, not just in reading and holding cattle but in stopping and turning them, too. That's why I ended up showing him so much in the cow horse classes. Plus, he had a great mother who was bred to work and did. People tended to overlook that just because his sire was so better known."

According to Christy, much of Major Bonanza's success as a show horse came from a trait that went beyond raw physical talent.

"Major was a trainable horse," she explains. "He wasn't conventional, to say the least, and he definitely had a mind of his own. If he got loose, for instance, you weren't going to catch him until he decided he was ready to be caught. But he was willing to learn and wanted to please, and if you gave him enough room to just be the horse he was, he would work his heart out.

"I loved Major," Christy adds. "Besides being a winner himself and a sire of winners later on, he was a unique character."

COURTESY QUARTER HORSE JOURNAL

Major Investment, a 1977 sorrel stallion by Major Bonanza and out of Rags Dandy, was his sire's first AQHA world champion.

PHOTO BY HAROLD CAMPTON, COURTESY QUARTER HORSE JOURNAL

Trained and ridden by Bob Avila, Major Investment was the 1981 World Champion Junior Cutting Horse and Reserve World Champion Junior Reining Horse.

All the King's Children

Major Bonanza's show career concluded in 1980. By that time, the Reeses had left Canada to build a home and breeding center a mile or so away from the Avilas' training operation in Oregon. As the two couples began to have and raise families, they also oversaw the raising, training and showing of the Major Bonanza family — one that totaled 786 foals in 24 crops and earned nearly $300,000 in show-ring prize money.

Major Investment, a sorrel stallion from his sire's third crop, got people's attention with his versatile performances at the 1981 AQHA World Show. Besides winning the junior cutting for Bob's first world championship, he also was reserve world champion in junior reining, placed third in junior western pleasure and was a runner-up for the show's Superhorse title.

"Even then," says Bob, "it was unusual for a horse to do that well in three such different events. People from other parts of the country, who hadn't seen Major show up in the Northwest, got interested in Major Bonanza as a sire after seeing Major Investment."

That interest grew after Bob won the junior cutting world championship again in 1982, this time on a Major Bonanza son named The Major Leaguer.

"That's when Major's career at stud went into high gear," the trainer notes.

That's something of an understatement. In the era before shipped semen could be used for breeding, Major Bonanza attracted enough mares to his court in western Oregon to be the sole source of income for the Reeses. In his 1983 crop alone, for example, he sired 102 AQHA foals.

Besides being popular with mare owners, he also drew an offer of $500,000 for half ownership from Alberta resident Gordy MacDonald. With their three children's future education needs in mind, the Reeses accepted. Major Bonanza spent his 1989 through '92 breeding seasons in Alberta, returning to Oregon and proximity to his original family in 1993.

The stallion's first two world champions were followed by others in events ranging from reining and working cow horse to western riding, roping and trail — "more events than any other sire in Quarter Horse history," notes Andy.

One of Major Bonanza's world champions, the 1983 sorrel gelding Boots Valentine, is remembered fondly by Steve Metcalf of Pilot Point, Texas. The trainer won the senior working cow horse title on him in 1990 and the senior reining title in 1991; Boots Valentine also won the 1990 youth world championship in working cow horse, was the 1992 reserve world amateur champion in that event, and claimed the 1994 national high-point title in reining.

"Boots Valentine was by far the greatest horse I ever rode," Metcalf states. "He was the easiest horse I ever rode, too. You'd show him how to do something once, and by the next day, it was in place — it didn't take a hundred repetitions before he understood what you wanted him to do. He was what we all dream of having, a horse whose mental ability was as great, or greater, than his physical ability."

According to Metcalf, who rode "quite a few of them," Major Bonanza's get had a number of traits in common.

PHOTO BY HAROLD CAMPTON, COURTESY STEVE METCALF

Boots Valentine, a 1983 sorrel gelding by Major Bonanza and out of Beauty Valentine, was another gifted performer.

PHOTO BY HAROLD CAMPTON, COURTESY STEVE METCALF

At the 1991 AQHA World Championship Show, "Boots" and Trainer Steve Metcalf teamed up to win the senior reining title.

COURTESY STEVE METCALF

Countryboy Bonanza, a 1978 chestnut gelding by "Major" and out of Pima's 'Gal, earned a Superior award in reining. That's Carol Carter up on the talented performer in this nice action shot.

Leaguerette, a 1987 sorrel mare by Major Bonanza and out of Cowboys Hi Dandy, was a top AQHA and NRHA reining competitor.

"They were pretty, good lead changers, big stoppers, and could do a lot of stuff," he says. "Whether you loved Major Bonanza himself or not, you had to respect him as a sire. We've all known studs that got better mares and didn't produce what he did."

Carol comments on the caliber of mares that came to her stallion's court.

"Major attracted great, proven mares from some of the biggest breeders, but it was people just like us — starting out with almost nothing except their focus and their dreams — that 'made' Major as a sire. So many of his best winning foals were bred by people who came to him with their one good mare, and pinned everything against that baby. Major made a lot of people's dreams come true, not just ours."

Among the many standouts from Major Bonanza's get list were such horses as these:

· Majors Silver Miss, 1985 Youth World Champion Western Riding, 1985 World Champion Junior Western Riding.
· Dust My Tucker, 1989 World Champion Junior Working Cow Horse.
· Cross Over Hannah, 1991 World Champion Junior Heeling, 1991 World Champion Junior Heading.
· Requested Major, 1993 Amateur World Champion Western Riding, 1995 World Champion Western Riding, 1996 World Champion Western Riding.
· Sgt Pepper, 1998 World Champion Senior Trail, 1998 Amateur World Champion Trail.

The stallion also sired 10 AQHA Champions, with the first, Whisper Bonanza, foaled in his second crop. As a sire of National Reining Horse Association competitors, he was a force to be reckoned with as well. At the end of 2003, 6 years after his death, he still ranked 15th on NRHA's top-20 leading sires list.

Major Bonanza's winning influence continued to the next generation. He was the maternal grandsire, for instance, of Hyline Billy Jack, AQHA's 1987 world champion in junior trail; Major Intuition, 1991 world champion in junior western riding; Zans Diamond Bonanza, 1995's high-point youth reining horse; and Major Sno Chex, 1998 world champion in junior reining.

Beauty and the Beasts

From the perspective of time's passage, Christy and Bob Avila both believe that Major Bonanza was largely responsible for changing the looks of contemporary performance horses.

"He prettied them up," she says, citing the lovely reining mare Leaguerette as an example. A full sister to The Major Leaguer, she was known to draw audible gasps of "wow, what a gorgeous horse!" from spectators the moment she walked into a show pen.

Bob elaborates.

"Before Major's day, we only expected halter horses to be pretty — it didn't really matter what a performance horse looked like as long as he could do the job. Once the Major Bonanza bloodline came along, that changed. Everyone loves a pretty horse, and judges are no exception. That gave the Major Bonanzas an edge. After a while, the performance breeders had no choice but to pretty up the horses they raised.

"I think that's Major's biggest legacy."

Major Bonanza died of colic in 1997, at age 25. His last 20 foals were born in 1998.

PHOTO BY HAROLD CAMPTON

Bob Avila built much of his fame as a trainer with the get and grand-get of Major Bonanza. In 1991, he rode Major Intuition to a world championship in junior western riding. The 1987 sorrel gelding was by George's Tonto and out of Whisper Bonanza by Major Bonanza.

PHOTO BY DON SHUGART, COURTESY QUARTER HORSE JOURNAL

Major Bonanza was endowed with both athletic ability and eye-catching good looks. He was able to capitalize on both attributes to found one of the Northwest's great Quarter Horse lines.

8 DOC QUIXOTE

He was known as the "Good Luck Sire."

Glory Ann Kurtz

"DOC QUIXOTE MADE MONEY for everyone that had anything to do with him," Pat Fitzgerald said.

And Fitzgerald should know. The Paoli, Okla., horseman purchased the legendary cutting stallion in 1989 and owned him until he died.

"I gave $75,000 for Doc Quixote," he continued. "He was 19 at the time, and no one was sure he would ever breed again. But he made enough money for me to pay for my place."

And Fitzgerald wasn't the only person who made money on Doc Quixote, the stallion a lot of people called the "Good Luck Sire."

Don Crumpler, Wichita Falls, Tex., paid $12,000 for the stallion in 1973 and won the National Cutting Horse Association (NCHA) Non-Pro Futurity on him. Then, in 1977, he made him the first cutting stallion to be syndicated and parlayed his initial investment into millions.

Doc Quixote, a son of Doc Bar, was nicknamed the "Good Luck Sire," because he seemed to make money for everyone who had anything to do with him.

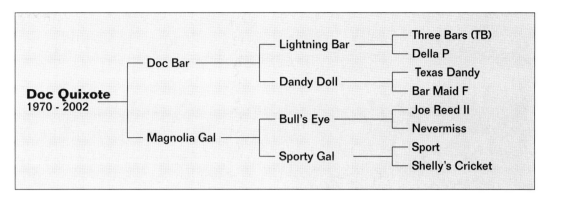

			Three Bars (TB)
Doc Bar	Lightning Bar		Della P
	Dandy Doll		Texas Dandy
Doc Quixote			Bar Maid F
1970 - 2002			Joe Reed II
Magnolia Gal	Bull's Eye		Nevermiss
	Sporty Gal		Sport
			Shelly's Cricket

In the Beginning

Doc Quixote, a 1970 bay stallion by Doc Bar and out of Magnolia Gal, was bred by Yvonne LeMaitre of Woodland, Calif. LeMaitre was a friend of the renowned West Coast horseman Charley Araujo, who owned Doc Bar at the time.

When the cross was made, Doc Bar—a 1956 sorrel stallion by Lightning Bar and out of Dandy Doll—was still known primarily as a halter horse sire.

Halter and Performance Record:
NCHA earnings of $3,728; 1973 NCHA Non-Pro Cutting Futurity—1st Place.

Progeny Record:

Foal Crops: 23	Performance ROMs: 85
Foals Registered: 1,032	Superior Performance Awards: 21
Halter Point-Earners: 6	World Champions: 0
Halter Points Earned: 27.5	High-Point Winners: 1
Performance Point-Earners: 270	NCHA Earnings: $9,247,994
Performance Points Earned: 4,016.5	

Don Crumpler and Doc Quixote won the 1973 NCHA Non-Pro Futurity, even though the stallion had a quarter crack in his hoof. He was shown very little after his Futurity win.

Doc Okie Quixote, with lifetime earnings of $638,000, was the NCHA Triple Crown Champion with owner Joe Heim in the saddle. The Triple Crown consisted of the championship of the 1983 NCHA Futurity and 1984 NCHA Derby and Super Stakes. The 1980 stallion died in 1986 following colic surgery.

Poco Quixote Rio, sired by Doc Quixote, is the high money-earning cutting horse of all time, winning $1 million at the Gold & Silver. The gelding is shown at the 1987 The Masters, with Bill Riddle in the saddle.

Beginning in the early 1970s, that would all change and the flashy ex-halter champion would go on to revolutionize the cutting horse industry.

Magnolia Gal, Doc Quixote's dam, was a 1953 bay mare by Bull's Eye and out of Sporty Gal by Sport.

Doc Quixote was speed-bred on both the top and bottom of his pedigree, and his stream-lined, athletic build showed it.

When Doc Quixote was three weeks old, he was purchased by Neil and Linda Mussallem, Gilroy, Calif., as a halter prospect. After the bay colt was weaned, he was taken to Morgan Hill, a Thoroughbred farm, and that's where he spent the first year of his life.

"He was so undisciplined, spoiled and unruly that when we unloaded him, the people at the farm couldn't believe he acted like that," Linda said. "He wouldn't even walk through a mud puddle — he'd just throw a fit.

"Neil took him to his first halter class, and it was like the clown and the puppy dog. He was all dressed up with his Western shirt with pearl buttons, but the colt was acting awful. I was afraid Neil was going to get hurt.

"Needless to say, he didn't win the class, but after that, we had a professional trainer, Russ Franklin, show him at Denver and he did pretty good with him."

The Mussallems were among the first lifetime members of the California

PHOTO BY PAT HALL

Cash Quixote Rio, a member of the NCHA Hall Of Fame, has lifetime earnings of over $604,700. The stallion was the 1990 and 1992 NCHA World Champion, owned by Heiligbrodt & Wood, ridden by Kobie Wood.

Reined Cow Horse Association, and they were starting to get involved in the performance horse industry, so they decided to send Doc Quixote to Leon Harrel, a top performance horse trainer who lived in Oakdale, Calif. Their goal was to have Doc Quixote show in the big NCHA Futurity, held annually in Fort Worth, Texas.

At the time, Harrel owned half interest in another son of Doc Bar named Nu Bar. According to Linda and Leon, as far as their cutting abilities were concerned, the two half-brothers were running "neck-and-neck."

"We were pretty ignorant about the cutting horse industry at the time," Linda said. "But we did know that, at the time, a trainer could only ride one horse in the Futurity. Since Leon owned

half of Nu Bar, we were sure that one horse would be Nu Bar."

So the Mussallems decided to sell Doc Quixote.

"If I hadn't owned half of Nu Bar, I would have bought Doc Quixote in a minute," Harrel said. "But since I already owned a son of Doc Bar, I put the word out that he was for sale."

One of the interested buyers was Paul Crumpler, Wichita Falls, Tex.

"I had a son of Doc Bar that Buster Welch was riding for me," Crumpler said, "and we went to the pre-Futurity works in Sweetwater, Texas. But I didn't like what I saw, so I decided to sell him and get a different one.

"I went up and sat with Shorty Freeman in the stands and told him that I was looking for another Doc Bar

Jazzote, a gelding owned and shown by George Glover, was the 1986 NCHA World Champion ridden by Sonny Rice. He was also ridden by Glover to the 1984 and 1985 NCHA Non-Pro World Championships. He is shown winning The Masters, where he won both the Open and Non-Pro divisions.

stud. I asked if he knew where I might find one."

"Shorty told me about Doc Quixote, so I hopped a plane and flew to California to check him out. I really liked him, but they were asking $12,000 for him and that seemed like a lot of money at the time."

However, Crumpler told Harrel not to sell the stallion to anyone else and just give him a little time to think. Every two or three weeks, Crumpler would give Harrel a call and ask how the colt was doing. But it wasn't long before Harrel was on the phone to Crumpler, telling him there were some other interested parties.

"I knew he was a big-time horse," Harrel said. "At the time, I was riding eight or nine Doc Bars, and he was as good as any of them.

Among the other people who had expressed an interest in "Quixote" was Gene Suiter of Los Olivos, California. When Suiter expressed a desire to come look at the stallion, Leon told him that Crumpler had first shot at the horse.

"You need to ask Paul if he does or doesn't want him," Suiter said, "because I'm interested"

Harrel called Crumpler and said "Time's up."

In April of his 3-year-old year, Doc Quixote was purchased by Paul Crumpler.

"The first thing he did was get a quarter crack in his hoof," Crumpler said. "But by September, he was sound. So I had Buster and Shorty prepare him for me to ride in the NCHA Non-Pro Futurity that fall."

Crumpler and Doc Quixote won the 1973 Non-Pro Futurity, pocketing $1,008 after marking 218.5 while showing against 19 other finalists. A total of 56 non-pros had entered the competition and the reserve champion was another son of Doc Bar, Doc Tari, owned and ridden by Dick Gaines. The winner of the open division, Doc's Marmoset, was also a Doc Bar daughter, ridden by Tom Lyons.

"I'm famous for not riding horses after the Futurity," Crumpler added. "I just like the aged events; I'm not a weekend person."

Because of Quixote's quarter crack and Crumpler's lack of interest in showing at weekend shows, the talented stallion was not ridden again for two years.

In 1976, Shorty and Crumpler got together and decided that Shorty would take Doc Quixote to Arizona and get him in shape to cut.

"Shorty got him ready and called me one day to say Quixote was ready to show," Crumpler said.

The duo's first show was the prestigious King Ranch cutting, They won both go-rounds and the finals on him, and the next day headed to the Wilson Ranch in Brenham, Tex., where they finished third.

That was the last time that Doc Quixote was shown. His career as a sire was about to begin.

Doc Quixote the Sire

In 1973, 11 mares were bred to Doc Quixote, and eight of the 11 offspring were entered in the 1977 NCHA Futurity. It was then that Crumpler knew he not only had a cutting horse, he had a sire.

Five of the eight left the Futurity with paychecks, with Crumpler splitting the Non-Pro Championship riding Chickasha Ann Doc. Spencer Harden was third on Doc's Wimpy and Lex Graham was eighth on Quixote Kitty. Doc's Wimpy also made the semifinals in the open division, as did Major Quixote and Chickasha Quixote.

Doc Quixote was such a hit that Crumpler took the advice of some friends and syndicated the stallion, making him the first cutting stallion to be syndicated. He offered 50 shares in Doc Quixote, selling 20 shares right away at $5,000 apiece, giving the buyers two years to pay for them at no interest. According to Crumpler, the

PHOTO BY FRED MILLER

Jazabell Quixote, a daughter of Doc Quixote, was not only a great performer but also one of the leading dams in the cutting horse industry. Ridden by her owner, non-pro Spencer Harden, she won the 1982 NCHA Non-Pro Futurity and finished 11th in the open. She won a total of $229,000 but is the dam of earners of $1.2 million.

last shares sold commanded a $30,000 price tag.

The pioneers investing in the syndicate included Jim Reno, Yvonne LeMaitre, Frank Richards, Bobby Shelton, Bob Sims, Gene Spaldings, Bill Talley, Spencer Harden, Joe Heim, Brent Layton, Dan Pearson, Rick and Janet Bellwood, Mike McBride, Dick Thompson, Boyd Summerhays, Lou Waters, Dave Brown, Denny Andrews, Don and Laney Crawford, John B. Connally, Richard Pope, Rod Edwards, Shorty Freeman, Dennis Funderburgh, Thad Gilliam and Jerry Dickson. Doc Quixote was moved to the breeding facilities of the B.F. Phillips Ranch in Frisco, Texas.

However, he wasn't there long. In 1982, the newly formed Super Syndicate purchased Doc Quixote and the shares issued in 1977 increased substantially in value. According to one source, the stallion brought a whopping $6 million.

"The last seven shares that I owned were purchased by Don Crawford for $700,000," Crumpler said.

The Super Syndicate was formed in 1981 by Robert Shelton, Crumpler, Possum Elenburg, Shorty Freeman, Dick Gaines, Don Parker, Jim Reno and Bud Sweazea.

Originally, the syndicate offered breeding rights to seven stallions, including Doc Quixote, Doc Athena, Doc's Hickory,

Doc's Lynx, Doc Tari, Leonard Milligan, Smokin Jose, Especial and Nu Bar.

The Super Syndicate made it possible to have the Gold & Silver—the first $1 million cutting. It was ultimately won by Poco Quixote Rio, a Doc Quixote gelding ridden by Bill Riddle.

The shareholders who had purchased shares in Doc Quixote for $5,000, saw their investment grow to $100,000 per share, while Crumpler's $12,000 investment had now parlayed into millions. Doc Quixote was now standing at the Shelton Ranch in Kerrville, Tex.

At the time the Super Syndicate negotiations were completed in 1981, Crumpler and his wife, Barbara, were weathering severe land and cattle losses; however, the money they got for their seven remaining shares lightened their financial burden and enabled them to buy into the Super Syndicate.

But Doc Quixote helped them even more. The following year, Crumpler had a horse sale, which pulled him completely out of debt.

In the July 13, 1982, issue of *Quarter Horse News,* the sale made the front page of Section B. The sale grossed more than $2.3 million, for a $21,335 average, and included more than 100 horses owned by Crumpler and 16 horses consigned by 11 guest consignors. The sale included many Doc Quixote offspring and several mares bred to him.

Doc Quixote's offspring continued to make him one of the most popular stallions.

While Crumpler still owned Doc Quixote, he bred a mare for Joice Heim of Thackerville, Okla. Even though Joice didn't have the money at the time, Crumple told her not to worry about it; that she could pay him later.

The mare that Joice bred to Quixote was Jimmette Too, and the mating resulted in Docs Okie Quixote, winner of the NCHA Triple Crown Championship. That title meant that the horse won the 1983 NCHA Futurity, and the 1984 NCHA Derby and Super Stakes. The stal-lion was also a finalist in the 1984 Gold & Silver Stakes, and earned close to $638,000 before his untimely death on Jan. 12, 1986, following colic surgery.

"I think that if Docs Okie Quixote would have lived, he would have been another Smart Little Lena," Fitzgerald said.

Topping Doc's Quixote's list of money-earning offspring was Poco Quixote Rio, the aforementioned Gold & Silver Cutting champion and recipient of the only $1 million paycheck ever paid in the cutting industry. His lifetime earn-ings amounted to $1,108,700

NCHA Hall of Fame inductee Cash Quixote Rio—the 1990 and 1992 NCHA Open World Champion Cutting Horse—won $604,742; and Jazzote took George Glover to the 1985 NCHA Non-Pro World Championship and then won the 1986 Open NCHA World Championship title with Sonny Rice in the saddle. His earn-ings totaled more than $586,000.

Laney Doc won $245,310 as Reserve Champion of the 1986 NCHA Derby and finished third at the 1986 Gold & Silver; and Docs Tivito won $234,043, including the Reserve Championship of the 1984 Non-Pro Futurity and the Championship of the 1985 Non-Pro Gold & Silver.

Jazabell Quixote collected more than $229,000, won the 1982 NCHA Non-Pro Futurity, tied for 11th in the Open Division and tied for second in the 1983 Non-Pro Derby and the 1983 Super Stakes. She also finished third in the Open Division of the 1983 Gold & Silver.

Betcha Moola earned $217,300, and was a finalist in the Open and Non-Pro divisions of the 1985 NCHA Futurity and the 1986 Super Stakes, as the co-champion in the Non-Pro Division of the 1986 Gold & Silver Stakes.

Miss Quixote Sails was a finalist in the 1986 NCHA Futurity, finished third in the 1987 NCHA Derby and won more than $189,600.

The list goes on and on, with 21 off-spring winning over $100,000, and sever-al of them are well-known stallions themselves, such as Docs Okie Quixote,

Cash Quixote Rio, Docs Tivito, Oh Cay Quixote, Holidoc, Captian Quixote, Alotofote and the World Champion Quixote Mac.

Super Syndicate Sells Doc Quixote

In 1988, the Super Syndicate started having cash flow problems due to the death of Doc's Lynx, in March 1985. The syndicate had purchased two new stallions to replace him, but the insurance company had not paid out on the $800,000 policy. Also, the resident veterinarian at the Shelton Ranch sent out a letter dated Feb. 11, 1988, to all the syndicate shareholders regarding Doc Quixote's semen production, stating that his quality had declined and until they came up with a solution, shareholders were requested to not send any mares to him to be bred.

In September, Mike Wells, chief operating officer of the Super

Laney Doc, a 1982 daughter of Doc Quixote, was an outstanding performer, earning over $245,300, including the Reserve Championship of the 1986 NCHA Open Derby, with Bill Riddle in the saddle. However, the mare is also one of the industry's leading dams, having produced 11 offspring winning over $1.2 million, including Cat Ichi, the winner of $303,271, and the championship of the 2004 NCHA Open Derby.

Syndicate, announced that two of their stallions had been sold—Doc Quixote and Doc's Hickory. Doc Quixote, at 18, had been sold to Heins Investment, which was the Top Gun Ranch of Whitefish, Mont., represented by Pat Fitzgerald, and Doc's Hickory had originally been sold to Robert Waltrip, Anderson, Tex., and Bobby Shelton of the Shelton Ranch in Kerrville, Tex. However, several days later, Top Gun Ranch also purchased the 16-year-old Doc's Hickory. According to Fitzgerald, the purchase price for Doc Quixote had been $75,000.

In November of the following year, Fitzgerald purchased Doc Quixote from Heins Investment, even though he knew about the semen problem.

In an article in the Nov. 24, 1989, issue of *Quarter Horse News,* Fitzgerald was quoted as saying that he didn't anticipate any problems.

"We had heard that, but we bred 30 mares to him," he said. "We have 30 mares in foal. Our vet, Dr. Joe Carter, feels we could breed as many as we want, but we are going to limit him. We probably are going to keep it to 30 or 40 mares."

But Fitzgerald went on to breed 57 mares that season, the most that had ever been bred to the stallion, with 38 foals being registered with the AQHA for the 1991 crop year and 51 for the 1992 crop year.

Fitzgerald bred the stallion for three more years, claiming the stallion more than paid for himself the first year.

With his last foals born in 1995 (10 were registered with the AQHA), Doc Quixote lived out his last years at the Fitzgerald Ranch in a big run with a girlfriend in the next run.

"He had the reputation of being mean and wanting to 'eat you alive,'" said Fitzgerald. "That's probably why I got him bought. At the very first, we had just one 'misunderstanding,' but after that, he was very pleasant to have around."

The Industry Loses a Great Sire

In May 2002, the Quarter Horse industry, especially the cutting industry, experienced a tremendous loss when Doc Quixote was laid to rest.

The morning of May 8, Fitzgerald noticed the 32-year-old stallion was not acting like himself.

"He acted like he had had a stroke," said Fitzgerald, "so we put him down right then. We didn't want to let him suffer."

Fitzgerald wanted to bury the stallion on his place so he called a man with a backhoe. When he told the man he needed someone to bury his stallion, Doc Quixote, the man surprised Fitzgerald by saying, "I judged him one time years ago when I was an NCHA judge."

The man arrived in 15 minutes and wouldn't charge anything for burying the great stallion.

"He was just kind of a big old pet the last few years," Fitzgerald said. "I hope I'm fortunate enough to have another one just like him."

Doc Quixote's Legacy

As of 2003—according to Equi-Stat, the statistical division of Cowboy Publishing Group—Doc Quixote was the seventh-leading sire of all time, with 437 offspring that have more than $10.3 million in lifetime earnings.

The stallion was also the sixth-leading broodmare sire of all time, with 141 daughters that have produced the earners of more than $10.5 million. Among his top producing daughters is Jazabell Quixote, dam of the earners of more than $1.2 million and the second-leading producer of all time.

9 DOC'S PRESCRIPTION

He was one of the performance industry's most versatile sires.

Glory Ann Kurtz

IF YOU HAD TO USE ONE WORD to describe Doc's Prescription's impact on the horse industry, that word would have to be "versatile."

Although the 1973 bay son of Doc Bar and Jameen Tivio was bred to be a cutting

Doc's Prescription was bred to be a cutting horse; however, following an injury, he became one of the Western performance horse industry's most versatile sires.

horse, he didn't remain sound, so he was never shown extensively. He did win some money in the National Cutting Horse Association, and was grand champion at halter, earning nine halter points. He also earned 16 Western pleasure points, earning his AQHA Performance Register of Merit in 1976.

However, the extensiveness of his versatility showed up in his get and grand-get. His beauty and athletic genes seemed to be "just what the doctor ordered."

Doc's Prescription was a strong breeder and one of the most talked-about facts about the stallion was the number of offspring he sired. During his lifetime, he sired 1,898 offspring from 22 colt crops, which translates to more than 86 registered offspring from every breeding season ... and this was before artificial insemination and embryo transfer became popular.

While most of his get and grand-get competed in the cutting arena, he sired winning get and grand-get that showed in the reining, reined cow horse, roping, pleasure, team penning and barrel racing arena, as well as AQHA competition.

In fact, it's debatable whether his legacy should be that he was one of the industry's greatest sires or greatest maternal grandsires. It's ironic how close the number and amount earned by his immediate offspring is to the number and amount earned by his maternal grand-get.

Doc's Prescription sired 274 offspring that earned more than $2.45 million in the performance arena. As a maternal

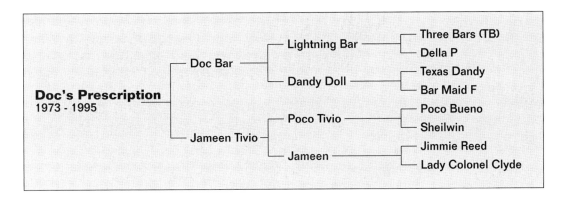

Doc's Prescription
1973 - 1995

Doc Bar
- Lightning Bar
  - Three Bars (TB)
  - Della P
- Dandy Doll
  - Texas Dandy
  - Bar Maid F

Jameen Tivio
- Poco Tivio
  - Poco Bueno
  - Sheilwin
- Jameen
  - Jimmie Reed
  - Lady Colonel Clyde

grandsire, he had 369 grand-get that earned more than $3.3 million.

While many sires have a "magic cross," Doc's Prescription seemed to nick well on a wide variety of broodmares.

In the cutting arena, he crossed especially well with the Poco Rip Cash daughters. But he also crossed well on Hollywood Buck, Beaver Royal, Gay Bar King and Black Gold Zan mares. He was bred to such a variety of mares that no single cross was really "magic" as far as offspring earnings are concerned.

Halter and Performance Record:
NCHA earnings of $106; Performance Register of Merit.

Progeny Record:

Foal Crops: 22	Performance ROMs: 138
Foals Registered: 1,898	Superior Performance Awards: 35
Halter Point-Earners: 23	World Champions: 3
Halter Points Earned: 75.5	High-Point Winners: 7
Performance Point-Earners: 295	NCHA Earnings: $2,022,290
Performance Points Earned: 8,583.5	

PHOTO BY DANNY W. HUEY

Demidoc, a 1980 daughter of Doc's Prescription, won over $135,150 in the 1980s, including the 1984 NCHA Non-Pro Derby, with owner Cindy Love in the saddle.

PHOTO BY JERRY

Docs Diablo, a 1976 stallion by Doc's Prescription, was destined for greatness. Ridden by Bill Freeman, the pair won the 1979 NCHA Cutting Futurity and were unbeaten until his untimely death in July 1980. The young stallion was reserve champion at a Texas Quarter Horse Association Show in Lufkin, Texas, the day he died.

And, although mostly known as a cutting horse sire, Doc's Prescription also sired Shy Prescription. A 1980 bay stallion out of Shy Dial, Shy Prescription was ridden by Steve Heckaman to the championship of the 292-entry 2-Year-Old Pleasure Futurity at the 1982 All-American Quarter Horse Congress. In addition, he earned a total of 53 open AQHA points, his Performance Register of Merit and a Superior in Western pleasure.

In the Beginning

Doc's Prescription was bred by Dr. and Mrs. Stephen F. Jensen, Orinda, Calif., own-ers of his legendary sire, Doc Bar. Born in 1973, he was part of the famous Doc Bar - Poco Tivio "golden cross." Prescription was out of Jameen Tivio, a daughter of Poco Tivio who was in turn out of Jameen by Jimmie Reed.

Jameen Tivio produced nine foals and all but two, Tivio Dandy and Docsens Me, were sired by Doc Bar. They included Doc's Cup Cake, Doc's Hotrodder, Doc's Vaquero, Doc's Lynx, Doc's Amador, Doc's Tom Thumb.

Glen Cantrell, Guymon, Okla., had purchased Jameen Tivio with Doc's Prescription at her side and bred back to Doc Bar. The noted producer died, however, before Cantrell was able to get another colt. He then sold Doc's Prescription as a yearling on June 5, 1974, to Glenn McKinney, Tulsa, Okla. One month later, McKinney took in a partner - horse trainer Louis Costanza, Sperry, Okla.

"We all went to the NCHA Cutting Futurity the year before and saw the Doc Bar horses for the first time," Cindy Costanza said. "That's what all of us wanted. Louis and I had a mare, so we decided to book her to Doc O'Lena. His stud fee at that time was $750, and to us, that was a very large amount of money.

"But fate stepped in, for in the June *Quarter Horse Journal* that I was looking at, there was a picture of Doc's Prescription with a 'for sale' on it. I showed Louis this and said, 'Here is a Doc Bar horse, so go and buy him.'

"Louis and Glenn were very close friends and he was also wanting this Doc Bar blood, so Louis called Glenn and asked him if he wanted to go look at this horse. Glenn had a friend that had a plane and he flew Louis and Glenn to Guymon, Okla.

"It was love at first sight and Mr. Cantrell gave them a few days to complete the paper work to make the sale final."

Doc's Prescription was soon nicknamed just "Doc."

"At that time, cutting was not as profitable (as it is today)," Cindy said. "So it was decided to show him at halter and perform him as well."

PHOTO BY PAT HALL

Dosey Doc was a full sister to Demidoc, the winner of the 1984 NCHA Non-Pro Derby. The daughter of Doc's Prescription won $154,252 in lifetime earnings, including the championship of the 1986 NCHA Non-Pro Super Stakes. She was ridden by Cindy Love.

At first, the general consensus was that Doc's Prescription did not have the necessary size to make it as a halter horse. But, as it turned out, he was too pretty to be overlooked.

Then it was found that he was a talented pleasure horse with a natural head set.

"You just showed him what you wanted him to do, and he did it," Cindy added.

Louis Costanza showed Doc's Prescription at halter, taking four grands and reserves, winning 18 of the 20 shows he entered and earning nine halter points.

Constanza also showed Doc on the rail as a 2-year-old, adding 16 western pleasure points to the bay stallion's resume. His biggest win came at the 1975 Tulsa State Fair where he placed first in a class of 62 horses.

"When Doc won the big Tulsa State Fair," Cindy said, "the judge kept the horses loping in the ring forever. Doc was just so relaxed that he never missed a beat. He had a won-derful mind and wanted to please you, and he was so smart."

From the pleasure arena, Constanza took Doc's Prescription to the cutting pen, with the intention of going to the prestigious NCHA Futurity held in December 1976. However, after only seven months of training, he had injured his hind leg and his cutting career was over before it started.

"We didn't have the money to get cattle," Cindy said, "so we did the best we could to get him trained. But it turned out he had a curb and couldn't take the constant stops and turn-arounds. Louis took him to our veterinarian and he said that if we didn't stop training on him, he would be ruined forever.

"Louis spent many hours rubbing that curb with this special salve that the vet mixed up, to help heal the curb."

So at the early age of 2, Doc's Prescription was retired to stand at stud.

Baker Prescription by Doc's Prescription shown with his owner, Merritt Wilson, winning the 1986 NCHA Non-Pro Futurity. The 1983 mare had lifetime earnings of over $97,600.

Docs Rerun that Louis trained and was later shown by Doug Lilly to the Congress pleasure futurity reserve championship.

As a Sire

Doc's Prescription was bred to four mares as a 2-year-old and, in 1976, his first three offspring hit the ground. One was Doc Juan, a stallion that went on to earn an AQHA performance Register of Merit. Another was Docs Diablo, a bay stallion out of Poco Christa by Poco Rip Cash.

Owned by Glenn McKinney, Docs Diablo was shown by Bill Freeman to a short but remarkable cutting career.

At the time Freeman got "Diablo" in September 1978, the trainer was 29 years old and lived in Pineville, Mo. Seven months later, Freeman and Docs Diablo won the 1979 NCHA Cutting Futurity. One week later, the pair won the Oklahoma Cutting Futurity.

They remained unbeaten, with earnings of $68,854, until the day Diablo died in July 1980 at a Tyler, Tex., Quarter Horse show, where he placed second. The young stallion also had 27 AQHA cutting points from the five shows he entered and won and had earned his AQHA Register of Merit.

At the time he was riding Docs Diablo, Freeman was asked how he felt about the Doc's Prescription colts.

"I think this is the premier line of the Doc Bar family," he said. "They seem to be more intelligent than any other Doc Bar colts, and I've ridden lots of them. I think they're destined to be the colts of the future."

The cross of Doc's Prescription on Poco Christa turned out to be one of the best, as she produced five offspring that won $137,828. Besides Docs Diablo, the list included Docs Cayenne, a 1979 mare that earned $46,249 in earnings; Prescription Rio, a 1985 mare the earned $22,037; and Docs Poco Julie, a 1978 mare that earned $20,000. Only Jinx's Li'

1 Squaw by Hollywood Buck produced offspring with more earnings.

Doc's Prescription made it to the 1976 NCHA Futurity though. But instead of performing in the arena, he stood in Stallion Alley.

"We had his stall all decorated," Cindy said. "It was a big thing and all the great stallions were seen there. He was a very special horse. He and his offspring paid for our place. We still have his show halter hanging in our office under his picture; he will always be loved by us."

The Costanzas raised several offspring of Doc's Prescription, including Docs Stylish, the dam of Doc's Stylish Oak; Docs Ceta, Docs Tempra, Sheza Prescription, Docs Sheik. They also owned part of

PHOTO BY G. WILLIS

George Smithwick, Lingleville, Texas, shown marking a 222.5 on Docs Royal Dancer to win the Championship of the 5-Year-Old division of The Non Pro, an event held in Oklahoma. The two were also champions of the 1985 NCHA Non-Pro Super Stakes and had lifetime earnings of over $148,700.

Five Years With Eddie Wilson

On March 15, 1977, McKinney sold Doc's Prescription to Eddie Wilson, with the registered owner being New Frontier Investments, Inc., Bowie, Tex.

Wilson owned Doc's Prescription for close to five years. During that time, the bay stallion sired 1,461 foals. Included among them were several of his best-known get.

Wilson's son, Merritt, was a non-pro cutter who took several offspring by Doc's Prescription to the winner's circle.

He won more than $20,000 on Docs Poco Julie and showed Baker Prescription, a 1983 mare with $97,646 in lifetime earnings, to the non-pro championship of the 1986 NCHA Futurity.

He also rode Koko Prescription, with earnings of $54,633, to the 1982 NCHA Non-Pro Futurity Co-Reserve Championship and the semifinals of the open division of the Futurity.

Finally, he rode Oro Prescription, with earnings of $64,097, to the reserve championship of the 1983 Harrah's Pacific Coast Futurity in Reno.

Cindy Love, an unknown non-pro cutter from Bowie, also had a hand in Doc's Prescription's success as a sire. She rode her mare Dosey Doc to win $154,252 and the Non-Pro Championship of the 1986 NCHA Super Stakes

In the article about her first-time win, she was called "Cinderella Cindy," as she seemed to come from out of nowhere to win the prestigious event. Cindy also rode Dosey Doc's full sister, Demidoc, to $135,152 in lifetime earnings.

Docs Royal Dancer, owned and shown by non-pro George Smithwick, won

PHOTO BY HACK

Koko Prescription had lifetime earnings of $54,633, including the co-reserve championship of the 1982 NCHA Non-Pro Futurity. Ridden by Merritt Wilson, the pair also placed in the open semifinals.

$148,729 in non-pro competition, including the Non-Pro Championship of the 1985 NCHA Super Stakes. Prescription Ten, owned and ridden by non-pros Reed and Claudia Laughlin, won more than $55,000. Docs Cayenne, with $46,249 in lifetime earnings, carried Sandra Cardwell to the Non-Pro Championship of the 1984 NCHA 5-Year-Old Classic.

Doc's Prescription also sired many high money-earning open horses in addition to Docs Diablo.

Neat Prescription, ridden by Kenneth Galyean, earned more than $64,000 in open competition and was the AQHA world Champion in Junior Cutting. Prescriptions Lena, ridden by Steve and Darla Miles, earned $61,330.

In AQHA competition, Dashing Doc was the AQHA High-Point Junior Cutting Horse with a Superior in cutting; Doctor Ceasar was the AQHA High-Point Cutting Gelding, with a Superior in cutting; Charge A Lotta Doc was the AQHA High-Point Amateur Cutting Horse; Root Beer Doc was the AQHA High-Point Junior Working Cow Horse and Docs Sheik and Sporting Model were both the AJQHA Reserve World Champion Cutting horses.

PHOTO BY DANNY HUEY

Neat Prescription, ridden by Kenneth Galyean, won over $64,000, including the AQHA World Championship in Junior Cutting. The two were also finalists in the NCHA Super Stakes and NCHA Breeder's Cup.

Docs Ceta was also the Canadian Cutting Horse Champion.

Skips Prescription was the 1983 AQHA High-Point Cutting Mare, an NCHA Super Stakes semifinalist, an Atlantic Coast Cutting Futurity semifinalist and earner of 44 AQHA cutting points.

Showing his versatility as a sire, Doc's Prescription also sired Pams Prescription, with 837 points and the Jeep Waggoneer Junior Champion, World Champion Amateur Western Pleasure Horse, High-Point Western Pleasure Horse and Horsemanship titles. Cindy Prescription, with 334 points, earned high-point honors and AQHA world championships in trail; Docs Dun Boy, with 195 points, earned high-point titles and his AQHA Superior in open and amateur trail; Miss A Rip, with 388.5 points, won world titles in horsemanship and western pleasure; Docs Poco Satin, with 231.5 points, had her Superior in open and youth western pleasure and horsemanship; and Daily Prescription, with 213 points, had a Superior in western pleasure and trail.

Spicy RX, was the National Snaffle Bit Association (NSBA) High-Point 3-Year-Old Western Pleasure Horse; Prescription Pokey was Superior in open and amateur trail. Peppy Attraction, Docs Rerun, Lucys Doc and Docs Wonder Drug all earned Superiors in western pleasure; TNT Prescription had a Superior in amateur western pleasure and Docs Azurelea was Superior in barrel racing and pole bending.

New Owners

In 1981, Glenn Neans, a building contractor from Round Rock, Tex., called it a "stroke of luck," when he purchased the 8-year-old Doc's Prescription from Wilson on Dec. 15. "He wasn't on the market," said Neans, owner of Redondo Roco Ranch. "We

PHOTO BY FRED MILLER

Oro Prescription had lifetime earnings of close to $64,400, including the open reserve championship title of the 1983 Harrahs Pacific Coast Futurity, with non-pro Merritt Wilson in the saddle.

just turned out to be at the right place at the right time."

Neans had used Hershel Williams, Fitzhugh, Okla., as his agent to express his interest in the horse.

"From there the deal was on," said Neans, who at one time owned a part of Doc's Lynx, a full brother to Doc's Prescription. He felt Doc's Prescription was the best breeding horse in the country.

Wayne Pooley, the ranch trainer at the time, recalled riding Doc's Prescription on cattle in an article in the *Quarter Horse News*.

"We needed some cutting photos of Prescription," Pooley said. "He hadn't been cut on in several years. I saddled him up and loped him about 30 minutes, then cut some cows. I can tell you I was amazed. I had no idea what kind of a cutting horse he was and very few people in the cutting horse industry have seen him work - probably not more than a dozen people.

"I've ridden colts sired by almost every Doc Bar horse and most of them are super horses. But without a doubt, Doc's Prescription has to be one of the very best siring sons of Doc Bar. His colts have unbelievable minds; they will accept training and they will allow you to train them. They are real athletes."

After the purchase of Doc's Prescription, Neans got into the cutting industry in a big way. In 1983, he bought out the interests of Georgetown Development Corporation, owned by Bud Sweazea and Don Parker, Georgetown, Tex. That was believed to be the largest cash transaction in the cutting horse industry at the time, with the assets including 360 acres of land and improvements, 250 top-bred cutting horses and 27 shares in the Super Syndicate. The acquisition made Neans the largest shareholder in the Super Syndicate, a group of popular breeding stallions, and, according to *Quarter Horse News,* the largest single investor in the cutting horse industry at the time.

Although Neans' dream was to be "one of the leaders in the industry for performance horses, as well as good-looking horses," he ran into financial problems and on Sept. 23, 1988, Doc's Prescription, at the age of 15, again changed hands.

This time, the stallion sold to Heins Investment, Whitefish, Mont., and joined a battery of four own sons of Doc Bar already owned by the Top Gun Ranch.

Pat Fitzgerald was the manager of the Top Gun breeding facility, located in Paoli, Okla., where Doc's Hickory, Doc's Wrangler, Doc Quixote and Double Tough Doc also stood. The stallion manager, Dr. Joe Carter, was previously the manager of Flag Is Up Farms, a California Thoroughbred breeding operation.

According to Fitzgerald, Doc's Prescription had been purchased while en route to California, where it had been planned that he would stand at the Rapp Ranch in Napa.

"We left him there (at the Rapp Ranch) for about 10 days," Fitzgerald said, "then we had him shipped back to Oklahoma."

Asked what piqued his interest in Doc's Prescription, Fitzgerald replied, "We've ridden some of his colts and really liked them. Also, we have several own daughters of Doc's Prescription."

Those daughters included Docs Stylish, a full sister to Docs Diablo and Docs Ceta, who was the dam of Docs Stylish Oak, who later became one of the country's leading cutting horse sires.

Doc's Prescription as a Maternal Grandsire

Many of those great mares ridden to championships in cutting competition became producing dams.

Dosey Doc produced 10 offspring that to date have won close to $390,000. They include Dash Rip Rocks, a 1996 stallion by Lenas Jewel Bars, with earnings of over $166,000; Freckles Playdough, a 1988 gelding by Freckles Playboy that earned more than $135,000 and Haidaken, a 1995 stallion by Haidas Little Pep, with earnings of more than $42,600.

Demidoc produced four offspring earning over $205,700. They included Young N Freckles, a 1995 gelding that earned $83,830; Sons Little Prince, a 1989 stallion that earned $51,850; and CL Winchester, a 1997 bay gelding that earned more than $49,000.

Docs Poco Julie was the dam of eight offspring earning more than $138,950, including Smart Poco Lena, a 1984 gelding that earned $131,358.

Docs Stylish was the dam of Doc's Stylish Oak, a 1984 stallion that earned $72,621.

The Twilight Years

In September 1989, Doc's Prescription was transferred to Tim O'Neill, Allen, Okla., and it was announced that the stallion would stand at the Oswood Stallion Station, located at the Rapp Ranch in Napa, Calif.

Six months later, the 17-year-old stallion was purchased by Benny Martinez's Sierra Oak Ranch, Porterville, Calif. Two weeks later, On March 30, 1990, the stallion was transferred to Jeff Oswood, Napa, Calif.

Four years later, on Jan. 1, 1994, Doc's Prescription, at 21 years of age, transferred to the Docs Prescription Trust and was leased to Pete Bowling, who stood him during the 1995 season for $1,250. Bowling's Horse Creek Ranch was located just outside of Gettysburg, Pa., north of Washington, D.C.

During the 1994 breeding season, Doc's Prescription covered 17 mares before he was put down. He died in May 1995, at the age of 22 and in the spring 1996, his final offspring, three fillies, were born: DJs Della Doc was out of a Doc's Sug daughter and In Dreams and This Docs A Lady, were both out of Thoroughbred mares.

Doc's Prescription will be remembered in the years to come as one of the greatest sons of Doc Bar, and more than likely, the most versatile...not only for what he did, but the talent he bred into the generations of offspring he sired.

Showing his versatility as a sire, Doc's Prescription also sired the great pleasure horse sire Shy Prescription. The 1980 bay stallion was ridden by Steve Heckaman to the championship of the 292-entry 2-Year-Old Pleasure Futurity at the 1982 All American Quarter Horse Congress.

10

JEWEL'S LEO BARS

Despite his registered name, he will forever be known simply as "Freckles."

Glory Ann Kurtz

THERE AREN'T TOO MANY legends in the performance horse industry that are recognized instantly by their nicknames. In the case of certain horses, however, the nickname gets used so often that it almost renders the formal name obsolete.

Such was the case with the cutting horse stallion known as "Freckles."

Registered with AQHA as Jewel's Leo

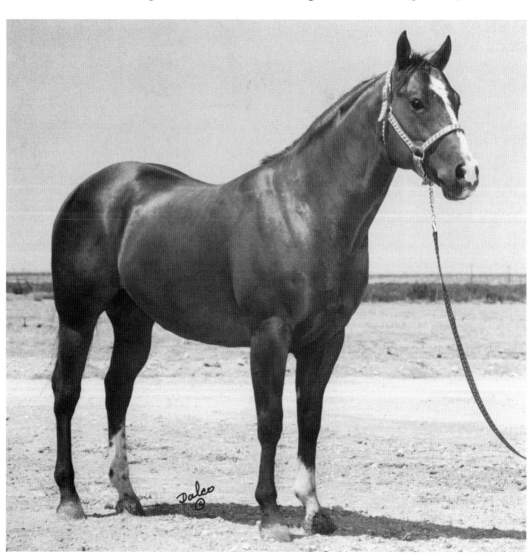

PHOTO BY DALCO

Bred to be a racehorse, Jewel's Leo Bars became a legendary cutting horse sire, more often called by his nickname "Freckles."

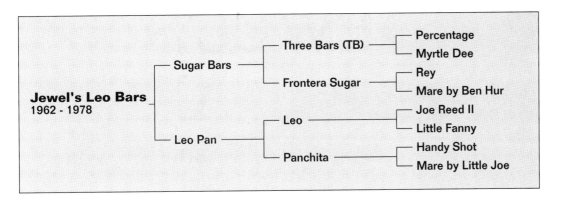

```
                          ┌─ Three Bars (TB) ──┬─ Percentage
           ┌─ Sugar Bars ─┤                    └─ Myrtle Dee
           │              └─ Frontera Sugar ───┬─ Rey
Jewel's Leo Bars          │                    └─ Mare by Ben Hur
1962 - 1978 ─┤            ┌─ Leo ──────────────┬─ Joe Reed II
           └─ Leo Pan ────┤                    └─ Little Fanny
                          └─ Panchita ─────────┬─ Handy Shot
                                               └─ Mare by Little Joe
```

Bars, Freckles was bred by A. L. Smith of Perry, Okla. A 1962 sorrel stallion by Sugar Bars and out of Leo Pan, he was a product of the renowned Bud Warren – Leo racehorse dynasty.

Sugar Bars and Leo Pan

Sugar Bars — Jewel's Leo Bars' sire — was a 1951 chestnut stallion by Three Bars (TB) and out of Frontera Sugar by Rey. Initially a AAA-rated racehorse and a grand champion halter horse, Sugar Bars went on to achieve AQHA Hall of Fame status as the founder of his own family of two-way champions — horses that were fast enough to achieve AAA times on the racetrack and good-looking enough to stand grand at halter at the biggest shows in the nation.

When Sugar Bars died in 1972 at age 21, he had more registered get than any other stallion; was the leading sire of AAA — AQHA champions and the leading brood-mare sire of ROM producers.

A few of his better-known get — all out of daughters of Leo — were Connie Reba, second in the Kansas Futurity and an AQHA Champion; Dan's Sugar Bars, seventh in the 1962 All-American Futurity and an AQHA Champion; and Counterplay, stakes winner and an AQHA Champion.

Leo Pan — Freckles' dam — came with her own set of impeccable credentials. A 1950 chestnut mare by Leo and out Panchita by Handy Shot (TB), she was a maternal granddaughter of the renowned Little Joe.

Halter and Performance Record:
NCHA earnings of $6,037; Performance Register of Merit

Progeny Record:

Foal Crops: 13	Performance ROMs: 21
Foals Registered: 101	Superior Performance Awards: 9
Halter Point-Earners: 4	World Champions: 2
Halter Points Earned: 4	High Point Winners: 1
Performance Point-Earners: 43	NCHA Earnings: $616,329
Performance Points Earned: 1,528	

Sugar Bars, the sire of Jewel's Leo Bars, was a 1951 son of Three Bars (TB), out of Frontera Sugar by Rey. He was a AAA-rated racehorse as well as a grand champion at halter. A member of the AQHA Hall of Fame, Sugar Bars was a leading sire of AAA-AQHA champions and a leading broodmare sire of ROM producers.

Leo Pan, the dam of Jewel's Leo Bars, was a 1950 mare by Leo out of Panchita by handy Shot (TB). She was one of the mares that helped establish Leo as the greatest broodmare sire of his era.

The combination of Marion Flynt, an oilman from Midland, Texas, and Jewel's Leo Bars produced a dynasty of cutting horses. It was his Jewel's Leo Bars/Rey Jay cross that was the "magic cross" for successful cutting horses.

Rey Jay, the legendary one-eyed cutting horse, shown being ridden by Tom Lee. He was purchased by Marion Flynt, who bred Rey Jay's daughters to Jewel's Leo Bars to create one of the first "magic crosses" in the cutting industry. He was an AQHA Champion and a Superior Cutting Horse. He earned 257 AQHA cutting points, as well as halter and Western pleasure points. He also earned his NCHA Bronze Award.

As one of the mares who helped establish Leo as the greatest broodmare sire of his era, Leo Pan was the dam of 10 registered foals. Included among them were five full brothers — Jewel's Leo Bars; Son O Sugar, a AA-rated racehorse and Bronze Award winning cutting horse; Sugar Again, an A-rated race winner; Sugar Still, with two performance horse points; and Sugar Pan, with one halter and five working points.

Early Influences

By the time Jewel's Leo Bars' registration papers were issued on Dec. 12, 1962, he was owned by Ira S. Lethco, Fort Stockton, Tex. He has been described by those who saw him as a yearling as being a deep-chested, deep-hearted, long-hipped colt that looked like he'd make a heck of a runner. With those credentials, Jewel's Leo Bars soon changed ownership again, being purchased by Ford Harris for a reported $5,500, a huge price for a yearling Quarter Horse in 1963, even if he was bred to run.

Kirk Coffman, Tomball, Tex., who was a son-in-law to Harris and partnered with him on Jewel's Leo Bars, was impressed with the colt's conformation and decided to show him at halter. He earned his first halter points by winning a class of seven at Rosenberg, Tex. Their second show was at Wharton, Tex., where Jewel's Leo Bars again took the first-place ribbon, this time in a class of four.

But Jewel's Leo Bars was bred to run, and it was time to start him under saddle. Billy Bush managed the horses on Harris' race operation and broke the young stallion to the saddle before he went into race training.

Billy nicknamed the stallion "Leo Bars," but it wasn't long before he was calling him "Freckles," because of all the spots in his white blaze and stockings.

The 2-year-old stallion had the best chance that a racehorse could have at the time. He was sent to Bubba Cascio, who would go on to train such legendary racehorses as Dash For Cash.

But Freckles wasn't destined to be a racehorse. After two race starts, he finished fifth once and second another time, winning only $30 and earning a paltry 55 speed index.

Bush was quoted as saying, "Freckles couldn't outrun me."

Cascio suggested that the young stallion be gelded since he wasn't going to make it as a racehorse. However, before Harris could decide what to do, he met a horse trader named Muscles Foster, who said he would be holding a horse sale in Coppell, Tex. Harris immediately solved his own problem and consigned Freckles. Little did he know that it also solved a problem for Marion Flynt of Midland, Texas.

According to Bush in Gala Nettle's book *Trendsetters* Vol. I, "Muscles always went around the country buying horses on credit and then selling them. Before he went by Ford Harris' place, he'd gotten some horses from Marion Flynt that way.

Then he got his finances all messed up and ended up owing Marion the money for them.

"Flynt, who was involved in the oil and gas business in Midland, Texas, knew he wasn't going to get his money out of Muscles, so the best thing he could do was to go to Muscles' sale and take a horse in exchange for the money Muscles owed him."

Flynt, who was 63 at the time, had gotten interested in cutting horses and had become the president of an ailing National Cutting Horse Association (NCHA), a position he held for 12 years. He had gone to the sale with Zack Wood, the executive director of the NCHA.

Flynt had left the ring for a minute when Wood saw a nice 2-year-old colt by Sugar Bars come in. Wood walked out into the hall and told Flynt about the horse and Flynt walked back into the sale ring, took one look at the good-looking Jewel's Leo Bars and raised his hand.

In 1974, Jay Freckles placed third in the NCHA Maturity and was in the top 20 of the NCHA. He won such honors as Champion of the All-American Quarter Horse Congress, King Ranch Championship Cutting, the Kentucky State Fair and the Missouri State Fair.

Freckles Gentlemen, a 1978 stallion by Jewel's Leo Bars out of Christy Jay, and a full brother to Colonel Freckles, is still owned by Kay Floyd, who owned Freckles Playboy when he died.

Colonel Freckles, sired by Jewel's Leo Bars out of Christy Jay, was bred by Marion Flynt, and owned by Bob McLeod when he won the 1976 NCHA Futurity, ridden by Olan Hightower.

Some say he paid $6,500 for the stallion; however, Wood and Kay Floyd, his ranch manager for 15 years, said he paid $5,600, which was a lot of money for a washed-up racehorse from someone who didn't even care about racing. But the price was irrelevant to Flynt because it had settled a debt.

Marion Flynt and the Square Top 3 Ranch

Flynt was born Sept. 8, 1901, in Winters, Texas. He was the son of a county sheriff. Following in the footsteps of some of his relatives, he became a car dealer and set-

tled in the oil-boom town of Midland, where he opened a car dealership. It was there that he met his future wife, Faye Holt, the daughter of a prominent ranching and oil family.

In an article in the October 1992 *Quarter Horse Journal,* Bruce Beckmann wrote that Buster Welch described the couple as "having enough money to burn a wet mule."

Flynt was a good businessman, but his true love was horses, especially cutting horses. In 1981, Flynt operated ranches north and west of Midland, where the couple maintained their home. Approximately 500 cattle and 75 head of quality Quarter Horses roamed the 60 sections of ranch

At the time Flynt bought Freckles, he was serving one of his many terms as president of the NCHA, headquartered in Fort Worth, Texas. He served as president from 1956-1958 and again from 1963-1971. He was then installed as President Emeritus.

Freckles Delite, a 1975 daughter of Jewel's Leo Bars out of Christy Jay, shown with Oaks Delite, her 1982 filly by Doc's Oak.

land, with each carrying the distinctive Square Top 3 brand.

He had tried riding cutting horses himself, but his thrill was in owning them. He owned Marion's Girl, who had won the 1954 and 1956 NCHA World Champion Cutting Horse titles with a young up-and-coming trainer named Buster Welch in the saddle.

At the time Flynt bought Freckles, he was serving one of his many terms as president of the NCHA, headquartered in Fort Worth, Texas. He served as president from 1956-1958 and again from 1963-1971. He was then installed as President Emeritus.

In an article by Sally Harrison in the 1993 NCHA Futurity program, Flynt said, "When I started with NCHA, they were three months behind in the rent. I'd

call for an executive meeting and maybe four (members) would show up. It was an uphill job."

Freckles Heads to the Cutting Arena

In 1965, Jewel's Leo Bars was a 3-year-old and had not been started on cattle, so obviously he was not a candidate for the high-paying NCHA Futurity. He was again shown at halter, winning one AQHA point in a show in Odessa in a class of five. In later years, he picked up an additional two points for a lifetime total of three AQHA halter points.

But Flynt was anxious to see if the beautiful stallion could cut, so he called Welch to see if he would train Jewel's Leo Bars.

In *Trendsetters,* Welch described Jewel's Leo Bars.

"He was green broke when we got him," he said. "He was a pretty sucker, though, and just a real smooth working horse.

"Greg (Buster's son) was a little boy then and he just loved him. We called Greg 'Freckles' a lot back then, because he had a bunch of freckles on his face. Since Jewel's Leo Bars had a bunch of freckles on his face, he and Greg had a lot in common. Those freckles attracted Greg to him and he'd say, 'I want to ride that freckled-face horse.' That's the one he spent a lot of time on."

So once again, Jewel's Leo Bars was nicknamed "Freckles," and this time the nickname stuck. In fact, it stuck so well that in years to come, many people knew the stallion only as Freckles, not realizing that his registered name was Jewel's Leo Bars.

Although young Greg spent most of the time on Freckles, Welch had teamed up with another cutting horse trainer named Shorty Freeman, and both of them spent time training and showing Freckles.

As a 4-year-old in 1966, Freckles won the 46-entry class at the Houston Stock Show and that fall won the Dallas State Fair, with 41 entries.

John Pergio also logged time on Freckles.

"I had ridden some futurity horses for Marion," John Carter said, "and one day he asked me if I'd ride Freckles. I rode him three months.

"When I rode him, he probably had as good an average as any horse for the amount of shows he went to. I won just over $1,000 a show on him," said Carter. "He was a good-minded horse and he was a real nice horse to handle."

According to Carter, Freckles stood 15.3 hands and weighed 1,250 pounds. Carter said he was "high-headed," but had "action to burn."

Even though he was shown very little in AQHA cutting competition, he managed to accumulate 25 lifetime AQHA cutting points.

But it wasn't long before Flynt, and the entire cutting industry, realized that Freckles' worth was as a cutting horse sire and the "magic cross" was Freckles crossed on daughters of Rey Jay.

Flynt Purchases Rey Jay

The Square Top 3 Ranch breeding program consisted of about 25 mares, which were mostly bred to Rey Jay, a stallion purchased by Flynt in the spring of 1966 from Tom and Delight Lee of Indiana. Delight had been at one of Buster Welch's clinics at the Square Top 3 Ranch, where she met Flynt.

Rey Jay was bred by the King Ranch, and sired by Rey Del Rancho, who was regarded as one of the best cutting sires the King Ranch ever raised. As a weanling Rey Jay injured an eye, which resulted in permanently clogging one of the stallion's tear ducts, leaving the eye inflamed and cloudy. He was sold to Loyd Jinkens, who traded him for three Holstein calves. Curly Tully ended up with the stallion and made a cutting horse out of him. Tom Lee saw the stallion compete in Michigan while Tully was visiting some relatives, and decided he had to own him. In fact, he wanted him bad enough that he traded his good Royal King mare, another horse and an extra $5,000 to own Rey Jay.

Rey Jay became known as the "one-eyed cutting horse," as Lee put a mock pair of eyeglasses on him when he cut to keep the sand and dust out of the stallion's eyes.

According to *Trendsetters,* there were rumors about what the mysterious eyeglasses did for the stallion.

"I was sitting on a horse near the stands at one show watching Tom and Rey Jay show," Delight said. "Two men sat in the front row near me and when Rey Jay started cutting, one of them said to the other, 'You know, I put one of those eye-things on my horse, but it didn't help him cut one bit better!'"

Tom and Delight had married in 1960 and spent a year showing horses in both NCHA and AQHA competition. Tom had

Rey Jay in the NCHA Top 10 when the year ended and also earned his AQHA Superior award in cutting. Delight rode him in Western pleasure, winning class after class, and Rey Jay soon became an AQHA Champion.

Delight also rode Rey Jay in cutting competition, but he was difficult to ride. According to *Trendsetters*, Delight remembers one incident when she fell off the stallion and still placed.

"One time Dale Wilkinson had a big cutting," she recalled. "Rey Jay and I were having a good run until he drew himself back, then turned real quick and dumped me on the ground. I don't guess he ever noticed I'd fallen off because he kept on working that cow, never quit cutting. He continued holding the cow until the run time was up and the judge blew the whistle.

"The judges didn't know what to do with the run since I'd fallen off but Rey Jay had-

n't quit cutting. They finally decided to score him and the score was enough to take us to the finals."

After that incident, the NCHA decided to create a new rule stating that if a rider fell off the horse, the horse was eliminated from the competition.

In 1964, tragedy struck the Lee family when, while riding alone, Tom fell from a horse and had brain damage. He never again recognized Delight who, needing money, sold Rey Jay to Flynt.

But Flynt kept Rey Jay less than four years. He didn't breed his stallions to outside mares; he only bred them to his own mares. He felt he was getting too many stud colts and not enough fillies, and it was fillies he was after to cross on Jewel's Leo Bars.

In 1970, Flynt donated Rey Jay to Texas A&M University's breeding program. But Flynt didn't abandon his Jewel's Leo

Freckles Playboy, a 1973 stallion sired by Jewel's Leo Bars out of Gay Jay, was one of the greatest cutting horse sires of all time. He is still a leading grandsire and maternal grandsire of cutting horses.

Mia Freckles, a 1973 daughter of Jewel's Leo Bars out of Catch Me Jo x Fourble Joe, carried Kay Floyd to the Non Pro Championship of the 1973 NCHA Futurity. That was the same year that Colonel Freckles won the Open title and Freckles Playboy was Co-Reserve Champion.

Bars/Rey Jay cross. He went out and bought some Rey Jay mares.

After the sale of Rey Jay, Delight didn't have a horse to ride, so while attending a Buster Welch clinic, she met Houston Clinton, who owned the great cutting mare Alice Star. Since there were no rules at that time about a non-pro owning their horse, he let her show Alice Star. But the great mare had to undergo surgery and Delight was again afoot. It was then that Flynt said she could come and get Freckles and show him.

In June 1966, Delight hooked up her trailer and headed for Texas to pick up Freckles. Delight showed the stallion during the summer, and in the fall she was thinking of returning to Texas to show in the Dallas State Fair. She was no longer

married to Tom, and she detested the northern winters.

Delight and her baby sitter, Kay Floyd, returned to Texas with Freckles, just in time for the B. F. Phillips complete dispersal sale held at his Frisco, Texas, ranch Oct. 17-19, 1966. Gay Jay was one of the 257 Quarter Horses that Phillips offered in his sale. Flynt had just purchased Rey Jay and really wanted Gay Jay. Both B. F. and his daughter Pam had won showing Gay Jay in NCHA competition. She was out of Georgia Cody by Sorghum Bill by Bill Cody, and was definitely the drawing card for the sale.

"Marion paid $17,500 for Gay Jay," said Kay Floyd in *Trendsetters* and who was at the sale when Flynt bought the mare. "Several of those guys worked to run her price up on him, but he just stayed hooked and bought her because he wanted her. Of course, she later became the mother of Freckles Playboy, so she was a good buy."

Back to the Cutting Pen

In 1966, Delight relocated to the Lone Star State and went to work for Marion Flynt. She showed Freckles at the Dallas State Fair, winning the AQHA Senior Cutting with a 148 score. The next stop for the duo was the NCHA World Finals.

The 1966 NCHA World Finals were held in November in Muenster, Tex., at Colonial Acres, owned by Mr. and Mrs. Earnest Medders. But neither Delight, riding Freckles, or Sheila Morris, riding Rey Jay, managed to place.

After the Finals, Welch and Freeman continued to show Freckles; albeit not very extensively. Welch won the 1966 Houston Stock Show Cutting on the aged competitor, and Freeman competed on him at the 1968 Stamford Rodeo and at a team cutting in Dallas.

In 1970, John Carter climbed on the back of the 8-year-old stallion, winning the Southwestern Livestock Exposition Stock Show cutting held in Fort Worth, Tex. The pair also finished fourth at the San Antonio Livestock Show and won a spring cutting circuit in Phoenix, Ariz. Following the Houston Stock Show in February, the stallion was not shown again; however, at the year's end, the pair finished 10th in the NCHA Top 10. During his lifetime, Freckles won a total of $6,037.24 in NCHA earnings.

Freckles in the Breeding Barn

Freckles was bred very little at first and like the rest of Flynt's stallions, never to outside mares.

"Freckles was an easy horse to breed," said Terry Riddle, who had become Flynt's ranch manager in 1974 at the suggestion of Riddle's father-in-law, Shorty Freeman. "Sharon (Terry's wife) could breed him."

"At that time, we were living in Gayle Borland's house and we had to haul water to it," said Sharon in *Trendsetters*. "Marion offered us $800 a month and told Terry he could bring his roping horse, so Terry decided he needed to try it. I thought we were going to be rich."

In the fall 1974, Riddle was breaking the coming 2-year-olds at the Square Top 3 Ranch. There were three sired by Freckles that he felt were "easy to break" - Freckles Playboy, Colonel Freckles and Mia Freckles.

(Note: Freckles Playboy and Colonel Freckles are profiled in the following two chapters.)

"As soon as I started breaking Freckles Playboy, he showed me he was special," Riddle said. "He was quick and a big stopper. In fact, when I first started driving him, he stopped hard and moved low, and it was all natural."

A Legend is Born

All Jewel's Leo Bars needed to establish himself as a bona-fide cutting horse sire was one event — the 1976 NCHA Futurity.

Prior to this, the Flynt stallion had already sired Jay Freckles, the 1973 Futurity Champion Stallion and fourth-place finisher.

By the time the 1976 edition of the gala affair was ended, Flynt-owned or-bred horses had literally swept the 372-entry field. There had been only nine horses that were sired by Freckles born in 1973, and one-third of them had taken the 1976 Futurity by storm.

A *Fort Worth Star Telegram* article said, "The $215,000 NCHA Futurity held Dec. 12 in Fort Worth might just as well have been held in Midland — that way Marion Flynt wouldn't have had to haul his awards so far home."

Colonel Freckles was the Futurity Champion.

Two Flynt owned-entries — Doc's Becky, ridden by Bill Freeman, and Freckles Playboy, ridden by Terry Riddle — were Co-

Reserve Champions. Yet another Flynt entry — Mia Freckles, ridden by Kay Floyd — was the Non-Pro Champion.

Although Flynt didn't own the winning horse, he had bred him and nominated him to the Futurity. Moreover, Terry Riddle had trained all four winners.

Many horsemen of today feel that futurity was probably the toughest futurity ever held, with many of today's top sires and grandsires competing. They included Doc's Hickory, Doc Wilson, Wyoming Doc, Doc's Mahogany, Doc's Remedy, Doc's Oak, Smooth Herman, Doc Athena and Montana Doc.

In 1978 the Riddles left the Square Top 3 to start their own training operation in Wynnewood, Okla. Only weeks later, after breeding a mare, Freckles, at age 16, colicked and died. He was buried at the Square Top 3 Ranch. His last offspring was a filly, appropriately named Freckles Legend.

But that definitely was not the end of the Freckles legend.

The Legend Lives On

During his 16 years, Jewel's Leo Bars sired only 101 offspring — averaging less than 10 a year during his breeding years.

Ten foals a year is hard to imagine in today's world of stallions siring hundreds of offspring in a year with the help of artificial insemination and embryo transfer. But over 50 percent of Jewel's Leo Bars' offspring were AQHA performers.

In 1974, Jay Freckles placed third in the NCHA Maturity and was in the top 20 of the NCHA. He won such honors as Champion of the All-American Quarter Horse Congress, King Ranch Championship Cutting, the Kentucky State Fair and the Missouri State Fair.

He only sired eight colts before an early death, with Jay Pepsan and Jays Freckle being NCHA Futurity semi-finalists. Jays Freckle also was the Oklahoma Futurity Champion.

"He died at a young age," John Carter said, "but I think Jay Freckles was one of the greatest horses there ever was. He was a real outstanding breeding horse and you

know when a horse can breed above himself, he is truly outstanding."

Mia Freckles, who had taken Floyd to the Non-Pro Championship of the 1976 NCHA Futurity, won more than $33,500 and is a producer.

Freckles also sired Freckles Flynt, a stallion that was in the Top 10 of the 1978 NCHA Futurity and won the NWCHA Open Championship. However, he too died at a young age, but not before he sired offspring winning more $236,000.

Freckles also sired Futurity finalist Freckles Maiden and Non-Pro Futurity finalists Freckles Date and Freckles Memory. I'm A Freckles Too was a California stallion that sired offspring earning close to $300,000, and his full brother, Mr Freckles Boy, was a leading sire in Australia.

"I rode Mr Freckles Boy in the first $10,000-added cutting they ever had in Australia," John Carter said. "I went over there and won the first go-round on him, marking a 150. Then he fell down the second go and marked a 140. I ended up marking 151 in the finals and won it. I got $10,000 and the next man got $260. I got all the added money and they got the entry fees."

Obviously the magic cross for Freckles was on Rey Jay mares. According to Equi-Stat, which has records that only go back to 1982 (with NCHA Futurity records going back to the first futurity), that cross produced nine head earning more than $223,817 for a $24,868 average.

According to Larry Thornton in a 2002 article in the *Pacific Coast Journal,* when asked what made the Freckles/Rey Jay cross so special, Welch said, "Freckles was a real smart horse, pretty-moving horse that moved with a lot of balance. Rey Jay was a little more of a rugged kind of a horse and I think the two of them just clicked. They were probably two of the better cow horses of the day. That's the reason they crossed so well. It was 'breeding the best to the best and hope for the best.'"

Flynt died in 1987 at the age of 86, but he lived long enough to see his dreams come true. Under his early direction, the NCHA had become a successful cutting horse association. He was also credited with creating the "magic cross" of the cutting industry — Freckles on Rey Jay mares. Freckles had become a legendary sire, and Rey Jay was a leading paternal grandsire.

He was even around to see both Freckles Playboy and Colonel Freckles become two of the industry's leading "next generation" sires.

Freckles Playboy and Colonel Freckles are now also gone. But their offspring, plus others, have made Jewel's Leo Bars a leading paternal grandsire and maternal grandsire.

Together, Marion Flynt and Jewel's Leo Bars — the original "Freckles" — wrote one of the most colorful chapters in the history of the cutting horse industry. And it was a story that was destined to be taken up and added on to by generations yet to come.

PHOTO BY MIDGE

Freckles Flynt, a 1975 stallion by Jewel's Leo Bars out of Miss Cocoa Jay by Rey Jay, was a 3/4 brother to Freckles Playboy, Colonel Freckles and Jay Freckles. He sired offspring earning over $236,300.

11

COLONEL FRECKLES

As both an individual and a sire, he was known as "the millionaire".

Glory Ann Kurtz

IN THE 1970S, who would have ever thought that a Quarter Horse stallion would create millions of dollars? And yet, Colonel Freckles did just that.

In fact, having once sold for $3.5 million, and having sired the performance earners of more than $4.4 million, the word "millionaire" seems to be synonymous with his name.

A Golden Cross

Colonel Freckles, a 1973 sorrel stallion by Jewel's Leo Bars and out of Christy Jay, was a product of the planned breeding program carried out by Marion Flynt at his Square Top 3 Ranch in Midland, Texas. The stallion's genes perpetuated the blood of such AQHA Hall of Fame ancestors as Three Bars, Sugar Bars, Leo, Joe Reed II and King.

Jewel's Leo Bars, Colonel Freckles' sire, was a 1962 chestnut stallion by Sugar Bars and out of Leo Pan by Leo. Christy Jay, his dam, was a 1967 mare by Rey Jay and out of Christy Carol by Leo Bob.

Colonel Freckles, a leading sire of cutting, reining and reined cow horse offspring, was a son of Jewels Leo Bars out of Christy Jay by Rey Jay. He died at the young age of 13 from acute colitis. The stallion was bred and raised by Marion Flynt.

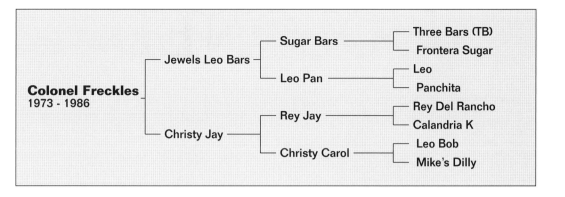

Colonel Freckles
1973 - 1986

- Jewels Leo Bars
  - Sugar Bars
    - Three Bars (TB)
    - Frontera Sugar
  - Leo Pan
    - Leo
    - Panchita
- Christy Jay
  - Rey Jay
    - Rey Del Rancho
    - Calandria K
  - Christy Carol
    - Leo Bob
    - Mike's Dilly

At one time, Marion Flynt owned both Jewel's Leo Bars, the original "Freckles," and Rey Jay.

Rey Jay, a 1955 King Ranch-bred stallion, was widely known as the "one-eyed cutting horse." An early eye injury left him with a permanently clogged tear duct and he competed in cutting in goggles, with the side for the good eye cut out.

Rey Jay's daughter, Christy Jay, earned three halter and two western pleasure performance points in an abbreviated show career. More noted as a producer,

Halter and Performance Record:
NCHA earnings of $46,305; 1976 NCHA Cutting Horse Futurity—1st place; AQHA Hall of Fame Horse.

Progeny Record:

Foal Crops: 10	Performance ROMs: 66
Foals Registered: 972	Superior Performance Awards: 9
Halter Point-Earners: 15	World Champions: 1
Halter Points Earned: 22	High Point Winners: 1
Performance Point-Earners: 265	NCHA Earnings: $3,724,933
Performance Points Earned: 2,696.5	NRHA Earnings: $126,513
NRCHA Earnings: $113,446	

PHOTO BY DALCO

Colonel Freckles, owned by Bob McLeod and ridden by Olan Hightower, won the 1976 National Cutting Horse Association (NCHA) Futurity, scoring a 223.

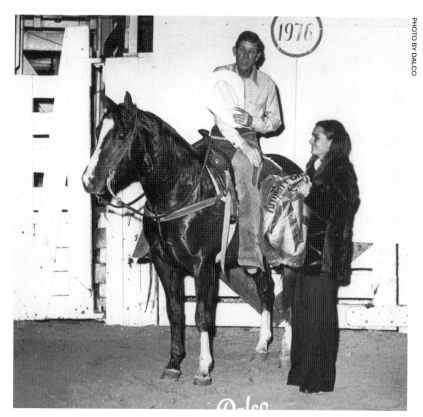

Colonel Freckles beat out some of the greatest stallions of our time in the 1976 NCHA Futurity, including Doc's Oak, Doc's Remedy, Doc Athena and Montana Doc.

she was the dam of 16 foals, including four full brothers and sisters to Colonel Freckles—He's A Freckles, the earner of more than $19,000; Freckles Delite, Flaming Freckles and Freckles Gentlemen.

Christy Jay was also the dam of C J Sugar, a great sire in his own right; Dox Molly O Grady, earner of $100,000; Christys Lena, earner of $64,300; and Colonel Rey Lena, reining earner of $24,000.

Getting back to Colonel Freckles, in the fall of 1976 he changed hands for what would be the first of several times when he was purchased by Bob McLeod of Brenham, Texas.

McLeod was a cutting enthusiast who had played professional football with the Houston Oilers for seven years. He became interested in the "Freckles" bloodline in 1975, after he had seen Jay Freckles score a whopping 152 at a Houston cutting. The ex-pro footballer decided then and there to go to Midland and see what Marion Flynt had for sale.

Freckles Fantasy won the 1983 NCHA open finals and earned a performance Register of Merit in 1984.

Colonel Freckles' dam was Christy Jay, a 1967 daughter of Rey Jay out of Christy Carol by Leo Bob.

"Back when I went to the Square Top 3 Ranch," he recalled, "Terry Riddle was working for Flynt. He had three 2-year-olds—Colonel Freckles, Doc's Becky and Freckles Playboy—in training for the 1976 NCHA Futurity.

"They just showed me Colonel Freckles that day. They didn't show me the other two. And I have to admit, if they would have showed me Freckles Playboy, I'd have bought him instead."

As it turned out, McLeod bought Colonel Freckles for $8,500.

When the South Texan got his new purchase home, he enlisted the aid of Olan Hightower, a Hockley, Tex., landscaper and cutting horse trainer, to put the final pre-futurity finishing touches on "Colonel."

The match-up was a good one, and the pair went on to win the 1976 NCHA Futurity.

In the process, they bested what is generally considered to be one of the strongest early-day futurity fields ever — a group that included Doc's Becky, Freckles Playboy, Doc's Remedy, Doc's Oak, Doc Athena, Montana Doc, Tip It San, Doc's Steady Date and Bardoc O'Lena.

Years later, Hightower was asked if he thought he could win the NCHA Futurity, even though he had been on the stallion only a short while.

"Yes, I knew I had enough horse," he said.

According to Hightower, he cut three cows in the finals.

"For my first cow," Hightower added, "I deliberately cut this one cow that everyone had stayed away from because it was 'wilder than a March hare.' The stands were full of people and I knew if I could keep my horse busy, I wouldn't have to worry. I was right, because the crowd went nuts.

"When I cut my second cow, the crowd got so loud that I couldn't even hear my horse moving. My horse wasn't weakening on the cow, but I felt I needed to quit because there was so much racket. Then I went for my third cow."

117

The maternal grandsire of Colonel Freckles was Rey Jay, the famous one-eyed cutting horse.

Colonel Lil, a daughter of Colonel Freckles, was the winner of the 1981 NCHA Futurity, with owner Joe Heim in the saddle. The win gave Colonel Freckles the distinction of being one of only two horses in NCHA history, up to that time, that had won the NCHA Futurity, then sired an NCHA Futurity Champion.

Colonel Freckles' win of the Futurity was a definite financial boon to McLeod.

"Prior to the NCHA Futurity," he said, "I had advertised Colonel Freckles for a $500 stud fee. I thought I might get 20-25 mares. After the Futurity, I felt like I should honor the $500 stud fee. It proved to be the wisest course of action, and Colonel Freckles bred more than 100 mares the next year."

A Short Career

Following Colonel Freckles' big win, McLeod felt the stallion was too valuable as a breeding sire to haul down the road. Hightower did ride the talented performer at the 1977 NCHA Derby, but Colonel's lack of seasoning showed up when a clod of dirt flew up, hit the black plastic on the wall and scared him.

According to McLeod, Hightower and Larry Reeder also showed Colonel Freckles at a few additional shows and he himself rode him in the NCHA Open World Finals held in Amarillo.

PHOTO BY DON SHUGART

Cols Lil Pepper, a stallion sired by Colonel Freckles, was co-champion of the 1988 NCHA Open Futurity, ridden by Doug Jordan. The stallion earned over $187,000 before his untimely death.

Curly Rode Her Ma, a daughter of Colonel Freckles, won close to $161,000 in lifetime earnings, ridden by a leading NCHA Non-Pro rider, Phil Rapp.

Colonel Flip, sired by Colonel Freckles, shown being ridden by Keith Barnett. The stallion was third in the 1983 NCHA Futurity and has lifetime earnings of close to $110,000.

A Promise of Things to Come

The stallion's best lick, as it turned out, would be in the breeding shed.

From Colonel Freckles' first foal crop consisting of 88 offspring, 36 would be entered in the 1981 NCHA Futurity.

Colonel Lil, a 1978 sorrel mare out of Two Rocks Lil, was the event's eventual winner. Ridden by Joe Heim, she netted $191,985.65 for her first place finish.

From that first "bumper crop," Colonel Freckles sired not only the NCHA Futurity Champion, but four Futurity finalists and seven semifinalists. Other members of the stallion's initial offspring offering were Colonel Leo Bar, the NCHA Super Stakes Reserve Champion and earner of $147,256; Freckles Fantasy, Co-

Champion of the 1984 NCHA Finals and earner of $107,368; and Lovely Freckles, earner of more than $73,000.

Freckles Fantasy was leading the NCHA 1985 World Championship standings when he was stolen from his stall at the July Abilene Summer Circuit and never found.

Colonel Freckles' life was filled with a certain amount of irony.

Just as he was sold prior to his becoming an NCHA Futurity Champion in 1976, he was again sold just two weeks prior to becoming a Futurity Champion sire.

His third owner was officially listed as Winmunn Quarter Horses — a Brenham, Tex., combine headed up by Houston-based commodity trader Winston Freeman and cutting horse trainer Don Munn.

PHOTO BY MIDGE

Nu Cash, a 1984 stallion by Colonel Freckles, won over $36,000 in cutting and reined cow horse competition. He is one of the performance horse industry's leading sires, siring offspring earning close to $1.8 million. Over $1 million was earned by horses in the reined cow horse arena.

In addition to purchasing Colonel Freckles from McLeod, the new owners also acquired four of the stallion's get and McLeod's 340-acre ranch in Brenham.

When asked what he got for Colonel Freckles in the 1981 deal, McLeod replied, "Let's say I valued Colonel Freckles at $2 million."

A Change of Venue

Two years later, on Dec. 8, 1983, Colonel Freckles' name hit the front pages of horse publications again when he was reportedly sold to Louis and Wanda Waters of Houston, Tex., for $3.5 million. At the time, it was believed to be the largest cash transaction by an individual to purchase a cutting horse.

The Waters had watched the stallion over the years, and he represented exactly the type of horse they were interested in breeding on their 5,000-acre Texas Hill country ranch. The Houston couple was already active in the cutting horse industry and, at the time, owned six Doc O'Lena syndicate shares.

They believed strongly in the potential of the Colonel Freckles-Doc O'Lena cross and further felt that their new purchase would be able to pass on his cooperative disposition, uncanny athletic ability and keen intelligence.

"I have admired Colonel Freckles as an individual for many years," Lou Waters declared shortly after acquiring the famous stallion. "One of the most impressive things about him is his ability to sire outstanding stallion prospects as well as performance champions. I expect Colonel to have a major impact on

Colonel Leo Bar, a son of Colonel Freckles, won over $147,000 in cutting competition ridden by Pat Earnheart. He is shown winning the Reserve Championship title at the 1982 NCHA Super Stakes.

the cutting industry over the next 10 years, through the outstanding stallions he is siring."

The Making of a Sire

Waters' prophecy came true, as Colonel Freckles sired not only prepotent sons but top-producing daughters, as well.

Today, Colonel Freckles has 10 offspring that have won more than $100,000, with six of the 10 being stallions that have sired winners in the performance arena.

While he is foremost known as a great cutting horse sire, Colonel Freckles also became a popular West Coast reined cow horse sire.

With Ted Robinson in the saddle, Nu Cash won the 1987 National Reined Cow Horse Association Snaffle Bit Futurity by a six-point margin.

Doc Jewel Bar won more than $7,800 in reined cow horse competition and was the co-champion stallion of the 1981 California Reined Cow Horse Association (CRCHA) Snaffle Bit Futurity. He was also reserve champion and champion stallion of the 1982 CRCHA Hackamore

Maturity, and the reserve champion of the 1982 Texas Reined Cow Horse Association (TRCHA) Snaffle Bit Futurity.

Reveille Bar was reserve champion of both the 1983 TRCHA Snaffle Bit Futurity and the 1984 CRCHA Snaffle Bit Futurity.

As a paternal grandsire of reining horses, Colonel Freckles has 436 grand-get that have won more than $1.2 million. Included among them are Colonels Smokingun, a.k.a. "Gunner,"an APHA-registered stallion who earned more $177,226; and Slide Me To The Bar, 1991 NRHA Futurity Champion.

High Sellers

By the late 1970s, Colonel Freckles' offspring were topping some of the nation's most prestigious cutting horse sales. The same held true for private treaty sales. Even before he had proved himself as a sire, it was advertised in the July 1979 Cuttin Hoss Chatter that Docs Colonel Sam, a yearling by Colonel Freckles, had been sold by Bob McLeod for $75,000.

At the 1980 NCHA Futurity Sale, a dozen members of "Colonel's" first colt crop sold under the gavel of Ike Hamilton. The two high sellers, Freckles Page Boy and Tassajara, brought $52,000 and $51,000 respectively. At the 1985 NCHA Futurity Sale, Colonel Ann sold for $53,000.

Through the changes of ownership, Colonel Freckles stud fee kept up with his rise in fame. It was $1,250 in 1978; $1,500 in 1981; $3,000 and $6,000 in 1983.

An Industry Loss

The horse industry suffered a severe blow in October of 1986, when Colonel Freckles died at the age of 13.

CJ Sugar, a 1982 stallion, was a full brother in blood to Colonel Freckles. While Colonel Freckles was sired by "Freckles," CJ Sugar was sired by his full brother Son O Sugar. Both stallions were out of Christy Jay.

Colonel Freckles was the maternal grandsire of Shakin Flo, one of the greatest cutting mares of all time. Owned and ridden by Sandy Bonelli, she won over $400,000 in Open and Non-Pro cutting competition.

"We had purchased some alfalfa," Wanda Waters said, "and one bale evidently had some blister beetle parts in it. Four horses, including Colonel Freckles, ate some of the bale and we lost all four of them."

Colonel Freckles was taken to Texas A&M for a week and just when it was thought he was through it, he succumbed to Colitis X, an inflammation of the colon.

On June 25, 1988, a complete dispersal was held of the Waters' horses at their Fulshear, Tex., ranch. A total of 190 horses went to 21 different states.

Two Colonel Freckles sons topped the event when Colonel St James, a 1986 sorrel stallion, elicited a final bid of $24,00 from F. J. Etchart of Tolleson, Ariz; and Chick Colonel, a 1986 stallion, went for $17,000 to Ralph Burchell of Cheyenne, Wyoming.

Colonel Freckles' Statistics

According to Equi-Stat, the statistical division of Cowboy Publishing Group, 316 of Colonel Freckles' cutting horse get have won more than $3.7 million

As of the end of 2003, he had also sired offspring earning $126,513 in NRHA reining competition and $113,446 in NRCHA-sanctioned events.

And, just as Lou Waters had predicted, several of Colonel Freckles' greatest get were stallions that went on to become great sires in their own right. This list is topped by Nu Cash, a stallion whose get have earned $1.7 million; and Just Plain Colonel, whose get have earned $1.3 million.

Other stallions sired by Colonel Freckles, which sired offspring with earnings over $100,000 in cutting, reining and reined cow horse competition, include: Colonel Flip, $803,396; Mr Kings Freckles, $375,390; Mr Freckles O Lena, $249,727; Colonel Barrachone, $194,986; Colonel Leo Bar, $181,117; Colonel Duhon, $180,774; Doctor Freckles, $148,265; Texas Kicker, $145,119; Master Jay, $144,359; Colonel Sal, $139,901; Arawans Freckles, $134,448; Colonel Hotrodder, $139,957 and Cutter Freckles, $113,392.

As a paternal grandsire, Colonel Freckles is responsible for the earners of more than $9 million. As a maternal grandsire, he is credited with the earners of close to $6.5 million.

Heading his list of top-earning maternal grand-get are such talented performers as Shakin Flo, earner of more the $400,000; Freckles Doc Oak, earner of $271,969; Von Reminic, earner of $180,218; and Freckles Son Ofa Doc, earner of $170,308.

Over the years, Colonel Freckles not only sired an NCHA Futurity champion and an NRCHA Snaffle Bit Futurity champion, but he also sired an AQHA world champion in junior reining, a Congress reining futurity champion and a four-time Best of America's Horse award-winner.

But regardless of all Colonel Freckles accomplishments, Wanda Waters said the best part of owning Colonel Freckles was the friendships he gave them.

"I really enjoyed talking to our 'telephone friends' from coast to coast and receiving letters from happy owners of Colonel Freckles offspring around the country and even internationally. It was a thrill to chat with the likes of Greg Ward, Smoky Pritchett, Ted Robinson, Bob Loomis, Dick and Brenda Pieper, Ralph and Mickey Gragg and Matt and Leslie Day."

In 2004, Colonel Freckles was inducted into the AQHA Hall of Fame.

Showing the versatility of Colonel Freckles, Slide Me To The Bar, a paternal grandson of Colonel Freckles, was the champion of the 1991 National Reining Horse Association (NRHA) Futurity. Sired by Freckles Solis, he earned over $110,200 while being owned by Frank Bolea and ridden by Todd Sommers.

12 FRECKLES PLAYBOY

He was living proof that, often-times, the best is saved for last.

Glory Ann Kurtz

FRECKLES PLAYBOY WAS BRED in the purple. But so are a lot of horses that never earn a dime.

At first, when he was tried at the racetrack and the halter arena, it looked as if "Playboy" wouldn't amount to much. Then, after winning the co-reserve championship of the 1976 NCHA Cutting Futurity, it looked as if he had found his niche as a cutting horse.

It took time and a shrewd and dedicated owner to find the stallion's true calling, however. And it was not as a performer, but as a sire.

Freckles Playboy, a 1973 sorrel stallion by Jewel's Leo Bars and out of Gay Jay, was bred by Marion Flynt of Midland, Texas.

Oil Money and a Keen Eye

Flynt hailed from the oil-rich boom town of Midland, Texas. Some people were

DON SHUGART

Freckles Playboy, a 1973 stallion by Jewel's Leo Bars out of Gay Jay by Rey Jay, was tried at the racetrack and in the halter arena before he found his niche as a cutting horse as Co-Reserve Champion of the 1976 NCHA Open Cutting Futurity. In 2004, he was the second leading sire of all time, siring 927 offspring winning close to $24.8 million.

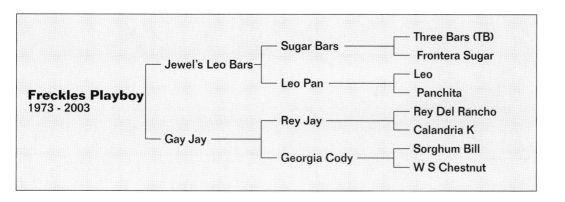

Freckles Playboy
1973 - 2003

- Jewel's Leo Bars
  - Sugar Bars
    - Three Bars (TB)
    - Frontera Sugar
  - Leo Pan
    - Leo
    - Panchita
- Gay Jay
  - Rey Jay
    - Rey Del Rancho
    - Calandria K
  - Georgia Cody
    - Sorghum Bill
    - W S Chestnut

of the opinion that his success in the cutting horse business was a direct result of his oil-based wealth. They maintained that he simply had the financial wherewithal to pay the country's top cutting horse trainers to haul his horses around the country.

But there were others who knew Flynt as a hard-working horse enthusiast, and they felt that a least a portion of his success was due to his keen eye for a good horse and his top-notch breeding program.

In the fall of 1966, Flynt purchased Gay Jay at a B. F. Phillips sale in Frisco, Tex.

Halter and Performance Record:
NCHA earnings of $59,975; 1977 World Champion Jr. Cutting; 1978 World Champion Sr. Cutting; Performance Register of Merit.

Progeny Record:

Foal Crops: 26	Performance ROMs: 129
Foals Registered: 2,079	Superior Performance Awards: 31
Halter Point-Earners: 5	World Champions: 11
Halter Points Earned: 6	High Point Winners: 6
Performance Point-Earners: 447	NCHA Earnings: $21,374,906
Performance Points Earned: 6,597.5	NRHA Earnings: $102,927
NRCHA Earnings: $174,358	

Marion Flynt, called Mr. Cutting Horse, shown with Rey Jay, the sire of Freckles Playboy. Flynt implemented one of the best breeding programs in the country and his Square Top 3 Ranch was the home of NCHA world champions, AQHA world champions and NCHA Futurity champions and reserve champions.

Gay Jay, the dam of Freckles Playboy, had 12 foals, with seven of the 12 having performance records. Four were full siblings sired by Jewel's Leo Bars, and included Freckles Playboy, Jay Freckles, Freckles Hustler and Freckles Pleasure.

Freckles Playboy was Co-Reserve Champion of the 1976 NCHA Futurity and finished third in the 1977 NCHA Maturity, with Terry Riddle in the saddle. With lifetime earnings of $59,975, he was retired in 1980. After he was diagnosed with navicular disease, Flynt gave the stallion to his ranch manager Kay Floyd.

Shesa Playmate, out of Lenaette by Doc O'Lena, was out of the first colt crop sired by Freckles Playboy. Ridden by Terry Riddle, she was a finalist in the 1981 Open Futurity and won the 1982 NCHA Derby.

Gay Jay, a 1958 sorrel mare by Rey Jay and out of Georgia Cody, was bred and raised by Mrs. Arthur "Curly" Tully of Azle, Texas.

Tully had sold Gay Jay as a yearling to Bill Riley of Fort Worth, Tex., for $400. After being taken back to her breeder as a 2-year-old for training, the mare changed hands several more times before being bought by B.F. Phillips for his daughter, Pam.

"I had several chances to buy Gay Jay back," Curly Tully said. "I could have had her once for $1,000 and once for $1,100, but I couldn't raise the money. I guess the reason she changed hands so many times was because she was such a cat, no one could ride her."

In cutting competition, Gay Jay earned $1,089.91. Retired to the broodmare band, she produced 12 foals and seven performers.

Freckles Playboy was the most renowned of Gay Jay's offspring. Two of his full siblings, however, also did their part to uphold the family name.

Jay Freckles, a 1970 stallion, was the 1973 NCHA Futurity Champion Stallion, the 1976 NCHA Reserve World Champion and the 1976 AQHA Reserve World Champion Senior Cutting Horse.

Freckles Hustler, a 1977 stallion, was the champion stallion of the 1980 NCHA Futurity and winner of the 1981 Atlantic Coast Cutting Futurity.

Freckles Playboy, a Champion Cutting Horse

As noted in the previous chapter, Terry Riddle started "Playboy" under saddle and trained him in preparation for the 1976 NCHA Futurity.

It was at this point in the famous stallion's life that Kay Floyd entered it.

Playboys Madera, out of Doc's Madera, is the highest money-earning offspring of Freckles Playboy, with over $570,800 in lifetime earnings. Owned by Kay Floyd, the mare was ridden by Terry Riddle to many titles, including winning $100,000 at The Masters. Floyd rode her to the 1988 NCHA Non-Pro World Championship.

Originally from Indiana, Floyd came to Texas by chance in the fall of 1966. Delight Lee, a close friend, had accepted a job at Marion Flynt's Square Top 3 Ranch. Floyd accompanied Lee to help with her young son, and wound up relocating as well.

When Lee ended her association with the Square Top 3 in 1970, Floyd took over as ranch manager. Floyd was serving in that capacity in 1973, when Freckles Playboy was born, and in 1976, when he was started under saddle.

"Terry broke and trained Playboy," she said. "The two were just alike. They reminded me of a light socket. One minute, they'd both be quiet, and then the minute Terry put his hand down in the herd, they would both come alive."

"One time Terry let me ride Playboy on cattle. I only got to ride him that one time, when he was a 3-year-old. It was fun, but I was afraid I was going to ruin him."

As previously noted, Flynt and Riddle had three horses—Colonel Freckles, Doc's Becky and Freckles Playboy—entered in the 1976 NCHA Futurity.

Colonel Freckles would go on to win the big event for owner Bob McLeod and trainer Olan Hightower of Brenham, Tex.

Freckles Playboy and Riddle would claim co-reserve champion honors.

The following year, Riddle rode Playboy to a third-place finish in the NCHA Maturity. In addition, Playboy also claimed honors as the 1977 AQHA World Champion Junior Cutting Horse. In 1978, he was the reserve champion at the NCHA Finals.

In 1979, Playboy placed eighth in the NCHA Top 10. At the Houston Stock Show cutting, held in conjunction with the finals, he scored the highest mark in both go-rounds and the finals of the 49-entry show. He also picked up the Open Championship year-end title of the West Texas Cutting Horse Association.

Kay Floyd claims that "Playboy" worked a lot like Rey Jay.

"And they both put a good hip and stifle on their colts," she added. "And they automatically wanted to stop."

Freckles Playboy was retired from cutting competition in 1980 with an NCHA Certificate of Achievement, Bronze award and $59,975 in earnings. In AQHA-sanctioned competition, he earned a cutting Register of Merit and 25 points.

In 1979, Freckles Playboy was diagnosed with navicular disease and Flynt decided

PHOTO BY T. JETT

Freckles Playboy is also a leading maternal grandsire. Playboy McCrae, a 1993 gelding by Dual Pep out of Playboys Madera, won the 1996 NCHA Open Futurity with Paul Hansma in the saddle. The gelding has lifetime earnings of $265,954.

to put the stallion down. But Riddle talked him out of it, saying that it was crazy to put such a good horse to sleep. So Flynt offered to give the stallion to Kay Floyd, thinking maybe she could make some money on him. It wasn't the first time the West Texas oilman had given her a horse.

"Mr. Flynt didn't pay me much of a salary," Floyd said, "so every once in awhile he would give me a horse - one that he didn't really want. And, even though Playboy was a great individual, that didn't mean he would be a sire."

But it wasn't out of character for Flynt to give away horses. Floyd remembers a time when legendary reining trainer Dale Wilkinson came to Midland and said he really liked one of Flynt's horses. Flynt gave him Freckles Date, who Wilkinson later sold for $100,000.

"One time he gave Keith Barnett a breeding to Playboy," Floyd said, "and the result of that breeding was Alices Rey Jay. He was always giving horses away. Someone could go to his place and say they wish they had a Playboy yearling. Marion would just say, 'Well, there's a whole pen of them out there. Just take your pick.'"

Floyd decided it was time to promote Freckles Playboy and stand him to the public. She stood him at Terry Riddle's ranch in Wynnewood, Okla.

She promoted the stallion with ads and passed out promotional freebies at the shows. She put her natural public relations talent to work, keeping track of all the earnings of his offspring and including them in her stallion ads. The owners of Freckles Playboy's offspring loved it.

But probably the biggest impact of her ownership of Playboy was that she cheered for his offspring - all of them.

In fact, she whooped and hollered so much when one of his offspring was having a good run at the major cutting events in Will Rogers Coliseum that she got a letter from the NCHA Executive Committee asking her to refrain from the practice because it was too distracting.

Playboy the Sire

Freckles Playboy's first colt crop of four hit the ground in 1978. From that small sampling came Shesa Playmate, a royally-bred mare out of Lenaette by Doc O'Lena. Lenaette had won the 1975 NCHA Futurity and her sire had claimed the same honor in 1970.

PHOTO BY DON SHUGART

Playboys Kid, a 1979 gelding by Freckles Playboy, has lifetime earnings of $445,018. In 1987, ridden by Mary Jo Milner in the 1986 NCHA World Championship Finals, the pair won all four go-rounds in the Non-Pro division, something that had never been done before or since.

Shesa Playmate lived up to her pedigree when, ridden by Riddle, she was a finalist in the 1981 Open NCHA Futurity. The following year, she was a finalist at the Las Vegas Futurity, the Atlantic Coast Cutting Horse Association Futurity, the NCHA Super Stakes and the AQHA World Show. But she gained her greatest fame when she won the 1982 NCHA Derby.

From Playboy's second foal crop of 32 in 1979 came Freckles Aglow, ridden by Terry's brother, Bill Riddle, to the semifinals of the NCHA Futurity.

People were starting to stand up and take notice; maybe Freckles Playboy was more than a champion - maybe he was a sire!

The 1980 foal crop of 48 confirmed the suspicion of many. Freckles Playboy offspring were popping up in the payout distribution column of many major events. Playboys Kid, out of Docsagin by Doc Bar, won $100,000 in 1983 ridden by Mary Jo Milner in non-pro competition and Larry Reeder in the Open division.

Mary Jo and the "Kid" were also the non-pro champions and top gelding at the 1983 ACCHA Futurity and the TQHA Classic, and the non-pro Champions at the Bonanza.

Freckles Aglow showed up in the winners' circle again, making the finals of the ACCHA Futurity, NCHA Super Stakes, TQHA Classic, and the Bonanza Cutting.

A Lenaette, out of Lenaette by Doc O'Lena, was a finalist at the ACCHA Futurity, NCHA Super Stakes, Bonanza Cutting, TQHA Classic and the NCHA Derby.

Casey Freckles showed in both open and non-pro competition and was a finalist at the ACCHA Futurity, Cutting Bonanza, Adrian Berryhill Maturity and the NCHA Derby.

Freckles Playboy had suddenly been elevated to the status of "super sire."

From 1978 through 2002, Freckles Playboy sired 26 crops of foals totaling 2,079. This was a time breeding 100 mares to a stallion was considered more than enough. Seven of his crops exceeded 100, with his largest colt crop being in 1990 when he had 168 foals.

"But I remember the time," Kay Floyd said, "when it cost $15,000 to subscribe your stallion to the NCHA Super Stakes and I wasn't even making close to $15,000 on stud fees."

As of the end of 2003, Freckles Playboy had 879 get that earned close to $24 million

132   LEGENDS 6

in cutting competition. That made him the second leading cutting sire of all time, following Smart Little Lena. As of the end of 2003, 18 Freckles Playboy get had won more than $200,000 and 56 had won more than $100,000.

Through 2003, a total of 67 of his offspring were either champions or reserve champions of a division of the three major NCHA-sponsored aged events—the Futurity, Derby and Classic Challenge.

Playboy's get also earned more than $98,000 in National Reining Horse Association competition and more than $174,000 in National Reined Cow Horse Association competition.

From the very beginning, Freckles Playboy geldings were in demand as great weekend, down-the-road horses.

Many were also in demand because they were hot contenders for NCHA World Championship titles. This was demonstrated by Playboys Kid, who took Mary Jo Milner to the 1986 Non-Pro World Championship and went on to win over $445,000 in lifetime cutting earnings.

Other great geldings sired by Playboy that earned more than $200,000 in lifetime earnings included Hyglo Freckles, $412,141 and the 1988 NCHA Open World Champion Horse; Playboy Bee Jay, $346,900; Dry N Freckled, $288,816; Power Player, $283,349; Playboy Olena, $250,800; Chicks Playboy, $243,338; and Crackerboy, $227,048.

As the years rolled by, Freckles Playboy became entrenched as one of the industry's leading paternal and maternal grandsires of money earners.

In 2004, he was the seventh leading paternal grandsire, with his grand-get earning close to $12 million. He was also the fourth leading maternal grandsire, with his second generation offspring earning more than $15.2 million.

The Last Years

As Playboy's great ability to sire top cutting horses was being discovered, Flynt and his wife divorced in 1983 and the horses were all sold. Floyd moved out and bought

Hyglo Freckles, a 1983 gelding by Freckles Playboy out of Miss King Hyglo, won lifetime earnings of $412,140. He is shown being ridden by Faron Hightower. Freckles Playboy geldings were in great demand as great weekend, down-the-road horses and several won over $200,000.

a 300-plus-acre spread near Stephenville, Texas. She hadn't ridden cutting horses for several years, but Flynt put a stop to that when he made another gift to her – the great mare Playboys Madera, a Freckles Playboy daughter who earned more than $400,000.

In the fall of 1987, Floyd won the NCHA Non-Pro Futurity riding Playfulena, a home-bred mare by Playboy out of Havealena. In doing so, she became the only woman to win the prestigious Non-Pro title twice. Retired to the broodmare band, Havealena turned into the cornerstone producer of eight offspring that earned close to $696,000.

In 1987, the cutting horse industry lost a great supporter and Floyd lost a dear friend when Marion Flynt died on Oct. 6 in an Abilene hospital. But it seemed to give Floyd the incentive to continue to prove that his breeding program was a world champion one.

Havealena, a daughter of Doc O'Lena out of Bar Socks Babe, produced eight off-spring by Freckles Playboy which won a total of $695,510. They included Play Like A Lena, $274,718 and Don't Hava Cow, $143,433.

Freckles Playboy was also a leading sire of stallions, with his highest-profile son being Freckles Merada, with 80 offspring winning close to $3 million. The 1990 stallion, out of Lenaette by Doc O'Lena, died at the early age of 12 in 2002, but not before he sired Meradas Little Sue, one of the greatest cutting mares of all time, with over $730,500 in lifetime earnings.

In 1988, she won the NCHA Non-Pro World Championship riding Playboys Madera and Freckles Play Girl. In 1992, 1993 and 1995, she won the AQHA Amateur World Championship in cutting riding Play Like A Lena, a full sister to Playfulena.

By 1995, Floyd had slowed down her participation in the cutting arena. That same year, Glen Blankenship went to work for Floyd and, in 1996, he rode Play Like A Lena to the NCHA Reserve World Champion and World Champion Mare titles. That same year, Paul Hansma rode Floyd's horse Playboy McCrae to the NCHA Open Futurity Championship.

That win again broke barriers for Floyd, as she became the only person to ever breed, raise and own an NCHA futurity champion and an NCHA reserve world champion in the same year. In 2000, Blankenship rode Dont Hava Cow to the NCHA reserve world chmpionship title.

The list goes on and on, with Dainty Freckles winning the NCHA Open Futurity in 1998 and San Tule Freckles in 2001. Two other Playboys - Maceys Playgirl won the Non-Pro Futurity in 1988, and

Playboys Lynnea accomplished the same feat in 1990. Playboys Perfecta won the Limited Open Futurity in 1993 and Playdox won it in 1998.

Play Who was the 1999 Reserve NCHA world champion and One Act Play was the 1999 NCHA non-pro reserve world champion. Tassa Mia Playboy was the 1996 NCHA Super Stakes open champion.

But it wasn't all about the titles and the money.

"With me owning and loving Playboy," Kay Floyd said, "and Terry training him, and everyone training his colts ... that's what made him the legend he is today."

The End of a Great Run

The year 2002 was the last year that Freckles Playboy would sire a foal crop. He was 29 years old, but still looked and acted great. He was standing at Raymond Beadle's R&B Stallion Station in Whitesboro, Texas, and Floyd would take the over 100-mile trip weekly to visit him. But try as they might, no mares got in foal.

The following year, Floyd took Freckles Playboy to Amarillo to Dr. Gregg Veneklasen, to see if there wasn't some way she could breed a few more select mares.

But nothing worked.

A successful, long-running race was about to come to an end. The following year, Floyd kept Playboy at her Stephenville ranch. While she was attending an AQHA convention in California, Playboy went into kidney failure and had to be humanely put down. He had just turned 30.

Playboy was buried on Floyd's ranch and a unique headstone, created and given to Floyd by a friend and Playboy admirer, was put on his grave.

As the third and longest-lived of the vaunted "Freckles" trio of cutting horse legends, Freckles Playboy served as living proof that, often-times, the best is saved for last.

PHOTO COURTESY AUGUSTA CHRONICLE

Playgun, a 1992 son of Freckles Playboy out of Miss Silver Pistol, won close to $186,000, including both the Open and Non-Pro championship at the 1996 Augusta Futurity, ridden by Jody Galyean and owner Dick Pieper. The gray stallion is also a million-dollar cutting horse sire, with 150 offspring winning over $2.7 million.

PHOTO BY PAT HALL

Kay Floyd rode Playfulena a daughter of Freckles Playboy out of Havealena, to the 1987 NCHA Non-Pro Futurity Championship. She became the only woman to win the prestigious title twice.

13 PEPPY SAN

As the first NCHA world champion to sire a world champion, he ushered in a new era.

Sally Harrison

PEPPY SAN WAS NOT THE FIRST stallion to win the National Cutting Horse Association World Championship. King's Pistol claimed that honor in 1957, 11 years after NCHA named its first champion. But Peppy San, foaled in 1959, ushered in a new era for the sport of cutting when he became the first NCHA world champion to sire a world champion. In the 55-year history of the National Cutting Horse Association, only one other stallion can claim the same

Peppy San, shown here with cutting horse legend Matlock Rose in the saddle, was the first NCHA world champion to sire a world champion.

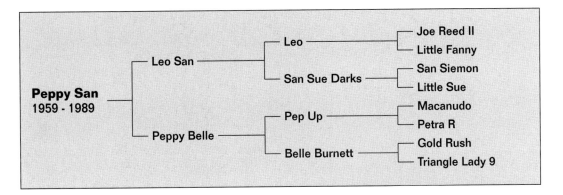

```
                                            ┌─ Joe Reed II
                              ┌─ Leo ────────┤
                ┌─ Leo San ───┤              └─ Little Fanny
                │             │              ┌─ San Siemon
                │             └─ San Sue Darks┤
Peppy San ──────┤                            └─ Little Sue
1959 - 1989     │             ┌─ Pep Up ─────┬─ Macanudo
                │             │              └─ Petra R
                └─ Peppy Belle┤              ┌─ Gold Rush
                              └─ Belle Burnett┤
                                             └─ Triangle Lady 9
```

accomplishment — Peppy San's full brother, Mr San Peppy.

As a young man, Gordon B. Howell, breeder of both Peppy San and Mr San Peppy, covered many miles a day in the saddle tending sheep and cattle on a New Mexico ranch. By the late 1950s, thanks to Texas oil leases, Howell was a wealthy man and served on the boards of numerous oil and gas companies. At one meeting in New York, so the story goes, when directors introduced themselves by noting their Ivy League credentials and business accomplishments, Howell proudly announced, "I'm Gordon B. Howell and I graduated from the sixth grade in Encino, New Mexico."

With money to indulge in leisure pursuits, Howell turned to horses. He already had a keen eye for conformation, owing to his days spent as a cowhand, and he soon became an expert on pedigrees, as well.

"Mr. Howell had been studying racehorses and he could recite Thoroughbred pedigrees," said leading Quarter Horse trainer Matlock Rose, who was introduced to Howell in the 1950s. "He didn't know Quarter Horses very well at the time, but he was an intelligent man, and it didn't take him long to figure out what was going on."

In 1957, Howell purchased Leo San, a 2-year-old stallion by the popular Quarter Horse sire Leo, and out of San Sue Darks by San Siemon, a well-regarded son of Zantanon. "I was looking for a sire that could raise a cutter, a racer, or a halter horse," Howell explained about his choice of Leo San in a 1984 article in the *Quarter*

Halter and Performance Record:
NCHA earnings of $49,478; AQHA Champion; 1967 NCHA World Champion; 1967 AQHA High-Point Cutting Stallion; Performance Register of Merit; AQHA Champion; Superior Cutting.

Progeny Record:
Foal Crops: 22	Performance ROMs: 58
Foals Registered: 493	Superior Performance Awards: 10
Halter Point-Earners: 16	World Champions: 8
Halter Points Earned: 37.5	High-Point Winners: 4
Performance Point-Earners: 153	NCHA Earnings: $3,026,915
Performance Points Earned: 2,272.5	

PHOTO BY GEORGE

Here's a vintage shot of Peppy San and Matlock, taken after the pair had won the open cutting at the 1963 Fort Worth Stock Show. That's NCHA founding father Marion Flynt presenting the winning trophy and legendary horseman George Tyler handing out the first place ribbon.

137

After being sold to the Douglas Lake Cattle Company of British Columbia, Canada, Peppy San continued his winning ways. With Matlock Rose in the saddle, the Hall of Fame stallion was the 1967 NCHA World Champion, World Champion Stallion and World Finals winner.

In AQHA competition, Peppy San was an AQHA Champion and Superior cutting horse.

Horse Journal. With Leo San in his barn, Howell began searching for mares, especially those with Old Sorrel bloodlines. It was during the Denver National Western Livestock Show and Rodeo, in 1958, that Howell sought the advice of Matlock Rose on the purchase of Peppy Belle, a daughter of Pep Up by Macanudo.

"Peppy Belle was a good mare with a pretty neck and good conformation," Rose remembered. "She looked like a Quarter Horse. I think those Macanudos were the best horses they raised on the King Ranch. They were cow horses and they had action."

Howell paid $1,600 for Peppy Belle, a bargain considering that he had forked over a reported $50,000 for the grand champion halter and cutting horse mare, Isis. Rose remembered Peppy Belle as being in foal when Howell purchased her. "She was bred to some horse in Wyoming," he noted. "I don't remember who it was, but we gave the colt away and started breeding her to Leo San."

Peppy San, by Leo San, foaled on Aug. 8, 1959, was 4-year-old Peppy Belle's first

Stardust Desire was another of the great Douglas Lake – Matlock Rose cutting horses that dominated the industry during the mid- to late 1960s. An NCHA World Champion and World Finals winner, the good-looking mare is shown here in open cutting action at the 1966 National Western Stock Show in Denver, Colorado.

registered foal. "Peppy San looked like a stud prospect when he was just a young colt," said Rose, whom Howell hired in 1959 to run his show and breeding operation. "He had a beautiful hip and a long neck, and his hind legs were set right. He looked like he could do something just standing still."

Leo San had never been shown, but Peppy San proved to be a natural cow horse and Rose entered him in the very first NCHA Futurity, which was held in 1962 in Sweetwater, Texas. Peppy San won the go-round and finished second to Money's Glo, ridden by Buster Welch, in the finals. It was Welch who would later ride Mr San Peppy to the NCHA world championship for King Ranch.

Although Peppy San excelled at cutting, Howell's main focus was showing halter horses. Between 1959 and 1963, when Howell held a Quarter Horse dis-

persal sale and turned to racing, Leo San's offspring, in the hands of Matlock Rose, never placed less than third in 66 get-of-sire classes. Some of his top winners included Leo San Susie, grand champion halter mare; Leo San Red, grand champion halter gelding and Superior roping horse; and Leo San Van, AQHA Champion and high-point cutting gelding.

"In those days, everybody showed in performance and halter," noted cutting horse trainer Jim Lee, of Iowa Park, Texas. "And there was a time when nobody could beat Matlock Rose. He'd come to a show with a semi-load of horses and do good with all of them."

When Howell sold his show horses in 1963, C.N. "Chunky" Woodward purchased Peppy San through Don Dodge, a top cutting horse trainer and good friend of Matlock Rose. Woodward, president of Woodward Stores Ltd., a Canadian department store chain, owned Douglas Lake Cattle Company of British Columbia, the largest privately held ranch in Canada, with more than 500,000 acres and 11,000 Hereford cattle.

Although Douglas Lake Cattle Company raised their own horses for ranch work, Woodward was interested in the American cutting horses he had heard about from fellow Canadian Cliff Ross. Don Dodge had outfitted Ross and seven other Canadians with horses used in a special cutting exhibition for Queen Elizabeth, and Ross hooked Woodward up with Dodge. Peppy San was Woodward's

Here's another great shot of Stardust Desire and Matlock, taken after the duo had won the open cutting at the 1966 Houston Livestock Show. Rex Cauble of Crockett, Texas, presents the trophy.

first cutting horse and between 1963 and 1967, he was shown sparingly, while Woodward pasture-bred him to Douglas Lake Cattle Company mares and acquired more mares - including Stardust Desire, a Macanudo granddaughter shown by Matlock Rose.

When Rose left Howell's employ in 1963, he set up shop in Gainesville, Texas, with well-known trainer and judge George Tyler. Rose and Tyler advertised their services in the *Quarter Horse Journal* under the slogan: "Our horses are broke and we are, too." Most of Tyler's and Rose's horses carried hefty price tags, including Stardust Desire, who Rose had placed fifth in the 1965 NCHA Top Ten standings.

Stardust Desire was 6 and had been shown with limited success by several riders when Tyler and Rose acquired her in 1964. Within months of the purchase, the scrappy mare and Rose began earning checks. They capped off the year with big wins at the Cow Palace and at the NCHA World Finals in Las Vegas, where Woodward first noticed Stardust Desire. "That was about as nice a mare as anybody ever rode," said Rose of Stardust Desire.

In 1966, Woodward backed Rose and Stardust Desire for another shot at the NCHA world championship. In January and February alone, the pair won the Denver, Fort Worth and Houston livestock shows. Late in the year, when they arrived in Muenster, Texas, for the NCHA World Finals, Stardust Desire ranked second only to the talented Vegas Boy, ridden by J.T. Fisher.

"That mare could always catch up if she got behind because you could call on her," pointed out Rose, who rode Stardust Desire that year for an unprecedented third consecutive World Finals win. The money she won in the World Finals nudged her year-end tally up $100 past Vegas Boy's total and also earned her the 1966 Open World Championship.

The following year, Woodward mounted Matlock on Peppy San with the same

PHOTO BY JIM KEELAND

Peppy's Desire, a 1969 sorrel mare by Peppy San and out of Stardust Desire, was the 1975 NCHA World Champion Open and Non-Pro Cutting Horse. Shown here with owner – rider Carol Rose of Gainesville, Texas, the talented mare won the non-pro cutting title at the 1975 Houston Livestock Show.

Chunky's Monkey, a 1970 sorrel gelding, was the last foal to be produced by the Peppy San – Stardust Desire cross. Orphaned at birth, "Chunky" went on to earn honors as the co-champion of the 1974 NCHA Derby.

Peponita, a 1969 black stallion by Peppy San and out of Bonita Tivio, was one of the cutting industry's all-time greats. Owned and shown by Matlock Rose, he was a two-time NCHA World Champion and a three-time NCHA Finals winner.

Shown by Rose in AQHA cutting competition, Peponita was a three-time world champion.

PHOTO BY LOUISE SERPA

Royal Santana, a 1971 sorrel gelding by Peppy San and out of Royal Smart, was an NCHA Non-Pro and Youth World Champion.

goal - to win the world championship. At 8, Peppy San was at the top of his form. Rose showed him 52 times and earned 50 checks. "I only lost a cow on him twice that whole year," Rose noted. "He was really cow smart and all cow horse. I could put him in a big pasture without a fence or ride him without a bridle. It was all the same to him."

Because he was an easy horse to show, Rose rarely needed to work Peppy San between events, but he did insist on personally attending to his daily care. Rose would brace, rub and wrap Peppy San's legs every night. On the road, he stopped every 300 miles to unload his horses and walk them a bit, unwrapping and rewrapping legs at every stop.

In addition to the 1967 NCHA Open World Championship, Peppy San and Rose won the prestigious Tournament of Champions, a six go-round event held in Vernal, Utah, and a third consecutive (the fourth for Rose) NCHA World Finals. Peppy San was also the AQHA high-point stallion and was the last NCHA world

champion to become an AQHA halter champion. In 1968, Carol Rose (at the time, Matlock's wife) placed second riding Peppy San in the NCHA Non-Pro World Finals. The win capped off Rose's successful bid for the NCHA Non-Pro World Championship, won primarily aboard Gay Bar's Gen. It was the second of three consecutive non-pro world championship wins for Carol, who would collect an unprecedented fourth title in 1975 aboard Peppy's Desire, Stardust Desire's daughter by Peppy San.

With Peppy San's world championship win came the demand for his services as a stallion. Rather than keep him in Canada, Woodward decided to stand Peppy San at Rose's ranch in Gainesville, Texas, in the heart of the cutting industry. It was there the stallion remained until his death at 30 years of age, in 1989. From his first foal crop in 1965 until his last in 1987, Peppy San sired 493 registered foals. Some of cutting's most enduring legends carry the blood of Peppy San, not the least of which is Smart Little Lena.

San Jo Lena, a 1984 brown stallion by Peppy San and out of Jo Olena, was the 1991 AQHA World Champion Senior Cutting Horse. Shown here being ridden by Pat Patterson, San Jo Lena earned $124,607 in NCHA competition.

Smart Little Lena, by Doc O'Lena and out of Smart Peppy, by Peppy San, was cutting's first Triple Crown champion and is the sport's all-time leading sire in terms of average earnings per performer ($29,118 per 681 head, through 1999). Rose had purchased Smart Peppy's dam, Royal Smart, from her breeder, Earl Albin, for $800. It was Albin who also owned Royal King, Royal Smart's sire.

"She was a pretty little mare," remembered Rose of Royal Smart. "She was small, about 13.3 hands, but she moved around good. I never rode her, but she was by Royal King and I knew he had some ability with a cow. That was my reason for buying her."

Rose eventually sold Royal Smart to Chunky Woodward, who bred her to Peppy San and got Smart Peppy in 1965. When Hanes Chatham acquired Smart Peppy and bred her to Doc O'Lena, he got

Smart Little Lena. Royal Smart's second foal sired by Peppy San, Royal Santana, earned $174,000 in cutting competition and was an AQHA world champion and Hall of Fame Horse.

When Woodward bred Peppy San and Stardust Desire, the results were spectacular. Peppy's Desire, foaled in 1969 and purchased from Woodward by Matlock and Carol Rose, became the first NCHA world champion produced by two world champions. And she set a record in 1975 by claiming both the open and non-pro world championships titles.

"Peppy's Desire favored Peppy San a little more than she did Stardust Desire," said Matlock Rose. "She was really cow smart like Peppy San, but there wasn't ever a better mare than Stardust Desire, either."

Chunky's Monkey, a 1970 Peppy San son, was Stardust Desire's last foal.

While running in a pasture with Chunky's Monkey at her side, Stardust Desire impaled herself on a tree limb and died instantly. Sonoita Queen adopted Chunky's Monkey and kept him at her side until the Douglas Cattle Company foals, including her own Peppy San foal, Sonoita's Last, were weaned. At 2, Chunky's Monkey was put in Rose's hands to train for the NCHA Futurity.

"Chunky's Monkey was really a good horse," said Rose. "But I couldn't keep him where he needed to be all the time. He was laid-back and he never went on to be the horse I thought he could be." Nevertheless, Chunky's Monkey was a finalist in the 1973 NCHA Futurity and was co-champion of the 1974 NCHA Derby.

While Rose was hauling Peppy's Desire for the NCHA world championship in 1975, Don Dodge was also on the road with Peponita, a coal-black Peppy San son owned by Marilyn Day, of Scottsdale, Ariz. Peponita edged out Doc's Starlight for fourth place in the NCHA standings that year and was named NCHA World Champion Stallion.

"Peponita was a stud and a very aggressive horse," said Dodge. "He was also quick and could do more, in my opinion, than Peppy San."

Rose often turned back for Dodge when Dodge showed Peponita, and even showed the stallion once or twice as Dodge's catch rider. "I thought Peponita had the potential to be one of the greatest," said Rose, who purchased the stallion from Day for $45,000, in 1976.

"I was in Phoenix when Matlock was there with Peponita," remembered J.T. Walters. "When he rode Peponita out of the arena and uncinched him, he said to

PHOTO BY T. JETT

Peppy Sans Pride, a 1982 sorrel gelding by Peppy San and out of Freckles Pride, amassed $97,055 in NCHA earnings. Pat Earnheart is up in this action shot.

PHOTO BY G. WILLIS

Wild Irish San, a 1982 sorrel gelding by Peppy San and out of Wild Irish Wasp, earned $95,096 in NCHA competition.

me, 'Here's my next world champion. Every time I ask him to do a little more, he can do it.'"

Peponita won the 1977 NCHA Open World Champion title with $38,695, a new NCHA record and more than double the earnings of reserve champion Doc's Starlight. Peponita also won the NCHA World Finals for the second consecutive year and was made AQHA senior world champion.

"Peponita was one of the nicest horses that I ever rode," said Rose. "He was a little prettier in front of a cow than his daddy and he had a little extra on a cow. He could really hold some bad ones. I thought he was about as cow smart a horse as you could get, but he wasn't any smarter than Peppy San. They were both good horses."

Peponita had somewhat of a respite in 1978, when Rose stayed close to Texas to show, but the stallion still placed in NCHA Top 10 standings and was AQHA champion for the third time. In 1979, Peponita and Rose again claimed the NCHA world championship and Peponita broke the NCHA lifetime earnings record with winnings of $120,400. At 10, Peponita was the world's richest cutting horse; he held two NCHA world championship titles, three AQHA world titles, and had won the NCHA World Finals three times. Incidentally, with his 1979 NCHA world championship win, Rose became the only rider to win five NCHA world titles and remains the only rider to win titles on four different horses.

Peponita helped prove Peppy San as a sire of sires when his son, Mr Peponita Flo, won the reserve championship of the 1991 NCHA Futurity. Mr Peponita Flo, in turn, sired Shakin Flo, NCHA Horse of the Year and many times NCHA open and non-pro limited-age event champion.

Sonita's Last, another great Peppy San son, was the 1978 NCHA world champion stallion. Sonoita's Last's daughter Sonita's Joy produced Sonitalena, the 1996 NCHA Open World Champion, sired by Doc O'Lena.

When Chunky Woodward held his first production sale at Douglas Lake Cattle Company, Rose purchased a gelded Peppy San son out of Royal Smart for $960. The horse was Royal Santana, whose full sister, Smart Peppy, would produce Smart Little Lena. Rose eventually sold Royal Santana to Tommy Moore of Fort Worth, Texas, who rode the gelding to win back-to-back NCHA non-pro reserve world championships, in 1979 and 1980. Royal Santana's career would span nearly two decades and include two AQHA world championships.

Booger San, another gelded son of Peppy San, was 1983 NCHA Non-Pro World Champion and earned nearly $180,000. Sanacee, a gelding by Peppy San out of Cee Miss Holly, was a three-time AQHA world champion.

In 1982, at the age of 21, Peppy San commanded a stud fee of $10,000. In 1984, Matlock and Carol Rose held a dispersal sale and Ike Hamilton, the legendary auctioneer, who presided over so many great Quarter Horse sales in the last half of the 20th century, recalled the highlight of the momentous event. "Matlock gave a demonstration on Peppy San," remembered Hamilton. "And while he was riding, he reached down and pulled off Peppy San's bridle and just kept cutting. There wasn't a dry eye in the place. I bawled like a baby."

Peppy San's last crop of foals took their first steps in 1987. By 1989, the grand old stallion's steps had slowed to a painful pace and Rose knew it was time to bid goodbye. "The life had gone out of his eyes and I couldn't stand to see him that way," said Rose. On April 26, Peppy San, who had remained with Rose throughout his illustrious show and breeding career, was put to sleep.

PHOTO BY DON SHUGART

Even at an advanced age, Peppy San displayed the well-balanced conformation and intelligent attitude that helped him establish one of the breed's premiere cutting horse families.

14 MR SAN PEPPY

He was the horse that built a dynasty.

Sally Harrison

IN 1985, KING RANCH advertised Mr San Peppy as "The horse that built a dynasty." At the beginning of the 21st century, Mr San Peppy's dynasty continues to grow. His son Peppy San Badger is the all-time leading sire of cutting horse money earners. His grandsons Dual Pep and Haidas Little Pep are among cutting's Top 10 all-time leading sires. And despite the fact that King Ranch has been out of the cutting horse business for over a decade, because of Mr San Peppy's progeny, it remains the leading breeder of cutting horses, with $6.5 million in earnings – nearly $3 million more than second-ranked Oxbow Ranch.

"When we bought Mr San Peppy, we thought our mares were of good enough quality… but we felt we needed a better

Mr San Peppy was both a world champion cutting horse and the founder of one of the breed's most-dominant performance lines.

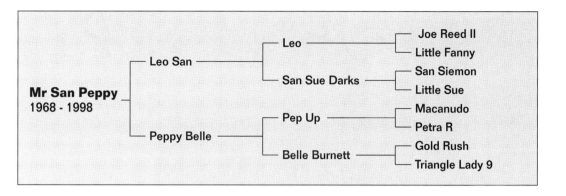

```
                                    ┌─ Joe Reed II
                          ┌─ Leo ───┤
                          │         └─ Little Fanny
              ┌─ Leo San ─┤
              │           │              ┌─ San Siemon
              │           └─ San Sue Darks┤
Mr San Peppy ─┤                          └─ Little Sue
1968 - 1998   │
              │                    ┌─ Macanudo
              │           ┌─ Pep Up┤
              │           │        └─ Petra R
              └─ Peppy Belle┤
                          │            ┌─ Gold Rush
                          └─ Belle Burnett┤
                                         └─ Triangle Lady 9
```

stallion than the mares, in order to improve their offspring," said Tio Kleberg, former vice president of King Ranch and descendant of the famous ranch's founder, Richard King. "Mr San Peppy was an outcross, except that on his dam's side he goes back to King Ranch (horses), and we were interested in that."

A Headstrong Pupil

Sired by Leo San out of Peppy Belle, Mr San Peppy was bred by Gordon B. Howell, of Dallas, Texas. Howell was also the breeder of Peppy San, Mr San Peppy's full brother, who Matlock Rose showed as the 1967 NCHA Open World Champion for Douglas Lake Cattle Company. In 1963, Howell dispersed his show horses and turned his attention to Quarter Horse racing at his stables headquartered across from Sunland Park, in El Paso, Texas. Howell, however, had retained Peppy Belle and her 1968 foal, Mr San Peppy, and when the time came to start Mr San Peppy on cattle, Howell enlisted the help of race trainer Bubba Cascio.

Cascio, who trained the legendary Quarter racing champion Dash For Cash for B.F. Phillips Jr., was no stranger to cutting. He had worked for Pinehurst Stables of Houston, Texas, in the 1950s, when Matlock Rose was the manager, and had shown Royal Jazzy, Calamity Jane, Poco Mona, Jessie James and Peppy San, among many other great early-day cutting horses. Mr San Peppy, however, was a challenge even for Cascio.

"He was a rogue," said Cascio of 2-year-old Mr San Peppy. "He'd buck and kick. I had a kid working for me that loved to ride and I put him on Mr San Peppy and sent him down to the Rio Grande, which at the time was all dried up. He rode Mr San Peppy in that deep sand about three miles out and back every day, and he finally got him to where he wouldn't buck everybody off. Then I built a little cutting pen and started him on cattle."

Cascio enlisted the help of leading Quarter Horse jockey Jerry Nicodemus as a turnback rider and began making progress with Peppy Belle's colt. "I had him running and turning with a cow," Cascio said. "He was a nice horse – a natural. And he had a lot of ability from the word go."

Halter and Performance Record:
NCHA earnings of $107,866; 1972 NCHA Cutting Horse Derby—1st Place; 1972 NCHA Non-Pro Finals—1st Place; 1974 NCHA World Champion; 1975 AQHA High-Point Cutting; 1976 NCHA World Champion; 1976 NCHA Finals—1st Place; 1976 AQHA World Champion Sr. Cutting; 1976 AQHA High Point Cutting and High Point Cutting Stallion; Performance Register of Merit; Superior Cutting.

Progeny Record:

Foal Crops: 23	Performance ROMs: 60
Foals Registered: 1,327	Superior Performance Awards: 15
Halter Point-Earners: 3	World Champions: 3
Halter Points Earned: 22	High-Point Winners: 3
Performance Point-Earners: 197	NCHA Earnings: $2,600,950
Performance Points Earned: 3,144	

COURTESY QUARTER HORSE JOURNAL

Famed cutting horse trainer Buster Welch likened Mr San Peppy's cutting style to "controlled violence."

The Welch Era Begins

When Cascio left El Paso for Ruidoso Downs, Howell sent Mr San Peppy to cutting horse trainer Buster Welch. Welch was immediately impressed with the colt's natural ability and strength. "His style was almost like controlled violence," Welch said. "He was very powerful and there wasn't any limit to what he could do."

Although Cascio had refined Mr San Peppy, he had not totally reformed him and the horse still looked for excuses to buck. Welch, however, was wise to his antics. "He bucked with me just one time," Welch added. "And when he did, he bucked into an iron fence and hit his head, and he never tried it again. Although I have a feeling he might have liked to."

Welch had a barn full of good 3-year-olds in 1971, including Poco Lena's last foal, Dry Doc, by Doc Bar. So Welch enlisted his son, Greg Welch, to show Mr San Peppy in the NCHA Futurity (Buster Welch and Dry Doc would win the event).

"Those were my college days and Mr San Peppy was as wild as I was," Greg Welch said. "I even had him with me at school for a little bit."

Once, Welch invited some young women to watch him ride the impressive young colt. While Welch was showing off, his jacket slipped off the right side of his saddle and Mr San Peppy seized the opportunity to dump Welch in the dirt. "I hit the ground before my jacket did," an embarrassed Welch remembered.

But for Greg Welch, putting up with Mr San Peppy's high spirits was a small price to pay for the opportunity to ride such a tremendous athlete. "He was one of the greatest horses I've ever ridden," said Welch, who today ranks among cutting's top five all-time leading trainers, in terms of earnings. "He was a cow horse deluxe – a big-moving, really physical horse. I kept telling Daddy that he was a better horse (than Dry Doc) and after the Futurity, Daddy decided he was too and he started riding him."

Mr San Peppy won the first go-round of the 1971 NCHA Futurity with Greg Welch aboard, but he lost a cow in the second round. "I had him a little too wild in the second go-round," Welch explained. "He taught me a lot about training. At the time, I knew the end results I wanted, but I had to learn patience to get there. He taught me a lot about that."

After the Futurity, Buster Welch began showing Mr San Peppy and Greg Welch rode Little Boy Rey for S.J. Agnew, of Centralia, Wash. In 1972, Buster won the NCHA Derby with Mr San Peppy and Greg claimed the reserve championship on Little Boy Rey.

In spite of his early reputation as a rogue, once Buster Welch started showing him, Mr San Peppy turned pro. He even responded to the lighter touch of women and children. Buster Welch's wife, Sheila, rode Mr San Peppy to finish seventh in the 1972 NCHA Non-Pro Top Ten standings and won the Non-Pro World Finals on him. Even Sheila's young daughter, Nina, liked to climb aboard Mr San Peppy after his workouts with Buster.

"One day when Nina was supposed to be cooling Mr San Peppy out, we looked up and she was working a steer," Buster recalled. "Her little feet didn't even reach the stirrups. There was a water trough in the middle of this long alleyway and Mr San Peppy jumped it and headed that steer. And before we could get to them, he turned around just as gentle and jumped and headed that steer again. I told Sheila, 'We really need to try to buy that sucker.'"

A Change of Owners

It was after the Derby that Gordon Howell decided to sell Mr San Peppy. He wanted $50,000, in those days a hefty price for a cutting horse. Welch scraped together a down payment, and S.J. Agnew, Welch's partner in several West Texas ranches, purchased half-interest in Mr San Peppy, after Buster and Sheila spent several sleepless nights wondering if they had made the right decision.

"The morning after we bought the horse, we both woke up at five and looked at each other and said, 'Fifty thousand dollars!'" Welch remembered. "The next morning we woke up even earlier."

When Mr San Peppy scored 76 points at one event with Matlock Rose as judge, Welch felt much more confident about his decision to purchase the horse. When Rose, who had trained and shown Peppy San, approached Welch with an offer to

With Welch in the saddle, Mr San Peppy was the 1974 and 1976 NCHA World Champion Cutting Horse.

COURTESY QUARTER HORSE JOURNAL

Peppy San Badger, a 1974 sorrel stallion by Mr San Peppy and out of Sugar Badger, earned multiple honors as a performer. Retired to stud, he became the industry's all-time leading sire.

COURTESY NCHA

TROPIC OTEL

Danny Huey

Miss Peppy Also, a 1977 sorrel mare by Mr San Peppy and out of Miss Dry Doc, was her sire's top money earner. After bankrolling $194,500 in earnings, the talented performer went on to become a top producer.

buy the stallion, Welch felt even better. "I knew that Matlock was a good judge of horses," Welch said.

In 1973, Welch and Agnew advertised Mr San Peppy's services for $600, at the Buster Welch Ranch in Merkel, Texas. The ad described Mr San Peppy as: "A true cow horse with superb action, balance and style; a modern horse at 15 hands and 1,135 pounds."

Mr San Peppy's first crop, foaled in 1974, consisted of 13 performers, among them Peppy San Badger, who would eventually eclipse Mr San Peppy and every other cutting horse stallion as the leading sire of money earners. As it turned out, 1974 was a pivotal year for Mr San Peppy and Buster

Welch in more ways than one. While Welch was hauling for the NCHA world championship and trying to promote Mr San Peppy to mare owners, Tio Kleberg, of King Ranch, called to inquire about Mr San Peppy. Kleberg arranged to fly to California, where Welch was showing the horse, to have a look.

"When we saw him and saw him work, I made up my mind that he was the horse we wanted," Kleberg said. "Buster offered to lease the horse to us for two years with an option to buy. It was a great suggestion because that way we could look at his foals. We sent some mares to him in 1974, and after we saw the foals in 1975, we decided to buy him. Up until that time, we had not

PHOTO BY LARRY GRAHAM

Tenino San, a 1976 sorrel gelding by Mr San Peppy and out of Tenino Fair, was the 1982 NCHA World Champion Cutting Horse. Here, he carries regular rider Greg Welch to a third place finish at the 1983 NCHA Finals.

Dual Pep, a 1985 chestnut stallion by Peppy San Badger and out of Miss Dual Doc, earned more than $300,000 in cutting competition. Retired to stud, he sired the earners of more than $12.7 million.

Little Tenina, a 1988 sorrel mare by Peppy San Badger and out of Tenino Fair, was the 1991 NCHA Futurity Champion.

competed in NCHA events. We had always used our horses on the ranch for working cattle, in general. All our horses were proven before they went into the broodmare band and the main priority was soundness. That's one thing that impressed us about Mr San Peppy - he'd competed and had done exceptionally well and had never taken a lame step. Of course, the key to his soundness was his overall conformation."

Greg Welch remembered looking forward to watching his father ride Mr San Peppy. "I always thought he was one of the greatest horses I rode, as far as physical ability," he said. "But watching Daddy show him, and watching him cut a bad Brahman cow, it was the greatest. Even after they retired him, I always worked him every time I went down to King Ranch. I loved riding him."

King Ranch Royalty

In 1974, Kleberg convinced Buster Welch to move to King Ranch as a consultant. In spite of the fact that Mr San Peppy was laid off four months to breed King Ranch mares, he still earned the title of NCHA world champion. "We bred Mr San Peppy while he was competing and it was not a problem for him, except that we had to stop showing from March through June," Kleberg said.

In 1976, Mr San Peppy won the NCHA world championship once again, earning $12,330 more than reserve champion Jay Freckles. He also claimed the AQHA world championship and became the first horse to garner both NCHA and AQHA world titles in the same year.

Mr San Peppy finished in the NCHA Top Ten standings again in 1977 and 1978 and became the first horse to earn over $100,000 in open competition. At 6, he became the youngest horse ever inducted into the NCHA Hall of Fame. "Mr San Peppy never took a tired step," Welch said. "He had so much 'try' and he was such a tremendous athlete."

In 1977, ridden by Buster Welch, Mr San Peppy's son Peppy San Badger made headlines by winning the NCHA Futurity.

Gradually, "Little Peppy," as Peppy San Badger came to be known, began to overshadow his sire, although ultimately, both horses became giants in the performance horse breeding industry.

Like Father, Like Son

Peppy San Badger was bred by Joe Kirk Fulton of Lubbock, Texas, out of the Grey Badger III daughter, Sugar Badger. It was Wayne Pooley, Fulton's ranch manager, who engineered Peppy San Badger's conception. In 1973, Pooley was at a cutting in Dallas where Welch was showing and trying to drum up breedings for Mr San Peppy. While he chatted with Welch, Pooley was called to turn back for another rider and realized that he had unsaddled his own horse. Welch immediately jumped in and offered Mr San Peppy as a turnback mount. "But that's a stud isn't it?" asked Pooley, who was concerned about "undoing" Mr San Peppy's show training.

Welch, who had used Mr San Peppy on a regular basis for ranch work, including roping and dragging calves, assured Pooley that using Mr San Peppy as a turnback horse would not affect his cutting performance. Pooley took Welch up on his offer and was so impressed with Mr San Peppy that he vowed to ask Joe Kirk Fulton to send a mare to breed to him.

Welch first glimpsed Peppy San Badger when the colt was a yearling. "He had distemper and he was all drawn up," Welch remembered. "I liked him, but he wasn't anything that just jumped out at me. I didn't see him again until Bruce Reeves, who broke him and started him on cattle, brought him to the ranch where I was and asked me to help him. When I got on him, I never was so impressed with a horse in my life."

Reeves left Peppy San Badger at King Ranch for Welch to ride. In the summer of 1977, upon Welch's advice, King Ranch struck a deal to buy the colt from Fulton. "Buster said that this might be Mr San Peppy's best son even though he was from his first crop," Kleberg said. "He thought we should try to buy him and Joe (Stiles, man-

ager of King Ranch's show horse division) and I agreed."

"Mr San Peppy was a fierce-working horse," Welch noted. "Little Peppy had that ability, but he also had a unique way, when the time came, to shut down and be soft and pretty right in the middle of something hard. He was so strong and yet so controlled; he never had to slam himself around. He reminded me of the golfer's prayer, 'Lord grant me the strength to hit the ball easy.' And he always had more in reserve."

With Welch aboard, Peppy San Badger won the 1977 NCHA Futurity and the 1978 NCHA Derby. Initially, King Ranch limited the stallion's breedings, but soon mare owners from coast to coast were eager to own a piece of Peppy San Badger. "Little Peppy was as well-balanced a horse as you could find," Tio Kleberg said. "If you could draw the perfect horse, as far as balance, it would be Little Peppy. His first crop was phenomenal. We bred him to 20 mares his 4-year-old year and out of those 20 mares, nine or 10 foals came back to the Futurity and six made the finals. Peppymint Twist (NCHA Derby champion) was from that first crop."

PHOTO BY DANNY HOEY, COURTESY NCHA

Haidas Little Pep, a 1980 chestnut stallion by Peppy San Badger and out of Doc's Haida, amassed lifetime earnings of $425,174.

155

Smart Peppy Lena, a 1984 sorrel Breeding Stock Paint gelding by Smart Little Lena and out of Two Ds San Peppy by Mr San Peppy, amassed $491,483 in the cutting horse wars.

Santa Belle, a 1985 bay mare by Doc's Hickory and out of Santo Peppy by Mr San Peppy, was the earner of $22,431.

Welch hauled Peppy San Badger for the 1980 NCHA world championship title, laying him up for four and a half months during breeding season; he concluded the year as NCHA reserve world champion. "In my book," Kleberg said, "Little Peppy is a world champion."

From his first crop, Peppy San Badger upstaged his sire, but Mr San Peppy still played a major role in King Ranch's breeding program, as well as the Quarter performance horse industry. Tenino San, sired by Mr San Peppy, was the first foal out of Tenino Fair, a Doc Bar daughter from one of S.J. Agnew's Thoroughbred race mares.

"Tenino San could be compared to Mr San Peppy," said Greg Welch, who started and trained Tenino Fair's colt and rode him as the 1982 NCHA Open World Champion for Bob and Patsy Brooks, of Whitesboro, Texas. "There were no small moves to him. It was all big, hard moves. He took a lot of riding - he was almost geared too fast, sometimes. But he had a really electric look about him when he worked."

Later, when bred to Peppy San Badger, Tenino Fair would produce NCHA Futurity winner Little Tenina, ridden by Greg Welch and earner of nearly $400,000. Tenino Fair's foals, sired by Mr San Peppy and Peppy San Badger, would earn more than $825,000.

Another Mr San Peppy foal, Miss Peppy Also, out of a Dry Doc mare, was co-reserve champion of the 1981 NCHA Derby with Buster Welch. The sorrel mare, owned by Silverbrook Ranch, earned $194,500 during her career and retired to become a successful broodmare. Soltera Peppy, by Mr San Peppy out of La Solitaria, placed third and fourth, respectively, in the NCHA Futurity and Derby, and produced Docs Lone Oak, earner of $234,635.

A Sire of Broodmares

It was daughters such as Miss Peppy Also and Soltera Peppy that assured Mr San Peppy's place among cutting's all-time leading maternal grandsires. Cutting

Mr San Peppy was not just an arena horse. Here, he and Buster Welch cut out a hefty King Ranch Santa Gertrudis calf while one of the ranch's Kineños looks on.

champions Mr San Peppy's daughters have produced include Smart Peppy Lena, $429,985; Santa Belle, $221,431; Rambo Oak, $185,150; and Tapeppyoka Peppy, $181,069, among others.

Primarily due to Peppy San Badger's progeny, Mr San Peppy also ranks among the top paternal grandsires of cutting horses. He is second only to Jewel's Leo Bars in average earnings per performer in this category. His sons' performers had earned more than $24.5 million through 1999, and include Little Badger Dulce, $668,461; Haidas Little Pep, $425,174; Little Tenina, $394,315; Dual Pep, $307,384; and CD Chica San Badger, $279,038.

Mr San Peppy's last crop was foaled in 1995. In 1998, at the age of 30, "the horse that built a dynasty" suffered a debilitating stroke and was euthanized. He is buried at the King Ranch where his most famous son, Peppy San Badger, still resides.

Through his own pre-potent efforts, and those of his sons, Mr San Peppy was truly "the horse that built a dynasty."

157

15 GREAT PINE

From his Midwestern home, the capable reining stallion helped define a fledgling industry.

Cheryl Magoteaux

LIKE THE NAMESAKE TREE that shades his grave, Great Pine's legacy is one of towering strength and endurance.

Eleven years after his death, Great Pine was still the No. 1 leading maternal grandsire of National Reining Horse Association money earners.

Great Pine has been honored by induction into the NRHA Hall of Fame, and the honor is appropriate, as the flashy stallion helped define a fledgling industry. From 1981 to 1988, Great Pine was a leading sire of reining horse money earn-

ers, and he was still listed as the No. 11 all-time leading sire in 2003. From 1993 through 2003, he was a leading maternal grandsire of reining horses.

In the 1960s and 1970s, the All American Quarter Horse Congress was a proving ground and the Columbus, Ohio, event became a showcase for Great Pine's sons and daughters. Although he would eventually be known as a great reining sire, his early winners were not limited to the reining pen. Great Pine sired Congress halter, western pleasure, and

As a yearling, Great Pine was a winning halter horse.

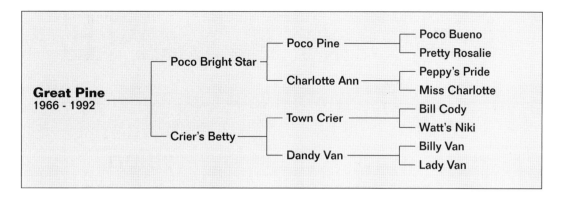

Great Pine
1966 - 1992

- Poco Bright Star
  - Poco Pine
    - Poco Bueno
    - Pretty Rosalie
  - Charlotte Ann
    - Peppy's Pride
    - Miss Charlotte
- Crier's Betty
  - Town Crier
    - Bill Cody
    - Watt's Niki
  - Dandy Van
    - Billy Van
    - Lady Van

reining futurity winners and even a hunt seat futurity champion!

A Blue Light Special

Great Pine was foaled in 1966 near Jacksboro, Texas. B.H. Wheelis bred his sorrel mare, Criers Betty, to Poco Bright Star, a 5-year-old stallion that Paul Curtner stood, along with his sire, Poco Pine. Criers Betty was by Town Crier — an AQHA Champion with 110 halter points — and out of Dandy Van by Billy Van.

Bill Lumm, president of the Ohio Quarter Horse Association and a founder of the Congress, had some mares in Texas being bred to Poco Pine. He visited Curtner and looked at some Poco Pine foals to take home to his Diamond L Ranch in Swanton, Ohio.

He remembers, "The Poco Pines were priced very high at that point. Paul showed me this Poco Bright Star weanling and said I could take him if I wanted. I thought he looked as good as the Pines and was less expensive than an own son."

With the purchase made, Great Pine and Lumm's bred mares were hauled to Ohio by Lumm's friend, Stretch Bradley. Later that year, Lumm was approached by Calvin Kohlman of nearby Port Clinton, Ohio.

"He said he was getting into Quarter Horses, and wanted to know if I had one that looked pretty good. I told him I had one that looked very good — and not as high-priced as some of the others."

Kohlman bought Great Pine and two

Halter and Performance Record:
Performance Register of Merit; AQHA Champion.

Progeny Record:
Foal Crops: 23	Performance Points Earned: 1,910
Foals Registered: 469	Performance Registers of Merit: 47
AQHA Champions: 1	Superior Performance Awards: 6
Halter Point-Earners: 15	World Champions: 1
Halter Points Earned: 75	High-Point Winners: 2
Performance Point-Earners: 200	NRHA Earnings: $658,904

mares, but his foray into Quarter Horses would be short-lived. Six months later he sold the lot. "I decided to concentrate on draft and miniature horses," he says.

COURTESY RON RENNER

Great Pine was, first, an AQHA Champion show horse and then an industry-shaping reining sire.

COURTESY QUARTER HORSE JOURNAL

After being purchased by Larry Rose, Great Pine's show and breeding emphasis was switched from halter to reining.

COURTESY LARRY ROSE

Great Pine's stopping style – extremely low in the back and soft in the front – was ahead of his time.

A Budding Halter Career

It was May of 1967 when he contacted Norm Gradel, a longtime horseman in Toledo. Norm and his daughter, Cathy, bought Great Pine and the other mares and Cathy claimed the colt. Although he was anything but fit, she and her friend, Benny Ann Harrison spent the summer showing him and Benny Ann's yearling in halter classes. She remembers, "He was just starting to look better when I took him to Columbus."

Ronald Renner was a new graduate of Ohio State University who had grown up showing in 4-H and local shows. In his words, "I wanted to step up a level and compete in AQHA shows. I was looking for a young gelding I could do reining and working cow horse on so I went to the AQHA show in late August at Columbus."

One of the colts in the yearling stallion class caught his eye. "I said to my wife, 'I like the way that horse moves.' I remember thinking how very balanced he was and that he had a kind of grace about him. He was a little scruffy, but I really liked him."

The colt got the gate, but by the time he walked through it, Ron was there.

"I told the young lady that was leading him that I was looking for a colt," he continued, "and asked if she'd sell him. She said she would, so we got together the next weekend. I gave her $400 and a 4-year-old mare for Great Pine."

Renner planned to geld his horse in the spring. He showed him in two AQHA halter classes that fall at Ashland, Ohio, and he won both. They were respectable wins with six and eight colts in the classes.

He fitted the horse through the winter and in March, took him to Columbus. When he placed third in an AQHA class of 37 yearlings, Ron decided to let Great Pine stay a stallion.

"Then my goal was to earn his AQHA Championship," said Renner. He showed Great Pine in halter, pleasure and trail.

"I rode him in a pleasure class a week or two after I saddled him the first time. He was such a good horse, he let me do that."

His voice softens as he remembers, "Pine was just a real proud horse. He always had such a quality look about him. He was a joy to be around."

Trainer Larry Rose, who had a farm south of Lexington, Ohio, towards Belleville, was familiar with the pretty, dark sorrel stallion. Rose remembers, "Great Pine looked so slow, and lazy and low-headed. Every time he'd beat me (in halter) I'd think 'I'd hate to have to ride that!'"

But as the horse began to be ridden, he looked better to Rose.

Rose had earned his first AQHA World Championship at the age of 15, with Nifty Bee in trail. A year later, he added another title on Nifty Baby Doll in western riding, and before he was 20, he had won a Reining World Championship on Nifty Della Bee. Forty years later, the swarthy Ohioan would be known for his offbeat personality and quirky training techniques. Controversial and opinionated, he nevertheless enjoyed vast success in the reining world. But in those days, Rose was an intense young trainer showing in halter, trail, pleasure and just about everything else to support his growing passion for reining.

The Rose Connection

Ron Renner sent Great Pine to Rose the first week in January of his 4-year-old year to get the reining points that would complete his Championship.

Eighteen days of training later, Great Pine was entered in an AQHA reining class in Paoli, Indiana. When the class was over, Great Pine had his first reining point and Rose had a new perspective.

He says, "When you have a great one,

you can tell it right off. He wasn't even that broke. He'd been ridden in a Tom Thumb in pleasure and would barely neck rein."

After four shows, Great Pine went home for the breeding season. When he returned, he quickly got the final points needed and at the age of 4 became an AQHA Champion.

Renner remembers, "Larry had fallen in love with him. After I got him back home, he'd call and ask if he could take him to this big show or that one. I'd haul him up there and he'd go show him."

A short time later, a divorce caused Renner to opt to sell his stallion. Rose remembers, "I had Nifty Bee and he was a leading sire of reiners at that time."

He muses, recollecting the still-fledgling days of the reining breeding industry, "Prior to that time, if they flunked everything else, they could be a reiner. We were just starting to see people breed specifically to get a reining horse."

Nifty Bee had sired Boggies Last and Mr Nifty Bee — both National Reining Horse Association World Champions and both eventual NRHA Hall of Fame inductees.

In Rose's words, "The last thing I needed was a stud, but I just had to have him. Ron wanted $10,000, and I managed to scrape together $9,500 and he took it."

Lady Be Great Pine, a 1976 chestnut mare by Great Pine and out of Tabano Mollie, was one of the first "Pines" to make it big as a reining horse. Here she is after carrying Kristie Rose to a win in the ladies reining class at the 1986 All American Quarter Horse Congress, Columbus, Ohio.

A New Home

Rose had the horse he believed in and he went on to win with him at the toughest reining events in the nation. In the early '70s there were few big NRHA Open reinings, but at the state fairs in Michigan, Ohio, Indiana, Kentucky and New York, the top five Junior and Senior AQHA reining horses would qualify for the $1,000 Reining Stakes.

Great Pine's style was ahead of its time. "He stopped like modern horses," Rose said. "Deep behind and soft in front. I didn't have a clue of how to get one to do that. It was just him."

Physically, Great Pine was light years ahead of the pack as well. His ability to pass on his good looks promised quick payback on Rose's purchase. The 1969 All American Quarter Horse Congress Halter Futurity Championship had gone to Tijuana Pine, a Great Pine son out of Amigoette by Amigo Man.

With some promotion and hard work, the 1971 breeding season looked to be a success and Rose found himself in the enviable position of having a stallion with 40 mares booked to him.

At $350 a mare in the days when pickups were selling for $4,000, life looked good. But when he took the horse he called "Old Star" to breed, Great Pine simply stared off toward the pasture, the barn or the arena.

Rose chuckles, remembering. "It's late January. I'm holding him and he's looking at everything but the mare and I'm thinking 'There went $9,500.' I'm one sick kid."

Great Pine would not breed that mare, or any mare. "I just kept trying every day," Rose noted. "I was desperate."

For the next six weeks, Rose continued to encourage his recalcitrant stallion. Around March 15, Great Pine changed modes and began to breed. A relieved Rose persevered and the season ended up with a high conception rate. But every year, the pattern would be the same, with Great Pine dormant sexually until the middle of March.

Tonya Lee Pine, a 1984 sorrel mare by Great Pine and out of Berts Lea Ann, was ridden by Kristie to a 4th place finish in the 1987 NRHA Non-Pro Futurity.

Great Red Pine, a stallion by Great Pine and out of Nifty Jodieann, had lifetime earnings of $60,952. He is shown here carrying Albert Burton to the 1992 NRHA Superstakes (4 & 5 year old) Reserve Championship.

Great Resolve (Einstein), a 1997 red dun stallion by Great Red Pine and out of Silversnow Pinestep, earned $147,283 in reining competition. Reining icon Tim McQuay rode the talented performer to a 3rd place finish in the 2000 NRHA Futurity.

163

Miss Tinseltown, a 1994 sorrel mare by Great Red Pine and out of Ms Holywood Showtime, amassed $114,375 in NRHA earnings.

Vic Clark of Shelby, Ohio, is a prominent accountant, as well as an NRHA and AQHA judge. Back then, he was a young college student, working for Rose, leading, riding and showing horses. Great Pine was pure fun. Clark remembers, "We'd take a piece of binder twine and ride him with it around his neck. He had this big mane that hung down on both sides of his neck, so you could hold on to his mane. That horse could stop eight or ten feet, barefoot and ridden bareback."

But Great Pine had a sense of humor. "He learned that when you'd spin him with that baling twine, you couldn't stop him," Clark explains. "He'd keep spinning until he spun you off. Then he'd stop and look at you."

Great Pine foals continued to excel in the halter pen and Rose was breeding 50 and 60 mares, mostly halter mares, each

year. Then, as the Ohio horseman recalls, "Some of those halter horses were started on reining and began to do well."

A Reining Sire is Born

Im Great Too, a Great Pine son out of Skippa Shoe by Skipper Jr, became the 1974 NRHA Futurity Reserve Champion with Paul Horn riding. It was on Im Great Too that one of the National Reining Horse Association's most legendary memories was made.

It took place at the 1975 Congress, in the days of 35- to 40-horse open reining classes. Million-dollar rider Bill Horn was showed Miss White Trash and catch-rode Im Great Too for his brother Paul, who was injured. Horn tied with himself to win the event and in the runoff, to the

Primary Pine (A Famous Amos), a 1990 sorrel stallion by Great Pine and out of Amie's Ace, was the NRHA earner of $38,463.

delight of the crowd, he won on his brother's horse — Im Great Too.

Rose was doing his part by starting colts for reining. 1975 was a watershed year in Great Pine's career, due as much to Rose's foresight as to Great Pine's prepotency. The previous fall, Rose had five 2-year-old Great Pines in training. "I was riding them for customers that were payers and I talked them into selling their Great Pines. I took the hit so they could go to other trainers."

He remembers, "My take on the deal was that if other trainers would brag on them, it would be better than me talking them up. People knew why I was bragging on them, but if they heard it from others, I thought they would believe it."

The 1975 NRHA Futurity structure took 15 horses to the finals, and that year five of the 15 finalists were Great Pines. "Bob Mac rode two, and John Amabile,

Bob Anthony and Paul Horn each rode one," Rose recalls.

In 1977, Rose rode Great Simon Sez to the NRHA Futurity Reserve Co-Championship. "I won $6,600 and sold him for $6,000 and thought I'd never have to work another day," he remembers.

Great Pine get continued to excel on the show front. He'za Great Pine became an AQHA Champion in 1977. Owned by Howard Lee of Unionville, Ohio, the palomino stallion out of Sugar Mora by Skip Mora earned a Superior western pleasure award as well.

But more and more reiners began making the trek to Great Pine's court at Rose's farm. "The NRHA bunch was still small at that time. I was still breeding about 70 percent halter/pleasure type mares. Then it kept switching over the years until we were breeding mostly reining mares."

Dry Sugar Rose, a 1995 chestnut mare by Primary Pine and out of Dry Sugar Lena, was ridden by Larry Rose to a 3rd place finish at the 1998 NRHA Futurity.

Great Pine was truly the working man's horse for the ages. Rose's accommodations were Spartan, and just the drive up the rutted driveway could be daunting. The clientele was seldom elite, and Great Pine's legacy was more that he produced scores of steady, consistent performers than a few superstars. His foals earned over three quarters of a million dollars in the age when the Futurity paid less than five figures.

Rose chuckles, "I bred anything that came up the driveway. I didn't have the luxury of culling mares or of buying a bunch of winning mares to breed to him. And it just didn't matter what the mare was. When Im Great Too did so well, people thought, "If he can sire a reiner out of that kind of mare, what can he do?'"

Rose's place is located next to an Amish community and the Amish boys he hired to clean stalls drove to work in a wagon each day. One day the wagon mare, hitched to the rail, still in harness, was showing obvious signs of heat. "The kid asked what I'd charge to breed to my stud. I had no mares to breed that day so I told him to get all that crap off her and we'd breed her."

A few years later the young man asked Rose if he'd like to buy a nice black filly. "I went to look at her and she didn't pace, so I bought her for $250. I named her Pines Dolly, got her trained, and she's probably the only horse with NRHA earnings that has a Standardbred mom!"

Great Pine's genetic strength let him cross successfully on just about any mare and that prepotency gave a new look to the reining horse world. Rose enthuses, "Great Pine brought conformation to reining. They used to be just horses, and then Great Pine introduced looks."

Vic Clark concurs with Rose's assessment. "That horse - with the exception of being a little more upright in pasterns than the ideal - and some of that kind of horses can turn around better - was living proof of the theory of form to function. He had a great big stifle, was well-balanced and low-necked. He sired that conformation, too. When his colts matured, they weren't big enough and strong enough for the big horse halter classes, but they were hard to beat as weanlings and yearlings."

Pretty is as Pretty Does

Clark pauses, thoughtfully, and continues, "Before Great Pine, I thought about halter horses as having the conformation to win a halter class. But he translated that correct form into performance as well. The other thing - I guess we took for granted his intelligence and what he passed on. I could train those foals to get on their feet and stand to look at you in a couple of days. I didn't appreciate it back then until I realized they weren't all like that."

He adds, "He also brought that graceful movement. There were several. Miss Doll Pine, the dam of Crome Plated Jac, was a gorgeous halter filly. Larry and I both showed her and she won at least 10 yearling filly classes. Then she went on to become an NRHA Non-Pro World Champion with Richie Greenburg."

Rose and Clark showed the Great Pine daughter Justa Great Pine as a 2-year-old in pleasure. Retired to the broodmare band and bred to Topsail Cody, she produced the NRHA Futurity Limited Open Reserve Champion, Top Gun

COURTESY LARRY ROSE

Rose's no-frills approach to handling Great Pine did not call for an excess of "spit and polish." Still, the legendary sire looked great even with just a lariat around his neck.

167

"The Great Pines were just gorgeous movers, said Clark. "They were talented, good-minded horses that had halter conformation back in those days. And the amazing thing was that, especially in the beginning, there were not any top reining mares bred to him. He gave his foals both the looks and the movement, no matter what kind of mare they were out of."

The pretty-boy sire was strictly working class and life was all about work for Rose and Great Pine. Clark shares stories of being at the shows, finishing showing, and driving a couple hours home to breed Great Pine, then back to the show in time for the morning classes.

Rose remembers, "In those days, there was no ultrasound or palpating to see where the follicle was. Everything was live cover."

Rose's attention was more easily captured by what was in the arena than in what was in the breeding barn. "I was riding a bunch of horses and I'd get involved - breeding would slip my mind - and at the end of the day I'd remember 'I've got mares to breed!' There'd be three to breed and I'd tie them to the fence in the indoor arena and half an hour later they'd be all bred - all live cover."

Rose admits, "I was the worst breeding manager there ever was. He was the kindest horse, not 'studdy' at all, but when he'd come down off that third mare, he'd be really mad at me."

At Rose's farm, there were often horses everywhere - tied to trees, even in the horse trailer. "If an owner called to see his mare, and she was in the trailer, we'd put her in a stall and put whichever one was in the stall into the trailer."

If the process of breeding was a chore, the product was all joy. "The babies all had a really good on-off switch. They could do hard things hard and then go right back to doing soft things soft. They could run and stop and go back to the center and lope off like a pleasure horse," says Rose.

Generation Next

The list of families that crossed well with Great Pine was diverse, but one that would produce branches that stretched through generations came when he was bred to Bennett Star Bar. After having four foals with no accomplishments, she was bred to Great Pine for the next six foals and a dynasty began. Not only did the ensuing foals perform, they produced. And the next generation included NRHA champions, AQHA ROMs and World Show finalists.

Rose made sure the Great Pines got into the right hands. An unabashed promoter, he knew the value of having the top trainers in the nation riding Great Pines. "Paul Horn did the most for him - riding his babies. Tim McQuay did a lot - he would buy one I'd trained and go on with him."

McQuay is the National Reining Horse Association's All-Time Leading Money Earner and he's garnered a substantial portion of his earnings on Great Pine get and grand-get.

"They're very gritty and very trainable," he commented. "The first one I rode was Great Nifty Fox. I won the first go of the 1985 NRHA Futurity on him and ended up fifth."

Another prominent win for a Great Pine son came in 1986, when Bill Horn rode Vincents My Way to win the NRHA Derby for owner Henry (Vincent) Uvino.

McQuay had even more success on second-generation Great Pines, initially with another magic cross, that of Hollywood Jac 86 on Great Pine mares. Crome Plated Jac, by Hollywood Jac 86 and out of Miss Doll Pine, won the Ohio State Fair Open Reining and was the Congress Opening Reining Reserve Champion three times. In 1984, Jack Little Pine - a full brother to Crome Plated Jac - placed fourth at the NRHA Futurity.

Although most of the spotlight has shown on Great Pine daughters as broodmares, there have been sons of Great Pine with superior production records. Great Red Pine was a son that sired winners and he was No. 20 on the NRHA All Time Leading Sire List in 2003.

McQuay won the 1999 National Reining Breeders Classic on the Great Red Pine daughter Miss Tinseltown. In 2000, McQuay rode the Great Red Pine son Great Resolve, a.k.a. "Einstein," to a win in the Congress Futurity and a third-place finish at the NRHA Futurity.

Rose muses, "Miss Tinseltown and Dry Sugar Rose, two Great Pine grand-daughters, are two of only about a dozen mares that had won over $100,000 in the NRHA through 2003."

Through the 23 years they were together, Rose's respect for Old Star grew. "It seemed when people came and opened the door and looked at him, he knew he was the center of attention. He was real docile and quiet, even as a young stud, but he was a proud horse."

He remembers his passing. "He was 26 and got some toxic hay that had been over-sprayed. He lived about 10 days and lost about 400 pounds He kept trying to live - and I just didn't have the heart to put him down."

Finally, the situation was so bleak, there seemed no other option. "We dug this big hole in the front yard, next to a big pine tree."

Rose led his stallion down to the freshly dug grave to meet the vet. "I'm not emotional, but I cried like a baby leading him down to that hole."

The feeble stallion walked slowly along with Rose. Then, amazingly, he put his head down and began to eat grass.

"I couldn't do it," Rose remembers. He told the vet to go home, then carefully walked Great Pine back to the barn, where the stallion died during the night.

Reflecting on the horse's impact on his life, Rose says simply, "He changed me from a pauper to a millionaire. I'd be working at McDonalds if not for him."

Over a decade after his death, Rose still honors Great Pine. "His stall has his name on it in walnut letters. It's still just like it was then. No one could replace him. There's been no horse in that stall since he died."

COURTESY LARRY ROSE

Larry Rose continues to look to the future with his proven line of reining horses. Here, he poses with the Great Pine granddaughters Dry Sugar Rose (left) and Miss Tinseltown. Both mares earned more than $100,000 as NRHA competitors and both will be given the opportunity to add to the Great Pine story as producers.

16 THE INVESTER

Endowed with overall balance and powerful hindquarters, he was built to move.

Heidi Nyland

POINTED FIRST TOWARD A CAREER as a halter horse, The Invester seemed destined to remain within that realm. And, while he and his offspring did well in that event, it soon became apparent that the stallion's true calling would be as a rail horse.

Endowed with overall balance, a powerful stifle, well-rounded croup and strong hocks, he was built to move.

The Invester, a 1969 sorrel stallion by Zippo Pat Bars and out of Hank's Peppy Lou, was bred by Eldon England, Oklahoma City, Okla.

Zippo Pat Bars, a 1965 chestnut stallion by Three Bars (TB) and out of Leo Pat by Leo, had been purchased by Paul Curtner of Jacksboro, Tex., to cross on his Poco Pine mares.

The AAA-rated racehorse's first foal crop hit the ground in 1969. Among its 12 members were The Invester and Zippo Pine Bar. Both colts would go on to achieve legendary

The Invester – one of the pleasure industry's first great sires – is enshrined in both the AQHA and NSBA Halls of Fame.

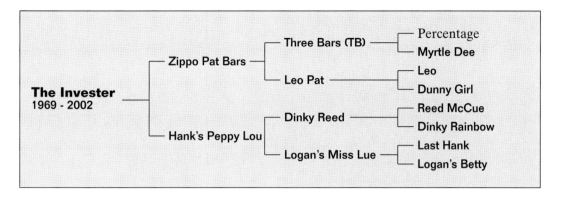

The Invester
1969 - 2002
- Zippo Pat Bars
  - Three Bars (TB)
    - Percentage
    - Myrtle Dee
  - Leo Pat
    - Leo
    - Dunny Girl
- Hank's Peppy Lou
  - Dinky Reed
    - Reed McCue
    - Dinky Rainbow
  - Logan's Miss Lue
    - Last Hank
    - Logan's Betty

sire status and, in effect, serve as each others' most formidable breeding pen rivals.

A Well Thought-Out Plan

The Invester first entered the show ring as a halter prospect named Hank Lou Bars. An up-and-coming young showman named Jerry Wells watched from the stands as the then-70-something England showed the sorrel weanling colt at the 1969 Oklahoma State Fair.

While the youngster did not place well in the class, Wells knew he had to have him. He followed England out of the show pen and asked him if he would sell the young horse.

"I thought he was the hand-made, prettiest colt out there," Wells recalled. "He had a very pretty head, a pretty neck, and about as pretty a hip and croup as you could put on one. And he had a nice stifle. He didn't carry a humongous gaskin or hind leg, but it fit him. He had correct feet and legs and he was made with overall balance.

"I asked England what he'd want for him," he continued, "and he quoted me a price. The biggest old tears came out of his eyes when I said I'd take him.

"I asked if he was sure he wanted to sell him. He said he didn't want to, but thought he should. The colt was going to be a yearling soon, and England didn't think he'd be able to handle him."

Buying the young stud for a modest $3,500 was an investment that would

---

Halter and Performance Record:
Open Performance Register of Merit; AQHA Champion; Superior Halter; AQHA Hall of Fame Horse.

Progeny Record:

Foal Crops: 29	Performance Point-Earners: 687
Foals Registered: 1,163	Performance Points Earned: 21,029
AQHA Champions: 11	Performance Registers of Merit: 341
Amateur Champions: 1	Superior Performance Awards: 143
Youth Champions: 4	World Champions: 4
Halter Point-Earners: 158	High-Point Winners: 3
Halter Points Earned: 1,476	NSBA Earnings: $313,220
Superior Halter Awards: 4	

---

jump-start Wells' horse-handling career. The native Oklahoman would go on to secure a firm reputation as a horseman capable of finding the proverbial "diamonds in the rough." Among the other legends he is credited with discovering and/or owning are Sonny Dee Bar, Te N' Te, Impressive and Conclusive (see chapter 18).

But Wells didn't keep the England-bred colt long enough to show him. Just two months after taking the youngster home to his new property and half-finished barn, Wells found a buyer for him.

"I knew I probably wouldn't have him that long because he was sure stud material," he said. "Plus, I was going into business for myself then. My barn was just about finished. I had room for a few horses in it, but I had to sell the new ones. I didn't have any place to keep him."

In December of 1969, George Pardi of Fredericksburg, Texas, was in the market for a new horse. He asked Jack Benson to

While owned by George Pardi, Fredricksburg, Tex., The Invester was shown by trainer George Benson to an AQHA Championship and Superior halter award.

find a perfect riding horse for him; an older horse ready to work under saddle. Two years earlier, Benson had bought Three Storms from Wells on Pardi's behalf. The horse had been a racehorse and Pardi successfully showed him to his AQHA Championship.

Unfortunately, Three Storms died soon after Pardi purchased him. Benson and Pardi were happy with Wells' horse selec-tion and went back to him for a replace-ment horse.

"Jack called looking for another horse for Pardi," Wells said. "He wanted an older horse he could get going under saddle. I had The Invester. I told him all about him. He said he wanted an older horse, but he'd look at him. I told him, if you look at him, you'll buy him. I priced him at $15,000. That's what Pardi gave."

Here's a nice circa late 1970s shot of three men who were instrumental in The Invester's development as a top performance sire. From the left, Jerry Stanford and Brad McCamy are mounted on a pair of young Investers and Jack Benson is astride of "the old man."

PHOTO BY JIM KEELAND, COURTESY QUARTER HORSE JOURNAL.

KEELAND HOUSTON

Vestida Moneca, a 1973 sorrel mare by The Invester and out of Muneca Mia, earned a Superior in western Pleasure.

Wells added that The Invester went to the right place in a deal that was good for everyone involved.

"That little rascal went a long way toward getting my barn finished," he said. "That was a lot of money at the time. And, he found his niche. I might not have done all that with him. I would have focused on showing halter. It worked out well for everybody."

In the short time between the Oklahoma State Fair and December 12, when Pardi signed for The Invester, Wells took time for one more thing. He changed the young stallion's name.

At the time, Wells considered the horse a solid and well-planned investment. Little did he know that when he changed the 8-month-old's name, he established a theme that would identify Invester-bred horses for years.

"Hank Lou Bars just didn't fit him," Wells recalled. "I didn't like that name at all. He was such a pretty son of a gun to have a name like that. I don't remember how we came up with The Invester, but I knew his name had to be changed."

With his new name and owner, The Invester headed to Texas.

Texas Unlimited

At the Pardi ranch, trainer Benson quickly bonded with the horse he nicknamed "Baldy." Under his care and conditioning, The Invester earned Superior halter horse status and was on his way to becoming an AQHA Champion.

Benson knew he had to keep his prized horse when Pardi dispersed his stock in 1973. Owner and trainer worked out a plan. Benson would buy The Invester for $25,000, paying $5,000 down and the remainder over time. Benson moved his training operation and his newly purchased horse to Irvin

Vester Vision, a 1975 sorrel stallion by The Invester and out of Miss Pocket Money, was an AQHA Champion and earned a Superior in western pleasure.

Catchman's ranch in Bellville, Texas. There, Benson stood The Invester and shared the profits with his landlord.

The move introduced Benson to new friends who would be instrumental in The Invester's future. Future co-owner Brad McCamy first saw The Invester while working at Catchman's. "He was running out in the pen," McCamy remembered. "Even if you didn't know much about horses, you'd know there was something special about him. He just had that presence."

McCamy began working for Benson a year later. He watched Benson's special bond with the stallion he worked with daily, the stallion McCamy called "Big Daddy."

"I never saw anybody else ride him," McCamy said. "Then Jack went away and asked me to ride him so he wouldn't be so fresh when he got home. He was big and strong, but he could stop and spin and work a cow. For Jack to let me ride that horse, that was something. He was special to Jack. He truly loved that horse. He promoted him and he knew what he had."

The Makings of a Sire

Two years later, in 1977, the Benson-McCamy pair founded Stallions Unlimited and co-owned The Invester. There, the sorrel stallion stood next to several of the day's top stallions, including Hobby Horse and Red Dee Hobby. The Invester quickly proved himself as a promising young sire.

"For his first four or five foal crops, The Invester was one of the leading sires of halter class winners every year," McCamy said. "Then, when those foals were old enough to ride, we found out it wasn't a fluke that a

PHOTO BY REGGIE RUSSELL, COURTESY QUARTER HORSE JOURNAL

Miss Balance Plus, a 1979 palomino mare by The Invester and out of Miss Gay Gold, was typey enough to win halter futurities as a weanling, and balanced enough to earn a Superior in western pleasure as a mature horse.

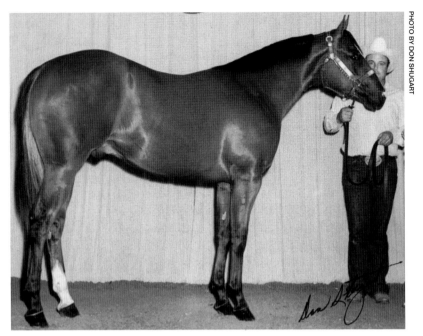

PHOTO BY DON SHUGART

PHOTO BY DON SHUGART

Invest In Ears, a 1979 bay gelding by The Invester and out of Miss Cozy Chick, was another great two-way performer. As a yearling (top), he won the 1980 TQHA yearling gelding halter futurity and placed in the Top 10 at the World Show. As a mature horse, he earned Superiors in open and amateur Western pleasure.

few of them were good movers. We changed what we were doing and focused on breeding pleasure horses. They were what pleasure horses should be."

McCamy immediately recalls names of The Invester's early and successful sons and daughters. El Cicatriz, a 1973 bay gelding out of Bar Moon Miss, was the 1974 AJQHA World Champion Yearling Gelding. The Pardi-bred gelding also earned Superior halter awards in both the open and youth division.

Later in life, El Cicatriz proved himself an excellent mover. With owner Jocelyn Wejroch-Williams in the saddle, the aged gelding won numerous dressage competitions.

Of The Invester's first successful get, a 1973 mare named Vestida Moneca topped McCamy's list. Nancy Cahill rode the mare to her AQHA Register of Merit in performance. Then the duo went on to become highly-successful in open western pleasure competition.

In 1980, The Invester served notice that he was a sire to be reckoned with when, at the 1980 All-American Quarter Horse Congress, six of his get placed in the 2-year-old snaffle bit futurity finals.

Trainer Marty Johnson successfully trained three of the finalists with help from her then-husband, Jerry Stanford: Sure Investment (first place), The Collateral (second), and The Matinee (sixth).

"Jack Benson made arrangements for us to ride and train three Investers while we were employed at Misty Acres in Lufkin, Texas," Johnson said. "The 1978 foals were broke in 1979 and shown as early as July 1980. They finished their 2-year-old careers at the 1980 Congress."

The Investers won $55,390, or 58 percent of the total class purse. Tommy Manion and Sure Investment placed first. Stanford rode The Collateral to a second-place finish. Keith Whistle and Double Vested claimed the third spot, and Barney Hinds on Miss Cash Ticket slipped into fourth place. Investers Reward and The Matinee stood by their family members in the finals lineup.

Sure Investment, a 1978 brown mare by The Invester and out of Sure Edith, was ridden by Tommy Manion to win the prestigious 1980 All American Quarter Horse Congress 2-year-Old Futurity.

Jerry and Marty Stanford of Lufkin, Texas, trained several of The Invester's earliest pleasure champions. In addition, the couple also mentored an up-and-coming young pleasure trainer named Cleve Wells in the art of making a winning rail horse. Here the trio is at an early 1980s Texas Classic horse show.

Impulsions, a 1987 chestnut stallion by The Invester and out of Randados Rosa, was ridded by Kelli McCamy to win the 1989 AQHA World Champion 2-Year-Old Snaffle Bit Futurity.

Johnson remembers watching the futurity class with Benson.

"It was a real proud moment," she recalled. "When Jack realized the first six were Investers he started down the stairs, from where we were sitting to where I had moved to congratulate the winners, and said 'We did it, Red!' That was a nickname he had given me.

"It was a special moment and something that hasn't been duplicated. It was the beginning of history. Soon after, if people didn't have an Invester, they wanted one."

In the next years, Johnson's patient training methods helped solidify The Invester's get as successful competitors. Johnson and Stanford worked with young Cleve Wells in Hempstead, Texas. Wells, an experienced calf roper, was anxious to learn Johnson's training methods and worked with them for nearly six years. Johnson's program consisted of training the disciplines of dressage in western form.

"The Investers were beautiful and pretty movers," Johnson recalled. "They presented an elegance in the arena. From the first one that I rode, I knew they were trainable horses, but not by the ordinary way. I did walking and stretching exercises along with a modified dressage program. They had to learn my program at the walk to apply it at the trot and then advance to the lope. Every day you'd regress back to the walk, progress to the trot, then the lope and try to add something new to keep their active minds from being bored. A lot of people were interested in the program.

"If people wanted to be successful on an Invester, they had to figure out how to be patient. These horses would try you, but with patience, they would always reward you."

Johnson remembers a special Invester son, Coys Investment, a 1979 gelding by The Invester and out of Bonanza's Bay Lady. Babs Bashore worked with Johnson and took on the colt as her special project. She showed him to win an Open Texas Classic Futurity Reserve Championship. Jerry Wells then bought the young horse for his daughter Nancy to show at the 1982 Congress. The horse went on to earn open and amateur ROMs.

"Nancy stepped on him for the first time at the Congress, practiced for two days, went in, and won the 13-and-under pleasure class," Johnson said. "He packed her around and was extremely broke. The crowd just loved him. To my knowledge, Coy was the only 2-year-old to win a Youth Western Pleasure class at Congress."

Johnson remembers her favorite Invester son from the 1980s. Invest In Ears was out of Miss Cozy Chick. The 1979 gelding known as "Ears" made his debut at the 1982 Silver Dollar Circuit in Las Vegas, Nev. He was circuit champion, winning all five days with Stanford in the saddle. Johnson also showed him in hunter under saddle classes at the 1982 Congress. "Ears" won NSBA money and earned a Superior in amateur and open western pleasure. He also earned his performance ROM as a 3-year-old.

While The Invester's first-generation get secured his reputation as a top sire, future generations assured that his legacy would live on.

Ten years after his first progeny claimed Congress titles, a new generation of Investers entered the 1990 Congress 3-year-old derby. Impulsions, a 1987 chestnut stallion by The Invester and out of Randados Rosa, won the prestigious event with Kelli McCamy in the saddle. Five more "Invester" get or grand-get placed in the top 10.

Syndication and Change

In 1979, the McCamy-Benson duo was encouraged to syndicate ownership of The Invester. Only a few Quarter Horses had been syndicated previously. Spreading ownership would up the stallion's advertising budget and limit the number of mares he bred. Benson and McCamy held onto 20 shares and sold the rest to breeders across the country.

"Each share guaranteed you could breed a mare a year for the life of the horse," McCamy recalled. "We limited the book and increased the quality of mares that bred to him."

The duo's plan proved sound. The Invester topped the AQHA's leading performance sire list and sired numerous AQHA high-point horses.

Then, a tragedy occurred in January 1989, that cast the 20-year-old stallion's future into uncertainty.

Benson was killed on his way to a Texas horse show. He stepped down from his truck and was hit by a passing semi. The tragedy left the horse without the owner who cared for him and loved him. After months of mourning, Benson's family agreed to sell the prized stallion.

Home for Good

In the late 1980s, Dan and Carol McWhirter of Doniphan, Nebraska, were searching for a breeding stallion The couple knew all about the aging sire because they had stood his son, The Big Investment, until his untimely death at age 6 in 1986.

PHOTO BY K.C. MONTGOMERY

Assets, a 1991 bay mare by The Invester and out of Miss Rebel Rita, won the 1994 NSBA 3-Year-Old Non-Pro Derby with Mary Carole Heckaman in the saddle.

PHOTO BY HARLOD CAMPTON

Vested Pine, a 1991 sorrel stallion by The Invester and out of Zippos Bay Lady, won the 1996 All American Congress Western Pleasure Maturity Limited Open with Alex Ross aboard.

The Big Investment, a 1980 sorrel stallion by The Invester and out of The Country Girl, sired 129 foals before his untimely death at the age of six. His get went on to earn 29 Superior awards, 64 performance ROMs and 4,554 points. In 1998, The Big Investment joined his sire in the NSBA Hall of Fame.

In his short life, The Big Investment sired 129 foals, which had earned 29 Superiors, 64 ROMs, a collective 4,554 AQHA points. The McWhirters knew winning was a family tradition.

"We were looking for a new horse for our breeding program," Carol said. "I had really wanted The Invester earlier, but in this business the good horses don't come up for sale very often. When Jack passed away, we waited a polite amount of time. Then I called up Jack's wife and told her I was interested in buying The Invester. She said the family just hadn't decided what to do. She'd put me on the waiting list and call when they were ready to sell."

The following September at Nebraska's Pitzer Ranch Sale, Carol heard that The Invester was up for sale. She was so excited she couldn't sleep. She called to ask for a price early the next morning. Acting as an agent for the family, noted horseman Dale Livingston priced the stallion. Carol called up her longtime customer and world championship halter showman Wayne Atchley, of Elkhorn, Neb., to ask if he'd partner with them to purchase the stallion. With a solid "yes," the McWhirters and Atchley formed The Invester Syndicate. All the pieces were fitting together to move the stallion north.

Then time stood still. Still rattled by their family's loss, the Bensons kept The Invester on their property for nearly three months. After legal setbacks surrounding the sale, the McWhirters finally moved the stallion to his new home on January 3, 1990. When he stepped off the trailer, the McWhirters were surprised to find a thin and neglected stallion.

"We were on a rescue mission," Carol recalled. "I truly believe that in another

PHOTO BY DON SHUGART

Principle Investment, a 1987 bay stallion by The Big Investment and out of Tiger Serena, was an AQHA Superior western pleasure performer and the NSBA earner of $35,566.

month, he would have been dead. We wouldn't let Wayne see him for two months - and he owned him with us. The Invester had big sores in his mouth. It took six to eight months to get to the point we didn't have to apologize for his appearance."

"We had spent a lot of money on a skinny horse," Dan seconded.

The McWhirters focused on getting The Invester back to top form. They had an equine dentist evaluate and form his teeth so he could better chew and process nutrients. Dan began feeding him a late-night snack of steamed rolled oats — a treat that was soon expected as part of The Invester's daily routine. Every night after the 10 o'clock news, Dan put on his coat and made a final trip to the barn. "He was always waiting for me," Dan says.

Analysis and Research

As The Invester fattened up, the McWhirters researched his siring trends and set up a plan to choose mares he would breed. Carol spent countless hours on the phone with McCamy, discussing his extensive experience standing the stallion. Pedigree analyst Larry Thornton worked with the McWhirters to review their new stallion's progeny records and study which bloodlines best crossed with The Invester.

Thornton found that mares with Three Bars breeding that also carried Leo, Joe Reed, Chicaro Bill, and Joe Moore blood crossed especially well with The Invester.

The Invester's Bonafide, Collectors Prize, El Cicatriz, Good Invester, Impulsions, Miss Balance Plus, Miss Cash Ticket, Mr Invester,

The Collateral, a 1980 gray gelding by The Invester and out of Sage Siemon, ranks as one of his sire's most durable offspring. In all, the versatile performer was ridden by 16 open, amateur and youth competitors to earn 962 points. The 26-year-old trooper is shown here in March 2004, with his latest partner – Shanaine Huck of Vincent, Ohio. That's trainer Don Jox with the good-looking pair.

ably, he passed on strong, low-set hocks, and a low tail set.

"There was no better hocked horse around," Dan said. "He could fix a mare's jog. He was the epitome of what a Quarter Horse should be."

McCamy focuses on The Invester's distinguishable legs.

"His biggest attributes were his hocks," he said. "He kept his foot on the ground when he loped and was just really powerful. That's a trait that hasn't diluted out."

The Boss

Life was good for The Invester in Doniphan. The McWhirters never saddled him and never put a chain over his nose. Stabled in the first stall, he stood next to his buddy, Good Asset, by Zippos Mr Good Bar.

"If Good Asset was outside too long, he was looking for him," Dan recalled. "The minute you'd bring him in, they'd touch noses through the bars. One day, Good Asset bit his nose. The Invester was mad for a week. He stood on the other side of his stall and didn't have anything to do with him."

The Invester showed off his management characteristics in other ways, too. When Brad McCamy visited the McWhirters shopping for broodmares, he went into The Invester's stall to see if he'd remember him.

After more than 10 years away from his one-time co-owner and manager, The Invester quickly recognized him.

"The Invester started dancing in his stall," Dan said. "When Brad led him out, he reached over and grabbed his sleeve. I apologized and told Brad he'd never done that before."

"He wasn't trying to hurt me,' McCamy said. "He just liked to do that. It was something he and I had always done. He was just different from any other horse I'd been around."

But while The Invester let you know he was the boss, he was never mean or pushy.

"Anyone could lead him," Dan continued. "He'd stand just like a halter horse. You could drop the lead rope, walk off,

Ms Big Spender, Ms Safety Deposit, Pardin Me, SR Market Invester, and Vester Vision are just a few Superior horses with this breeding scheme.

Carol says the syndicate established careful breeding criteria. If a customer's horse didn't fit the criteria, she'd simply tell them about the research they had done. With education, the McWhirters were able to help The Invester pass on top traits to mares and stallions.

"The Invester is a true curiosity because not only is he the sire of siring sons, he's the sire of producing daughters," Carol said. "We don't understand why. It's unusual. So many horses in the business are sire-line horses or maternal-line horses. He was equal."

The Invester passed on traits that were easy to see in his offspring. Most notice-

come back and he'd be standing right where you left him."

Some have said The Invester's get can be difficult to work with. Those close to the horses say they are smart and incapable of being intimidated. McCamy suspects that The Invester and his progeny helped redefine training, requiring trainers and riders to ask before demanding.

"It wasn't that the horses were tough," McCamy explained, "If you had an Invester, you had high expectations. Some people fought with them and tried to change them by pulling their faces. They just weren't going to take it. If you pulled and poked, they would fight. The Invester was like that, too. You could correct him, then you had to leave him alone. If you jerked him when he didn't do anything wrong, he'd paw your hat off. The Investers would not be intimidated. You had to train them by thinking, not by intimidating them. They taught us all how to be better horse trainers."

It's The Invester's personality and presence The McWhirters miss most. He easily bonded with those who worked with him.

One day in early 2002, when The Invester struggled to get up, the McWhirters knew it was time to say goodbye. He had lost weight and his eyes appeared tired. Wanting to keep him comfortable and healthy as long as possible, the McWhirters monitored his organs' function for more than a year.

On Feb. 28, 2002, The Invester was euthanized.

"The morning that we made arrangements to put The Invester down, out of the clear blue sky Jerry Stanford called," Carol said. "We hadn't talked to him in six months. He didn't have an agenda, he just knew he had to call. Something was wrong. I was crying. I'll never be convinced it was just coincidence."

It was no coincidence. The Invester made his presence known in and out of the show pen. His good looks, smart demeanor, and strong, flowing movement secured his place in Quarter Horse history as a top Quarter Horse performer who was able to consistently pass on his strong characteristics to future generations.

PHOTO BY FAYE ZNEK

Faye Znek (c)

Here's a circa 2000 shot of The Invester at his final home in Doniphan, Neb. Shown with the 31-year-old legend are (from left) Carol, Daniel and Dan McWhirter. Also pictured is "Roy" the Corgi.

17 SPEEDY GLOW

He is widely considered to be the first true western pleasure sire.

Heidi Nyland

FROM HIS START IN TEXAS to his promotion in California, Speedy Glow and his get topped judges' lists as calm, smooth pleasure horses. The red roan stallion is generally recognized as one the first true western pleasure sires. His flat-kneed movement influenced future judging standards and helped create the specialized western pleasure industry in the late 1970s and early 1980s.

Speedy Glow, a 1962 red roan stallion by Poco Red Bar and out of O's Linda Lee, was bred by Cotton Marriott of Seagoville, Texas.

Poco Red Bar, a 1958 sorrel by Three Bars and out of Poco Maria, earned two AQHA performance points and sired 20 point-earning sons and daughters. Of those few competitive offspring, three went on to be AQHA Champions, two earned Superiors, and nine earned ROMs.

PHOTO BY KAY VILLAS

Speedy Glow earned lasting fame as the West Coast sire of a top western pleasure line.

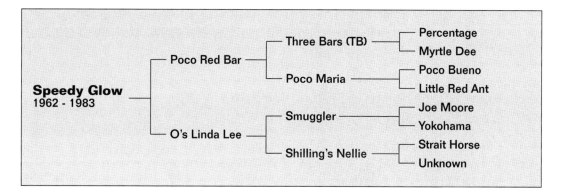

Speedy Glow
1962 - 1983

- Poco Red Bar
  - Three Bars (TB)
    - Percentage
    - Myrtle Dee
  - Poco Maria
    - Poco Bueno
    - Little Red Ant
- O's Linda Lee
  - Smuggler
    - Joe Moore
    - Yokohama
  - Shilling's Nellie
    - Strait Horse
    - Unknown

O's Linda Lee, a 1947 mare by Smuggler and out of Shilling's Nellie, was a foundation-bred mare that traced to such AQHA Hall of Fame horses as Joe Moore, Little Joe and Traveler.

A Glowing Start

Speedy Glow spent his first five years in Seagoville. In 1967, he was purchased by Orville Sims, Plano, Tex. Seven years later, Ken Grantham, Plano, Tex., became the colorful stallion's third owner.

The stallion was not heavily promoted during this time. However, a few of his get did well. Old Glow Pal, a 1970 chestnut gelding out of Miss Peppy Jo, was the 1972 All- American Quarter Horse Congress Pleasure Futurity Champion, and the 1973 AQHA high-point junior western pleasure horse.

As a young horse, Speedy Glow was trained and shown by Shorty Parks, Princeton, Tex. Parks was convinced the roan stallion had potential and focused his training on the western pleasure event.

Noted reining and cutting trainer Al Dunning was competing in western pleasure events at the time Speedy Glow appeared on the scene. He liked the stallion's movements and later trained several of his top performing get.

"I did western pleasure and had a lot of success at it," Dunning said. "There were a few sires that stood out in the beginning — The Invester and Speedy Glow were two. The first time I saw Speedy Glow, he was in Texas with Parks showing him. He won.

Halter and Performance Record:
Performance Register of Merit.

Progeny Record:

Foal Crops: 18	Performance Point-Earners: 326
Foals Registered: 433	Performance Points Earned: 16,912
Youth Champions: 5	Performance Registers of Merit: 190
Halter Point-Earners: 51	Superior Performance Awards: 92
Halter Points Earned: 547	World Champions: 7
Superior Halter Awards: 2	High-Point Winners: 3

"When you see the winner, you always want to know what they had. Watching him ride, I found out he was a quiet, level mover. Parks didn't have to do anything mechanical with him. That was the greatest horse Parks had. It was his bond. He was a gentle kind of trainer and he did a nice job on that horse.

"Later, I had some customers who were interested in pleasure horses," Dunning continued. "Parks had some of the Speedy Glows and, gosh, they looked good. They were quiet, low headed and good movers.

"There were a lot of roans - real pretty roans. All this was about the same time The Invester was coming on the western pleasure scene, too. The Invester was the first big time pleasure horse sire in Texas and Speedy Glow was the first big time pleasure horse sire in California."

In the breeding department, Parks noted Speedy Glow's ability to "fix" a mare - contributing strong genes that could diminish a mare's less desirable characteristics.

Miss Peppy Two, a 1973 red roan mare by Speedy Glow and out of Miss Peppy Jo, was one of her sire's first top performers. Shown here with youth competitor Suzanne Scott aboard, Miss Peppy was an open and youth Superior western pleasure horse.

"We mostly got little, ol' cheap mares to breed back in those days, but Speedy Glow helped them all," Parks told Doug Carpenter in a *Performance Horse* article. "His colts had straight legs and good minds, but most importantly they looked completely different through the head, neck, shoulder and even the tail. Their necks came straight out from their shoulders so they had a flatter top line; they carried their heads with their faces more straight up and down as opposed to having their noses pushed out like the horses from earlier years; and they carried their tails flat which created a totally new look."

Al Dunning wasn't the only trainer to realize the pleasure-pen potential of Speedy

Glow and his get. California-based trainer Stan Fonsen and his family traveled to Texas to follow the stallion's progress and find Speedy Glow offspring. Speedy's sons and daughters weren't yet in demand — or easy to find. After taking sons and daughters to California's open circuit futurities, Fonsen realized the horses' values.

Fonsen got hooked on the Speedy Glow horses after training Speedy Kilkenny, a 1971 gray gelding out of Darter's Chockie. "I called him 'Puff of Smoke' and he was the first Speedy Glow I had," Fonsen recalled. "I loved his temperament, so I did a little research on his sire. He was a big, red roan stud. He was a well-balanced, good-bodied horse. He had an average head. He produced a lot of roans, which became quite a trait in California for years.

"I bought quite a few of his colts to train for pleasure. They weren't popular at first. I got some printouts and found out where some of those colts were. He didn't have many on the ground. I found some in back yards, in the bush. I told some friends of mine down there I was looking for some Speedy Glow colts and they just looked at me funny and asked 'Speedy Glow, what is the matter with you?' I bought two or three of those colts, brought them back, and

they were big timers. They didn't know what they had down there. I kept going back for more."

Quick Changes

In 1977, Fonsen returned to Texas for more – in fact, to purchase Speedy Glow for his clients, Jim and Kay Villas of Healdsburg, Calif. But the Villases hadn't planned on buying a stud horse. They moved to California's Sonoma County wine country to start a vineyard. Horses were to be a hobby; they had two young Quarter

PHOTO BY DICK WALTENBERRY

Glowing Debutante, a 1974 red roan mare by Speedy Glow and out of Little Ernie, was a Superior western pleasure horse.

April Fawn Glow, a 1975 red roan mare by Speedy Glow and out of King's Evelyn, earned seven halter and 45 performance points in open competition. Shown here as a yearling with Shorty Parks, Princeton, Tex., "Fawn" went on to earn a Youth AQHA Championship.

Horses for pleasure — not business. All that changed when the 1970s wine market took a downward turn. The Villases changed businesses and quickly learned about the horse industry - and Speedy Glow.

"I took one of the two-year-olds to Stan Fonsen to divert from the thought of wine and get a horse trained," Kay Villas said. "He said I should be thinking about shows. I got the bug. We went to Texas and bought a yearling Speedy Glow filly named Silky Speed for a 1975 pleasure futurity. I won the futurity on her a year later, and we were hooked on the bloodline."

The Villases owned horses for a year and a half when Jim and Fonsen discussed buying a stallion. The couple was new to the industry and hadn't bred horses before, but was eager to learn. Because they already had a Speedy Glow daughter, looking at the stallion seemed a perfect fit. Plus, his known calm disposition suited the new horse owners.

"Stan called Parks and told him he had a client in California who was looking for a proven stallion," Kay recalled. "He told Parks we wanted to look at a whole package — the stallions, their foals, and mares bred to them. Jim and Stan went down to look at Speedy Glow. Grantham threw out a price that at the time seemed outlandish. Jim wasn't sure he was ready to pay a lot of money for a stallion when we didn't know much about it. We would have to be the ones that were breeding him. This was all on the learning curve. Finally, we decided to purchase him."

Fonsen recalls the deal that finally moved Speedy Glow to California. "We put a deal together and got him bought," he said. "Grantham didn't know what he had. He always thought the stud was a really good horse, but he didn't really want to promote him like the Villases did. He named a price and we didn't barter. We bought that horse for about $30,000 — which was a lot at the time. Not long after that, his foals were selling for almost that price. We also bought some mares and yearlings at the same time. We wanted something to show to people. California needed a pleasure horse sire and it worked."

Kay didn't see the horse until the deal was done. She remembers her first thoughts about the stallion. "Speedy Glow was a handsome horse; I'd never call him gorgeous," she said. "He was prolific in breeding his personal charm and attitude. Those were two strong points, as was the fact that his babies were very pretty movers. He did not have a gorgeous head. He stood 15.3 hands high; a big-bodied horse, but not a halter horse. He had a long back."

In January of 1978, the Villas family had their stallion; they still needed to learn about handling him. The family built a barn on their 120 acres of vineyard land.

PHOTO COURTESY KAY VILLAS

Sissy Glow, a 1975 palomino mare by Speedy Glow and out of Spanish Coin, earned 41 open performance points. That's Shorty Parks aboard the beautifully-headed mare in this shot.

Speedy Glow would soon be at home in his large stall and run-out. But for his first year in California, the couple sent Speedy Glow to Big Oak Ranch for breeding. Jim and Kay headed to Colorado State University for a short course in stallion management.

"We learned all the technicalities," Kay says. "We spent time handling him that year. He was easy to handle. We were very fortunate in that respect. He knew how to breed, but he had never worked on a phantom breeding dummy. He had never been collected; he had always done live cover.

"It took a time or two and then he was right with the program. We did put a chain under his chin just in case. I left slack and if he did whinny, I only had to jiggle the chain. I never had to correct him. We also didn't baby him. He wasn't a horse that cared for a lot of attention. And, he didn't like it if anybody was sweet and wimpy.

Glow Maker, a 1980 red roan stallion by Speedy Glow and out of Spanish Coin, earned 31 western pleasure points.

Speedy Kilkenny, a 1971 gray gelding by Speedy Glow and out of Darter's Chockie, was one of the first of his sire's get to be shown on the West Coast. Stan Fonsen – who was instrumental in procuring Speedy Glow for Jim and Kay Villas of Healdsburg, Calif. – is up in this nice side profile.

You could just tell by the look in his eye. He'd look at you with disgust if you didn't treat him with respect. He demanded it."

The Villases bred 60 to 100 mares each year they handled the stud. They also formed a plan to market the aged horse whose reputation was finally building. Speedy Glow produced winners with Skipper W mares as well as many other bloodlines.

"We had a big promotion when we first got him called 'Did you know?' Kay said. "He had babies that were already on the winning circuit so, in our *Quarter Horse Journal* ads, we asked 'Did you know how many points this horse had?' That was a focus. We wanted people to know what his get had already done."

Unfortunately, the Villases didn't breed Speedy Glow as long as they hoped. The couple owned the stallion only five years before he unexpectedly colicked and died when the family was away. A hired caretaker left the stallion without water for too long.

"We sent him to University of California at Davis," Kay said. "He was up there for a week and died. It was a very difficult time because it was just so unnecessary."

The Villases found it difficult to think about a replacement stallion. "We had two of his sons at that time, but we didn't know if we had the heart to start over with a youngster," Kay remembers. "As a yearling, we had an offer of $100,000 for Glowmaker, one of Speedy's sons. My husband turned that down because we needed him as a replacement sire. We had a working ranch that was active. We had broodmares that were in foal to him, but our hearts weren't really in it."

The Villases buried Speedy Glow at their Tramountane Ranch in Healdsburg. He's buried on a hillside that overlooks the vineyards and a river.

"No one agreed that he was a beautiful horse," Kay reflected. "People agreed he was handsome. They were amazed at his gentleness. He was a true gentleman. That was the common comment from anybody."

Generation Next

Speedy Glow's get carried on – and kept winning for years. Their smooth movements combined with longevity to help them gain points in many show rings. In 1998, 16 years after he died, four of his sons and daughters qualified for the world show; two placed in the top ten. What's more, trainers enjoyed working with the colts and fillies that were easy to train and required few "tune-ups."

After Speedy Glow died, the Villases continued to show Seven S Speedy Glow and Glowmaker, both stud colts, and Glowette, a young mare. The horses carried their father's celebrated traits – temperament, color and movement. Knowing that the AQHA circuit was growing, the couple took their horses to Dunning, who was already known on the breed circuit. The couple felt Dunning's easy-going attitude matched well with their horses' laid-back dispositions.

"At the time we had Seven S Speedy Glow, he was one of the most notable young stallions," Kay said. "You could tell all the sons and daughters from their movement. Plus, a lot of them were roans and black pointed. They could move. When they were all tacked up, they became beautiful. Their movement and head carriage was so natural. Everything about the package, people couldn't take their eyes off them. My show mare, Glowette, was huge on the winner's circuit. She was a big mare; she was elegant and beautiful in a stately manner."

Dunning fondly remembers working with Glowette, then later Seven S Speedy Glow and Glowmaker. "Kay sent me Glowette first," he recalled. "I was third at the Texas Classic with her and won the Congress. My wife, Becky, showed her, too and won nine in a row in hunt seat.

"What was cool about her was she was bigger than most of the pleasure horses out there, and she was pretty. It was hard for her to stay behind all the little bitty horses. I thought it was a problem, but the judges liked her and no one really hurt her for passing a horse. I showed her bridled

By the late 1970s, the Speedy Glow horses were a West Coast pleasure force to be reckoned with. At the 1978 WCQHA Pleasure Futurity, Stan Fonsen rode Sissy Glow to win the maturity and Kay Villas rode Silky Speed and Miss Speedy Twist to win the 3- and 2-year-old futurities.

up, but kept slack to her. We called Glowette a daisy clipper. She just clipped along like she was happy. She kept her ears up and had a great expression — characteristics that people still look for in a western pleasure horse."

Becky Dunning also remembers Glowette's championship form and attitude. "She was just so easy," she said. "There wasn't a trick to her. You just saddled her, took a few laps around the warm-up pen and went on in. Plus, she had huge, beautiful eyes. She was aware and communicative. She was a deep red roan, then had a black mane and tail and black legs. I've never seen another horse colored like her. She was a bigger horse and fit well in the English classes, too."

Al Dunning says most of Speedy Glow's get were flat kneed and drove up well from behind when they loped. "They also had sweet attitudes and they didn't want to go fast," Dunning said. "They were all different, but they all were really good movers and had good minds. The ones I had were excellent lopers. There weren't enough of them."

Although none of Speedy Glow's sons proved themselves as breeding horses,

Seven S Speedy Glo, a 1978 sorrel stallion by Speedy Glow and out of Seven S Pussycat, was chosen by Jim and Kay Villas as their junior stallion. Shown at halter (top), he earned a Superior and 52 points. Shown in western pleasure he won several top futurities and earned 37 points.

Dunning said a few of the stallions were noteworthy as show horses.

"Seven S Speedy Glow was a neat horse," he recalled. "He was natural as can be. He didn't want to pass a horse. He'd gauge himself. He was really smart. I won the Sun Circuit, the West Coast Circuit and the Las Vegas Circuit, and put 50 or 60 points on him in three or four months.

"Glowmaker didn't have the attitude that Seven S Speedy Glow had. I never did get him how I wanted him, but I still won on him. He was such a pretty horse and a big mover. I won so much on the horses Kay sent me that she gave Becky and me a free week's trip to Hawaii."

Shesa Special Glo was another one of Speedy Glow's champion-earning daughters. Much like her champion sister, Glowette, Shesa Special Glo was long-legged and capable. Patsy Calegari of Healdsburg, Calif., purchased the mare to show as a three- and four-year-old.

"She was a very elegant mare; her nickname was Legs," Calegari said. "I bought her as a yearling from the Villases and fell in love with her. My daughters were getting bigger, and were starting to ride Glowin Cinder, another Speedy Glow mare. Shesa Special Glo was for me. She was a sweet mare and a good producer."

But of all of Speedy Glow's sons and daughters, no horse's record compares with Hazardous Glow. The gelding earned $8,286.97 in world show money and claimed more than 60 titles. Tim Goode of Vancouver, Washington bought the gelding to show during his last AQHA youth year in 1988. He found the gelding had many of his sire's qualities including handsome looks and a kind, but standoffish attitude.

"I figured I'd show him for a year, take him to the world show, and probably sell him after that," Goode recalled. "Then I decided he was a family member and wasn't going to leave. He has a heart of gold. When it was show time, he was ready. He's business oriented. We retired him after the world show in 2000. You couldn't really do any better than what he did there. He was 20-some years old and won his second

PHOTO BY MIDGE, COURTESY QUARTER HORSE JOURNAL

Glowette, a 1980 red roan mare by Speedy Glow and out of Tipsy Girl, was a youth AQHA Champion and earned Superiors in hunter under saddle, and open and amateur western pleasure. Speedy Glow owner Kay Villas is aboard the elegant mare in this winner's circle shot.

PHOTO BY HOWARD CAMPTON, COURTESY COWBOY PUBLISHING GROUP

Cotton Eyed Glow, a 1977 sorrel gelding by Speedy Glow and out of Cotton Top Glory, was the 1980 High Point Western Pleasure Gelding and the 1982 World Champion Senior Western Pleasure Horse. That's owner Paula Swank, Agoura, Calif., and trainer Dale Livingston with the world champion in this curtain shot.

PHOTO BY K.C. MONTGOMERY

Here's Hazardous Glow, a.k.a. "Munroe." A 1982 chestnut gelding by Speedy Glow and out of May Belle Reed, Munroe was a 2-time reserve world champion performance horse, an AQHA Champion and AQHA Performance Champion, and earner of 12 open, amateur and youth Superior awards. The venerable performer is owned by Tim and Carol Goode, Vancouver, Wash.

youth AQHA Champion title. Speedy Glows go forever. I could take him out right now and do just as good. He's still in great shape."

Broodmare Mark

Although Speedy Glow's relatively small number of foals did well, this stallion is best-known for his grand-get. His mares produced many foals that carried Speedy Glow's best traits — calm disposition and flowing strides. By 2004, Speedy Glow's sons and daughters produced foals with 19 AQHA Champion and performance champion titles. Showing their lineage, top horses kept Speedy's "glow" as part of their names: This Te Glows, Te Too Glo, Mr Zip Glow, Mis Pretty Glow, and Small Town Glow.

Speedy Glow's grand-get earned more than $151,270.89 in National Snaffle Bit Association (NSBA) competition.

RD Speed Stick, a 1984 sorrel gelding by Red Dee Hobby and out of Miss Glow Van, was responsible for more than $45,900 of that amount. In addition, he was the 1987 AQHA world champion junior Western pleasure horse with Alex Ross in the saddle, who later became AQHA Executive Director of Judges .

Bobbie Hodges of Hodges Ranch in Herald, Calif., stands Zippo Pine Glow, one of Speedy Glow's maternal grandsons.

Zippo Pine Glow, a 1986 roan by Zippo Pine Bar and out of Sher Glow, earned $2,368.89 in NSBA competition. The stallion earned his Superior in western pleasure and holds amateur and open ROMs. Hodges and her husband selected the stallion for his pedigree — they owned his mother — and swift movement.

"Zippo Pine Glow's dam was a great show mare," Hodges said. "Speedy Glow seemed to pass on quite a bit of size. Zippo

PHOTO COURTESY KAY VILLAS.

PLEASURE FUTURITY WCQHA

The Speedy Glow horses continued to win on the West Coast for years after the patriarch of the line was gone. Just A Glow — a double-bred Speedy Glow granddaughter — won a mid-1980sWCQHA pleasure maturity with Marti Fonsen aboard.

Pine Glow is 15.3 hands high, and his dam was 16 hands high."

Hodges believes the roan color helps high-quality horses stand out. The color passed down for generations by Speedy Glow still attracts show-ring attention. "When I showed this stallion, I'd show with 190 other horses," she recalled. "It was an advantage because they saw me. You got seen, but you had to be phenomenal."

Hodges is hooked on breeding horses with Speedy Glow's bloodlines.

"Zippo Pine Glow was a top money earner," she said. "He came about as a result of a good breeding cross that has worked many times. We've even taken own daughters of Speedy Glow and bred them back to Zippo Pine Glow.

From obscure beginnings in Texas, to national acclaim and recognition in California, Speedy Glow founded a line of pleasure horses that floated into the west-ern pleasure show rings and demanded attention with their standout color and movement.

As a maternal grandsire, the big red roan achieved even more success. His daughters produced champions, not only in California, but across the country as well. In 1987, *Quarter Horse News* published its first pleasure-related maternal grandsire list. Speedy Glow officially entered the record books when he topped that list.

In AQHA competitions, Speedy Glow's 399 maternal grand-get have amassed 11 AQHA World and Reserve World Championships, 9 AQHA Championships, 122 Superior awards, 260 performance Registers of Merit and earned 19,443 points.

The numbers continue to shine and serve to establish Speedy Glow as one of the breed's enduring performance sires.

18 CONCLUSIVE

In the span of a few short years, he changed the face of the halter horse industry.

Heidi Nyland

ALTHOUGH HE LIVED ONLY HALF a normal life-span, Conclusive impacted the Quarter Horse halter world as few horses ever have. His influence on the breed was immediate, dramatic and it continues to reverberate throughout the industry years after his passing.

Conclusive, a 1977 sorrel stallion by Impressive and out of Night Pacer, was bred by Richard Brown of Brown Quarries, Inc., Washington, Mo. To say that the colt was a line-bred Three Bars

(TB) would be an understatement. Impressive - his sire - traced three times to the AQHA Hall of Fame stallion, and Night Pacer - his dam - went an additional two times to him.

A Must Have

From an early age, Conclusive stood out as a bona-fide halter prospect. Top halter fitter and showman Denny Hassett of Ulysses, Kan., chose the youngster — first

Conclusive, the 1981 AQHA World Champion Aged Stallion, was known for his "up, off-the-ground" profile.

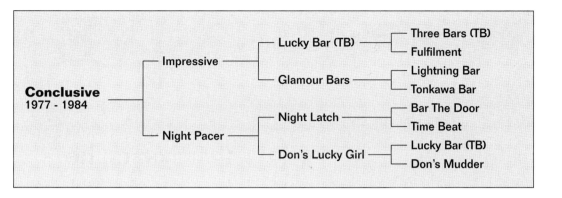

			Three Bars (TB)
		Lucky Bar (TB)	Fulfilment
	Impressive		Lightning Bar
		Glamour Bars	Tonkawa Bar
Conclusive 1977 - 1984			Bar The Door
		Night Latch	Time Beat
	Night Pacer		Lucky Bar (TB)
		Don's Lucky Girl	Don's Mudder

named "Sikes Impressive" — from a field of Impressive foals.

"Sikes Simmons of Greenwood, Mo., and I went to Brown Quarries to buy a weanling," Hassett said. "We looked at 25 or 30 foals down there, and he was the one we chose. I thought he looked like a good one and he turned out to be a great one."

Hassett showed Sikes Impressive — whose name had been changed to "Impressive Pace" — in 15 halter classes as a yearling.

The promising youngster's first outing was May 15, 1978, at Kansas City, Mo., where he earned honors as the grand champion stallion. Next up was a May 20-21 affair at Topeka, Kan., which resulted in two more blue ribbons.

Halter and Performance Record:
1981 AQHA World Champion Aged Stallion.

Progeny Record:

Foal Crops: 6	Performance Point-Earners: 53
Foals Registered: 368	Performance Points Earned: 1,044
AQHA Champions: 2	Performance Registers of Merit: 24
Halter Point-Earners: 162	World Champions: 14
Halter Points Earned: 3,809	High-Point Winners: 1
Superior Halter Awards: 27	National Snaffle Bit Earnings: $18,735

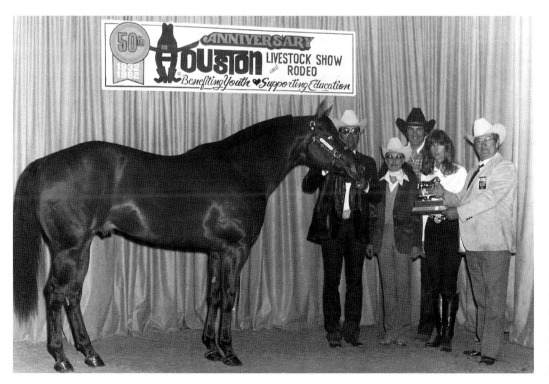

In his last trip into a show ring, Conclusive earned honors as the grand champion stallion at the 1982 Houston Livestock Show and Rodeo.

197

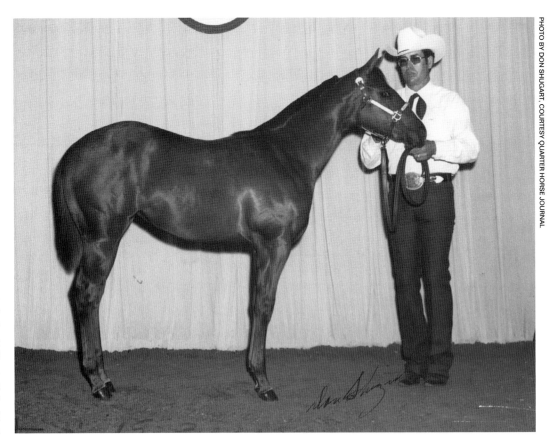

Conclusive Maiden, a 1980 sorrel mare by Conclusive and out of Splash Bar Maid, was a two-time reserve world champion halter horse. She is shown here with Jerry Wells after winning a weanling halter futurity.

Go Lucky Maiden, a 1975 sorrel mare by Sonny Go Lucky and out of Splash Bar Maid, the 1976 World Champion Yearling Filly, was bred to Conclusive. Prestigious Maiden, the result, won multiple world championships.

From Topeka, it was on to the big Des Moines, Iowa, show circuit. Shown four times at halter, the yearling stallion notched one first and three seconds. It would mark the last time that the Impressive – Night Pacer son would ever taste defeat.

"He was a fireball," Hassett recalled. "Not a mean horse, but one with a lot of go. You could handle him. He wasn't a horse that you had to show with a lip chain or a chain in his mouth."

It was while Hassett was showing Impressive Pace at Des Moines that Jerry Wells of Purcell, Okla., got his first glimpse of him.

"I was at the seven-day run in Des Moines," Wells said "Denny had this colt up there. I saw him approaching the show ring and thought, 'what in the world is that?' So I followed him up to the in-gate and told him I'd like to get a price on the colt.

"Denny said he'd show him, and then take me down to talk to Simmons. When we went to the stalls, Simmons said the colt was probably for sale, but he wanted a lot of money for him. I asked how much was a lot, and he said he needed to think about it. I told him if he wasn't interested in selling him, that was fine, but I was leaving the next day and I'd like a price."

Finally, Simmons threw out a number – $200,000.

"I told him that was a lot of money," Wells continued. "And he said that's why he priced him like that. He kind of wanted to scare me off. I thanked him and asked for some time to think about it. I couldn't come up with $200,000 on my own, so I called Jim Swink of Little Rock, Ark. Jim was a friend of mine, and I told him about this colt. He said if I liked him that much, he'd partner with me."

For the time being, Impressive Pace remained under the ownership of Simmons.

From Des Moines, Denny Hassett hauled the colt to shows in Bonner Springs, Kan., Kansas City, Kan., and Sioux Falls, S.D. Exhibited 10 times, the yearling notched one grand, four reserves and 10 firsts.

PHOTO BY HAROLD CAMPTON, COURTESY QUARTER HORSE JOURNAL

Prestigious Maiden, a 1982 sorrel mare by Conclusive and out of Go Lucky Maiden, was a five-time world champion open and youth halter horse.

Wanting to get a first-hand look at the colt, Jim Swink flew to Sioux Falls.

"Sikes and Jim met and agreed on a price," Hassett recalled, "and then Jim said he had to call his banker. It was Sunday so you knew he wasn't calling a banker. He was calling Jerry. He and Jerry talked it over, and Jim came back and said he'd take him."

Transferred to the ownership of Swink and Wells – and re-named Conclusive – the yearling earned honors as the grand champion stallion at the 1978 Oklahoma State Fair.

The Long Road to the World

With one big win under his belt, Wells decided to take Conclusive to Columbus, Ohio, for the All American Quarter Horse Congress. Although the experienced horse hauler stopped and rested his horses in St. Louis, Mo., standing in the trailer proved to be too much for the young stallion.

"I pulled onto the Congress grounds and we had to sit out there for six hours," Wells said. "It was all backed up with people waiting to get horses unloaded. There were so many in front of us, that I was worried sick about having Conclusive in the trailer that long. The next morning he was really sore on his front feet. He just got worse, and finally he foundered."

Wells didn't show Conclusive again as a yearling or as a two-year-old. When the horse was three, he was re-fit for halter competition.

Wells and Conclusive went back on the road in early 1980. In February, the 3-year-old stallion won his class at the Southwestern Livestock Exposition and Fat Stock Show in Fort Worth. Shown eight more times that year, he won them all.

The 1981 show season began in January. Exhibited at the big stock shows in

Denver, Colo., and Fort Worth, San Antonio and Houston, Tex., Conclusive recorded three grands and four firsts.

Qualified to go to the AQHA World Show, the 4-year-old was allowed to rest until fall. In October, he was shown at the Texas State Fair in Dallas, and the American Royal in Oklahoma City, Oklahoma. He stood grand on both occasions.

Next up was the AQHA World Show, held in early November in Oklahoma City, Oklahoma. There, Conclusive solidified his claim as one of the most dominant halter horses of his era by being named as the World Champion Aged Stallion.

In February 1982, the 5-year-old entered the show ring for the last time. Hauled back to the Houston Livestock Show and Rodeo, he stood grand.

Conclusive's final show ring tally was one to be proud of. Shown 31 times at halter, he recorded 14 grands, six reserves, 28 firsts, three seconds and earned 42 points.

By this time, the slow-maturing stallion had rounded out into quite an impressive specimen.

"Conclusive was a big horse; about 16 hands," Wells recalled. "He was a pretty-headed son of a gun and he was made right. He wasn't overly muscled, but he had plenty of strength. He put more muscle on his offspring than what he carried. A lot of that was because of foundering. He was rocked back on his hind legs for about a year."

Changing Hands

With a world championship to his credit, Conclusive's breeding book filled quickly. In 1982, Swink and Wells bred 235 mares to him. Conclusive was becoming a profitable and in-demand horse.

In 1981, Swink sold his interest in the horse to Robert Shelton and Robert Finger, Kerrville, Tex. The popular stallion remained under the ownership of Wells, Shelton and Finger for two years. Then, in July of 1983, he sold for the fourth and final time.

Obvious Conclusion, a 1982 sorrel stallion by Conclusion and out of Buz's Baccarat, was a two-time world champion at halter. Retired to stud, he sired the earners of 56 world halter titles.

PHOTO BY DON SHUGART. COURTESY QUARTER HORSE JOURNAL.

Ms Conclusive Jack, a 1983 chestnut mare by Conclusive and out of Two Jeff's Jill, was the 1985 Amateur World Champion 2-Year-Old Mare. Well-known halter exhibitor Chip Knost is at the typey halter mare's head in this three-quarter front shot.

The Final Destination

Edgewood Farms, Inc., Pilot Point, Tex., was a joint venture owned by Joe Edge and Russell Wood. To begin with, the pair was deeply involved with Appaloosas. Their program, which was headed by the Appaloosa Horse Club (ApHC) Hall of Fame stallion Roman's Strawman, was renowned for its world-caliber spotted horses.

In the late 1970s, Edge and Wood decided to change their focus and enter the Quarter Horse breeding industry. They successfully marketed "Strawman" for close to $1 million, and commenced a search for the perfect Quarter Horse stallion to showcase a new facility in Pilot Point.

"I looked around and watched for a stallion," Edge said. "In 1981, I went to a Jerry Wells sale and Conclusive was there. He caught my eye. He wasn't for sale, but I had Jerry get him out. We went over him and talked about his bloodlines. I bought two mares that day that were in foal to Conclusive — Buz's Baccarat and Go Lucky Maiden — and both of the resulting foals went on to become world champions.

"I gave $100,000 for Go Lucky Maiden," he added, "and that was the highest price paid for a broodmare at the time."

Edgewood Farms was happy with their Conclusive foals and decided to get serious about owning their sire. They returned to Wells' and made an offer. In June of 1983,

SR Elusive Dancer, a 1983 sorrel mare by Conclusive and out of I'ma Dancing Dude, was the 1984 Youth World Champion Yearling Mare. Shown here as a yearling with Ted Turner, the elegant halter champion was bred by the Shelton Ranch, Kerrville, Tex.

the negotiations were finalized and transfer papers were signed.

"We sold Conclusive for a lot of money," Wells said. "Let's just say it was more than $1.5 million."

Conclusive had spent the 1983 breeding season at the Shelton Ranch in Kerrville. In July, Joe Edge and Edgewood ranch managers Bill and Ann Lanning traveled to the Texas hill country to pick up the stallion. The Lannings would be responsible for the stallion's day-to-day handling.

Over-Coming a Bad Rap

By this time, the word was out that Conclusive was hard to get along with. Throughout his founder recovery period, he had been confined to a box stall.

"When you have a stud in a stall that long," Edge said, "he'll get a little rank. Conclusive got to where he had an attitude in his stall. But once you put a halter on him and took him out in the aisle, he was perfect. He just didn't want anyone messing with him in the stall, because he

had been messed with so much when he was younger."

When Edge and the Lannings picked up Conclusive, his handlers provided safety advice. "They told us you couldn't give him shots or do anything in his stall," Bill Lanning recalled. "If you were going to do anything, you had to take him out in the aisle. They were very up front about that."

So the Lannings established a strict regimen for Conclusive. They alone would handle him. If they weren't immediately available to show him to visitors, the ranch staff was instructed to politely ask company to stay until they returned.

"We had all these dreams that Conclusive was going to be the breed's next great sire - we wanted to write his name in the stars," Ann Lanning said. "But we knew we had to change his attitude. He was coming to a new place, and he was going to be around new people. If we established some guidelines, and everybody knew how he was going to be handled, then maybe he would relax and conform to our set of rules."

The Lannings, who currently stand 20 horses at their facility in Pilot Point, expect all their stallions to behave.

Conclusive was treated no differently. The couple began by outfitting him in different gear depending on what his job was to be.

"If we were going to show him to people, he had a cotton lead rope on," Bill Lanning said. "If we were going to the breeding barn, he had a chain in his mouth. If he went out the back door, he knew he was going to the breeding barn. He was allowed to squeal then. If he went out the end of the barn, he was going to be turned out and he was to behave."

New Image

Conclusive arrived in Pilot Point just after the 1983 breeding season. The Lannings structured guidelines helped him know what was expected. In no time at all, a transformation took place.

"When we brought Conclusive home," Joe Edge recalled, "we took him in the stall, hooked him up and were going to take his leg wraps off. Then we decided to take him back out in the aisle. He stood there like a gentleman. We took his leg wraps off, put him back in and left him alone."

The next morning, Conclusive was ready to test his new handlers. "I went to his stall and he challenged me," Bill Lanning said. "He came at me with his mouth wide open, ready to bite. I corrected him, let him know who was in charge, and from that day on he never offered to bite anybody. It only took once."

Conclusive's change in demeanor did not go unnoticed. People began stopping by Edgewood Farms just to see if the rumors were true. The Lannings showed Conclusive more than 700 times in the nine months Edgewood Farms owned him — each time in a cotton lead rope and without a hitch.

Sculptor Lyle Johnson asked to sculpt Conclusive and stayed at the ranch while he created the stallion's image in bronze. The artist watched his subject for hours.

"Lyle would sit in the daytime and watch Conclusive out in his pen," Ann Lanning said. "And then he'd work on the clay at night. He'd always say to us, you live with him, you need to critique him.

"Conclusive had a muscle separation in his neck and he wanted to know if we wanted it taken out for the bronze. He had a little indention you could lay your finger in - a long skinny indention in the muscle. We said to leave it. It was part of the horse."

Ann Lanning asked for the artist's opinion, as well. She knew Conclusive had a different look, but couldn't explain why.

"Lyle said 'look at his eye,'" she recalled. "His eyebrow went up into an arch. You can still see that unique look in Conclusive's offspring. It's a defining look."

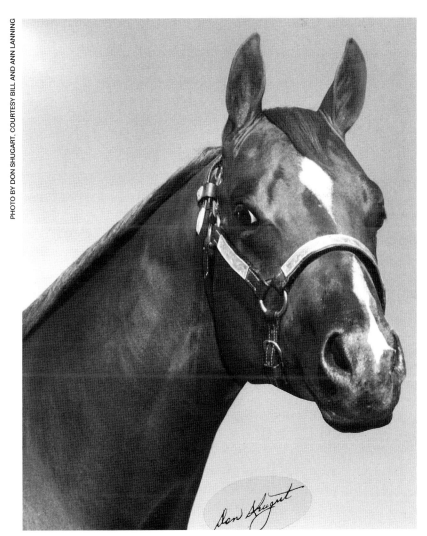

PHOTO BY DON SHUGART, COURTESY BILL AND ANN LANNING

Conclusives Choice, a 1983 sorrel stallion by Conclusive and out of Peppy Bar Benton, was the 1983 World Champion Weanling Stallion.

Fantastic Finale, a 1983 sorrel stallion by Conclusive and out of Fantastic Jackie, was the 1986 World Champion 3-Year-Old Stallion.

Changing Guard

The horse Edge, Wood and the Lannings thought they would have for years was only at his new home for nine months; barely long enough to settle in and prepare for the 1984 breeding season. In February, those close to the horse noticed something was wrong.

"We had just started the breeding season, and the farrier was shoeing him," Joe Edge said. "When he was done, he tracked him down the aisle. I noticed he was gimping a little. I asked if he'd check it. He did and said he hadn't quicked the horse. But Conclusive was still gimping a little. He took the shoe off, re-set it, and the horse seemed better."

The Lannings also noticed the horse's slight limp.

"We had collected him and turned him out in the stud pen," Ann Lanning said. "Bill was watching him and asked me to come watch, too. He thought Conclusive acted sore on his back leg. He'd walk, then trot, eat some grass. Bill went to the barn, and I sat and watched him for another 20 minutes. I thought I saw him short step with his back leg, but it was so fast I couldn't really tell. The next day you could tell he was a little off. Bill and I thought he was sore from getting up on the breeding dummy. It was a different one than he was used to. The vet came out and thought the same thing; he was just sore."

Conclusive's soreness didn't get better. In just a few days, his condition worsened until he couldn't stand. The Lannings never left his side during his last three days.

"The vet came back out the next day," Lanning continued. "He watched him and remarked that he thought it might be Equine Protozoal Myeloencephalitis (EPM). He said, if it was, it was only the fourth case he'd seen at that time.

"Each day Conclusive got a little worse. The vet said he'd start turning in one direction and act almost like he had a stroke. He said that, finally, he'd get down and wouldn't be able to get back up."

Conclusive's EPM progressed quickly. In five days he couldn't stand.

"On February 24, he laid down about 5 p.m.," Lanning said. "We had a big window in the office where we could see into his stall. He stretched out like he was sleeping. At 7 p.m. he had his front feet spread out but he couldn't get up. He didn't panic, but he nickered. He quit trying and folded his feet underneath him. I looked at Bill and said, 'This is it.'

"We called Joe and Russell, and the vet. Nothing worked. That night he'd look at us and nicker. We went in to pet him and talked to him. He never acted grouchy, even when the vet had the needle out, ready to put him down. He never looked defeated. He looked as regal and majestic as ever."

All this happened while 96 mares waited on the property to be bred. More were on the way. At the start of breeding season, Conclusive had only been bred five times. As the vet performed the autopsy and prepared Conclusive for burial, trailers were lined up to enter Edgewood Farms. The Lannings sent a ranch hand down the driveway to close the gate.

"We thought he'd always be a part of this ranch," Ann Lanning said. "We asked if we could pull his shoes. We had them silver-plated and they hang here on the wall in our office. He had a blanket that had his name on it and he was laid to rest on top of that. He had a sheet with his name on it and that was draped over him. Then we put his halter back on his head. He was buried at the former Edgewood Farms, which is now Reata Ranch."

With Conclusive gone, the Edgewood Farms brain trust had tough decisions to make. "We had a bad setback. I only bred out two of my 60 mares," Joe Edge recalled. "I left them all open. I was just discouraged."

Bill Lanning also remembers that winter. "It was a huge loss," he said. "We didn't do anything that winter. We ran the ranch, but we didn't have any foals the next year. Then we gathered our thoughts and started to look for another stud. What was a tragic situation turned out to be something good."

A Mirror Image

In due time, Edgewood Farms started thinking about a new stallion. From the very beginning, the intent was to stay within the bloodline. All four principals involved felt a Conclusive son would be the best fit.

Finally the time was right, and the perfect horse became available.

"In the summer of 1984, I called Ted Turner and told him to meet me at the airport," Edge says. "I rented a Lear Jet and we went to five or six states that day and looked at every young prospect available. We ended up in Mason, Mich. at a horse show. Mr Conclusion, a 1982 sorrel stallion by Conclusive and out of Miss Amber Charge, was there.

"I saw him in the stall and decided he was the one I wanted. And we were lucky enough to get him bought. After we got him home, a lot of people didn't want to breed to him because of his age. So I decided I'd just breed my own mares. His first foal born was Ican Handle The Heat — a five-time world champion."

Prior to being acquired by Edgewood Farms, Mr Conclusion had been named as the 1984 AQHA Reserve World Champion Yearling Stallion. In 1986, he became a third-generation world champion when he won the aged stallion title under all five judges.

"Mr" then went on to eclipse his sire as an all-time leading sire of halter horses — albeit with the luxury of living a full life. AQHA records reveal that – in open, amateur and youth competition – he sired the earners of 121 world championships, 113 reserve world championships, 17 high-point wins, and the earners of more than $1 million in AQHA Incentive earnings and World Show earnings, and National Snaffle Bit Association earnings.

Like his sire and grandsire before him, Mr Conclusion led a "legendary" life.

Still, it remains the obligation of all concerned to give credit where credit it due.

"Mr Conclusion did change the whole halter horse scene," Ann Lanning said. "But it really all started with Conclusive. His get were the first of the up, off-the-ground profilers."

The Legacy

As a sire, Conclusive's record was nothing to be ashamed of.

From only six foal crops and 368 foals, 14 of his get earned 18 world championships, and 16 of his get earned 17 reserve world championships. A number of his world champion get are pictured. Also among his most accomplished offspring were:

· Conclusive Leo - 1982 sorrel stallion out of Sunbeam Cactus - 1983 World Champion Yearling Stallion.
· Hint of Conclusion - 1982 sorrel stallion out of Hintons Lucky Bill - 1988 World Champion Aged Stallion.
· A Pretty Conclusion - 1983 red roan mare out of Little Red Roanie - 1986 Youth High-Point Halter Mare; 1986 High-Point Junior Halter Mare.
· Conclusive Win - 1983 sorrel stallion out of Miss Wendy Chick - 1987 World Champion Aged Stallion.
· Ms Conclusive Jack - 1983 chestnut mare

out of Two Jeff's Jill - 1985 Amateur World Champion 2-Year-Old Mare.
· Silent Conclusion - 1983 gray stallion out of Silent Frost - AQHA Champion; AQHA Performance Champion; Superior Halter, Calf Roping, Heading and Heeling.

Despite his short life, Conclusive's impact on the AQHA show horse world was far-reaching. What's more, the stallion made his mark as a prolific, second-generation sire.

"The hardest thing in the world for a stallion to do," Joe Edge observed, is to produce top-siring sons and top-producing daughters. "Most stallions can do one or the other. Conclusive did both.

"He sired such great breeding stallions as Mr Conclusion and Obvious Conclusion, and he also sired a number of mares that went on to become great producers.

"The Conclusive daughters were very good-headed, pretty-necked and big-hipped, and they crossed on just about anything. They were really well-developed, the way a show horse should be."

Finally, Conclusive's get weren't limited to showing at halter. Many of his granddaughters and grandsons have proven themselves as roping, hunter under saddle and western pleasure mounts.

"A lot of people looked at the horses' pedigrees, saw Conclusive, and thought they were only halter horses," Edge said. "We didn't have a whole lot by Conclusive, but horses by him and Mr Conclusion qualified for roping, and won the Congress in English and pleasure."

"Conclusive added to the breed," Ann Lanning summed up. "He was the first one that I remember having a great profile and height. And that look is still out there; and still winning."

From foundered halter horse with a chip on his shoulder to acclaimed champion with the world at his doorstep, Conclusive accomplished more in his short span of years than most horses do given a full lifetime. More so even than his renowned sire, he re-defined the conformation standards of an entire industry.

That was his legend, and that is his legacy.

As these two classic side profiles graphically illustrate, Conclusive (top) and Mr Conclusion were mirror images of each other. After the premature death of his famous sire, "Mr" more-than-adequately picked up the family torch and ensured that the line would live on.

19

DYNAMIC DELUXE

He passed on his trademark "sit back and lope" gait to an enduring line of pleasure horses.

Juli S. Thorson

DYNAMIC DELUXE WAS DIFFERENT — so different in build from the other Quarter Horses of his era that he might easily have been brushed aside to become an obscure, forgotten gelding rather than a memorable leading sire. Yet the very thing that made him incongruous in terms of conformation is what gave him his ticket to fame.

Thanks to such features as withers that stood higher than his hips, a level neck that tied in low to his chest, a shallow heart-girth and stilt-like front legs that sat well back beneath upright shoulders, the 1981 brown stallion could deliver a slow-motion, rock-back-and-lift lope the likes of which no one had ever seen. It came so naturally to him that he could do it from a dead standstill, with or without a rider.

What's more, he was consistently able to pass that lope—the "money gait" for winners in longe line, western pleasure, western riding and hunter under saddle competition—to his get. In arena events where quality of movement matters, Dynamic Deluxe's trademark lope could put one of his get at the top of a judge's card, and did so with regularity. By the end of 2003, his sons and daughters had earned over $163,000 in National Snaffle Bit

Endowed with a unique set of physical attributes, Dynamic Deluxe was custom-made to be a top western pleasure performer and sire.

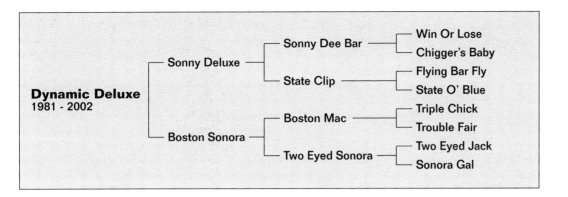

Dynamic Deluxe 1981 - 2002	Sonny Deluxe	Sonny Dee Bar	Win Or Lose
			Chigger's Baby
		State Clip	Flying Bar Fly
			State O' Blue
	Boston Sonora	Boston Mac	Triple Chick
			Trouble Fair
		Two Eyed Sonora	Two Eyed Jack
			Sonora Gal

Association monies and nearly $344,000 from the American Quarter Horse Association's Incentive Fund. He also was 2003's leading sire of AQHA youth performance horses after ranking on various leading sire lists for the better part of a decade.

It was his offspring's ability to lope with natural style and grace that brought Dynamic Deluxe himself to the attention and into the hands of the young couple who promoted him to prominence. Stephen and Cindy Stephens, married just two years and still in their 20s, first became aware of "DD" in 1987 after purchasing a yearling daughter from his first crop whose lope they'd seen on a video. That filly, the diminutive Socially Acceptable, did so well for the Stephenses in western pleasure futurities that they sought out and bought several more prospects by her sire.

"The ones we had were out of mares bred completely differently, ranging from cutting and reining blood to halter and old foundation lines, but they all could do the same lope. So we thought, 'This isn't just a coincidence; it's got to be coming from the daddy,'" recalls Stephen.

The Stephenses, both graduates of the horsemanship program at Meredith Manor, were doggedly determined to establish themselves in the horse business — so much so that in order to save the down payment for their first "ranch," in reality an old dairy farm in Sultan, Wash., they lived in their four-horse trailer for almost a year following their 1985 marriage.

Halter and Performance Record:
NSBA earnings of $1,534; Open Performance Register of Merit; Amateur Performance Register of Merit; Superior Western Pleasure.

Progeny Record:
Foal Crops: 18	Performance Point-Earners: 326
Foals Registered: 433	Performance Points Earned: 16,942.5
Youth Champions: 5	Performance Registers of Merit: 326
Halter Point-Earners: 51	Superior Performance Awards: 92
Halter Points Earned: 547	World Champions: 7
Superior Halter Awards: 4	High-Point Winners: 3

PHOTO BY DALCO

Dynamic Deluxe, shown here with Jerry Stanford, earned a Superior in western pleasure.

PHOTO BY DON SHUGART

"DD," as the popular stallion came to be known, was ridden by Cleve Wells to win the senior western pleasure at the 1987 Fort Worth Stock Show.

PHOTO BY DON TROUT

Dynamic Duplication, a 1986 bay gelding by Dynamic Deluxe and out of Dark Rerun, was the 1997 Youth All-Around High-Point Horse, and Youth High-Point Showmanship and Hunter Under Saddle horse.

By 1989, after fixing up the farm and renaming it Riverside Ranch, their stated goal was to own a top western pleasure stallion. One day, Cindy happened to open a magazine to a stud-services ad for Dynamic Deluxe, then standing in Mississippi. Figuring she had nothing to lose, she picked up the phone to call the owner, Mickey O'Connor, asking if the horse was for sale.

Coincidentally, he was. O'Connor had decided that very morning to put the then 8-year-old Dynamic Deluxe on the market. The Stephenses had nowhere near the five-figure asking price in their bank account, but just as they'd done in pursuit of their horse property, they didn't let a negative fiscal fact get in their way.

The next day, armed with a short-term loan from friends and plans to remortgage the ranch, Cindy was on a plane to get her first look at the stallion she and Stephen were destined to own until his death 13 years later.

Stephen remembers his wife's account of her first impression.

"Cindy called me after she got there and said, 'I was so relieved when I walked up to his stall. He turned to look at me, and his head, everything about him, is drop-dead gorgeous!'

"It was a relief to all of us, let me tell you!" exclaims Stephen. "All we knew about DD at that point was that he was a major, major imprinter of lopers. For all we knew, he could have looked like a donkey. We had all but agreed to buy this horse that we had only seen in a few pictures, and he turned out to be the type of horse that was gorgeous from any angle — beautiful, no matter how you looked at him. He wasn't like some horses that only look good from a certain angle or in a certain pose."

Stephen hasn't forgotten his own first impression, either.

"I had never seen anything like him. Cindy and her mom drove to Mississippi to get him, and I'll never forget when he first got off that trailer. I was in total shock just over the way he walked, with this elegant, stand-up gait. I'd never seen a horse stand up so straight in his shoulders, and walk like he was on stilts, so flat in the knee that it had hardly any bend.

"And you know how when a horse gets to a new place and puts his head up to look around? DD could never do that because of the way he was built, with that low-set neck. He just swung his head from side to side, like a special-effects creature from a movie, because it was physically impossible for him to lift it."

The Route to Renown

Bred by the late Verlin Jackson of Galva, Ill., Dynamic Deluxe was a blend of bloodlines with proven ability to produce top western pleasure horses.

His sire, also bred by Jackson, was Sonny Deluxe, a 1975 gray by AQHA hall of famer Sonny Dee Bar. Out of the gray mare State Clip, a granddaughter of Sugar Bars, Sonny Deluxe was an outstanding show horse who went on to sire more of the same. Along with being the nation's high-point western pleasure stallion in

Sweet Dynamics, a 1989 bay mare by Dynamic Deluxe and out of Impressive Valentine, was an AQHA Performance Champion and earned six Superior awards.

1978, he earned an AQHA Championship and Superiors in western pleasure and halter. Of his 140 Quarter Horse foals, 54 were AQHA point earners for a grand total of 4,789.5 points, four AQHA Championships, 12 Superior performance awards (mostly in western pleasure) and one Superior at halter.

Dynamic Deluxe's dam, Boston Sonora (Boston Mac x Two Eyed Sonora, by Two Eyed Jack), had no show record of her own, but made up for it by becoming almost a factory for the production of winning show horses. The 1976 brown mare was bred by Raymond Sutton of Gettysburg, S.D.

Eight of her 10 foals earned AQHA performance records. Six, including Dynamic Deluxe, were Superior western pleasure horses. Sudden Inclination, her 1992 son by Zippo Jack Bar, was the 1997 AQHA World Champion in junior western riding. He earned a Superior in that event in addition to one in western pleasure.

Although the Stephenses never had an opportunity to see Sonny Deluxe, they did have the chance to view Boston Sonora in person when she was acquired by other breeders in Washington.

"She was a big mare, about 15.3, and very short-coupled. I think DD got a lot of his qualities from her," Stephen remarks. "She had his stood-up shoulders, the balance in the body, the naturally level neck and the ability to just pick up and lope anywhere. Even though she wasn't shown, when you look at her production record and see how consistent she was, it's pretty clear she was no ordinary mare."

Nevertheless, her second foal — Dynamic Deluxe — failed to impress the man who bred him. According to Stephen, Verlin Jackson "took DD and a couple of other early yearlings to a sale and just got rid of them." He thinks he understands what may have been behind that move.

Isadorable Gal, a 1988 sorrel mare by Dynamic Deluxe and out of Mananas Mystique, was an open and youth Superior western pleasure horse.

"I'm sure DD had a pretty head as a yearling, like most of his babies did, but in those days, you wanted that big, Two Eyed Jack-type hip hanging off one, and DD didn't have that. He was dainty and didn't have that big, round, AQHA Champion kind of butt. He had a totally different look," Stephen says. "Jackson said, 'I didn't think nothin' of him — he was all head and neck and no rear end.'"

Indianan Rick Pasea purchased Dynamic Deluxe at that 1982 auction and sold him a few months later to Illinois resident David Johlin. Johlin didn't care about the yearling's lack of a big rear end. To him, the almost-black colt's unique way of moving more than made up for it.

"If the average person would have gotten DD at that age," says Stephen, "I think he would have gelded him in a heartbeat and not waited it out to see how he'd mature. David was so amazed by DD's movement that he put up with his other idiosyncrasies."

Recalling that "there was really nothing to breaking him," Johlin started Dynamic Deluxe under saddle, and then took him to the All American Quarter Horse Congress in the fall of his 2-year-old year. With western pleasure at the zenith of its popularity in the early 1980s, the Congress, in Columbus, Ohio, was considered to be Mecca for pleasure enthusiasts, attracting throngs of spectators and prospect speculators as well as hundreds of exhibitors.

This, relates Stephen, is where Dynamic Deluxe "got found out about." A group of trainers, including the late trainer Jerry Stanford and Marty Johnson (then Marty Stanford), created a partnership to buy the horse from Johlin for an undisclosed sum. Though reluctant to part with his pride and joy, Johlin recognized that proceeds from the sale would allow him to realize his dream of relocating from the Midwest to Texas.

"Dynamic Deluxe was entered in the 2-year-old pleasure futurity at the Congress," Marty Johnson said, "But we decided that he would not be shown. We were deeply involved with The Invester

Dynamic Fashion, a 1992 brown mare by "DD" and out of Pocos Unique Fashion, was an All American Congress winner and an open, amateur and youth Superior western pleasure horse.

Marty Stanford (now Marty Johnson) was instrumental in Dynamic Deluxe's early training and showing career. Here she is up on the talented rail horse as a 3-year-old.

PHOTO BY HAROLD CAMPTON

Dynamic In The Dark, a 1994 brown full brother to "Fashion," was the NSBA earner of $12,849.

horses at the time and wound up placing them first, second and sixth in the futurity. We felt it wound be to DD's benefit to take him back to Texas and put him through our own training regimen before showing him.

"Dynamic Deluxe's lope was effortless, but he needed flexibility developed in his pasterns at the trot. Cleve Wells was Jerry's assistant trainer at the time. He and I spent numerous hours on DD, preparing him for the upcoming show season."

The two trainers wasted little time in proving Dynamic Deluxe's prowess in the show ring. They showed him to win 73 AQHA western pleasure points in 17 shows, along with about $26,000 in futurity monies.

According to trainer Steve Heckaman, who showed Dynamic Deluxe later in the horse's career, Stanford was a natural-born promoter who enjoyed impressing people with the stallion's abilities.

"Jerry used to take him in the arena during noon breaks, saddled up and wearing a set of driving lines hooked to a snaffle,"

Here's Have A Smooth Trip, a 1994 brown gelding by Dynamic Deluxe and out of Smoothies Fancy. The elegant English horse earned a Superior in Hunter Under Saddle and an amateur performance Register of Merit.

remembers Heckaman. "Dynamic Deluxe would lope with that unique way of going he had, going so slow and collected that Jerry would just walk alongside him. He could even get Dynamic Deluxe to change leads while he was doing this, and it amazed everybody to see how talented the horse was, how he could lope collected up like a finished horse, with nobody on his back."

After Dynamic Deluxe earned his AQHA Superior rating in western pleasure early in 1985, the partnership opted to retire him to stud. Although he attracted a respectable number of mares his first two seasons, the partners determined he'd need more show-pen exposure to give his book a boost. In December of 1986, they gave him to Cleve Wells to be prepared for the '87 show season.

Wells got Dynamic Deluxe, then 6, qualified for the AQHA World Show in just a few weeks. Even though he'd had a two-year layoff from being shown, the horse hadn't lost his ability to out-lope the competition.

"He was a very, very good show horse," says Wells, "just exceptional to show, and real pretty on top of it. He was a nice jogger, but when he rocked back into that awesome lope, he pretty much had the class won."

The partners called upon Heckaman to show Dynamic Deluxe at that year's Congress, where he won the senior western pleasure in a class of 65 entries. The horse made his final show-ring appearance later that fall, placing ninth in the senior pleasure finals at the World Show. He concluded his competitive career with 111 western pleasure points.

In 1988, Dynamic Deluxe changed hands again to become the property of Mickey O'Connor. Then came the coincidental 1989 phone call from Cindy Stephens.

At age 8, Dynamic Deluxe had found his last owners. First from a converted dairy barn near the Canadian border, later from a showplace ranch in Weatherford, Texas, he embarked on his path to becoming a leading sire.

PHOTO BY K.C. MONTGOMERY

Dynamic Discovery (PT), a 1991 sorrel overo gelding by "DD" and out of Quincy Tinkerbell, carried youth competitor Leanne Forestiere to three world championships and one reserve world championship at the 2001 APHA World Championship show.

Dynamic Traits

Promoted by the Stephenses as "the king of pleasure," Dynamic Deluxe tended to pass on several traits in addition to his spectacular lope. Most, such as his large, almond-shaped eyes, level neck, elegant profile and profuse tail, are considered to be assets by those who breed for such events as yearling longe line and western pleasure. Such qualities are among the definitive physical characteristics of the contemporary rail horse.

"Another huge thing that DD stamped on his foals was balance," asserts Stephen. "They never really grew high-low, high-low between their front and rear ends like a lot of horses do. I think that's why they had such success in the longe-line world and in the 2- and 3-year-old pleasure futurities. They didn't grow high in back, so you weren't constantly working to pull them up in the front to get that lifted lope."

According to Stephen, most of Dynamic Deluxe's offspring were on the smaller side, with his slender heart-girth and long legs.

Deluxe Like Daddy, a 1993 bay gelding by Dynamic Deluxe and out of Im Impresiv Music, was one of his sire's most versatile get. Shown here with Bob Avila, the gelding amassed 402 points in open, amateur and youth competition. In addition, he earned Superiors in open western riding and youth halter.

"There were exceptions, of course, but the majority were dainty, very much like ballerinas," he says. "That's part of what made them such elegant athletes. What gymnast do you ever see who's tall, heavy-boned and coarse?"

Besides certain physical attributes, the stallion also passed a mischievous personality to many of his offspring, the colts in particular.

"DD had a Dennis the Menace personality, with some Eddie Haskell (a character from the Leave It To Beaver TV show) thrown in," says Stephen. "If he knew you were watching and paying attention, he'd be the most perfect gentleman. But if the opportunity was sitting there to do something mischievous, he'd take it. It was like he never stopped scheming, but he knew how to turn on the charm, too. He knew when he had to do something and when he didn't.

"He would have been the bad boy that every little girl likes to hang out with, but he had that bring-him-home-to-mama quality, too. You could just imagine the mothers going something like, 'My, what a perfect gentleman; handsome, too!'"

According to Stephen, Dynamic Deluxe had a quirk that illustrates the good boy-bad boy aspect of his personality. He liked to stick his tongue out one side of his mouth.

"Some of our funniest moments were when Cindy or I would go to his stall to bring him out for visitors. On one side, there would be this gorgeous horse, and then you'd put on his halter and turn him around, and he'd be hanging his tongue out that other side of his mouth, looking like a drunken sailor. We'd roll our eyes and go, 'Jeez, DD, don't embarrass us now!' It was like taking your kid to the grocery story and being red-faced about his naughty behavior."

Occasional eruptions of naughty behavior notwithstanding, Dynamic Deluxe proved to be a powerhouse as a performance sire. Of his 593 AQHA foals, 354 earned performance records. As of March 5, 2004, they'd piled up 21,671.5 lifetime points, with nearly half that total earned in youth classes.

Stephen discusses possible reasons for Dynamic Deluxe's success as a youth-horse sire.

"Kids are innocent," he says. "They don't get up there and play trainer, they just go show what they have. That's where the natural lope comes into play. The lope separates the first- and fifth-place horses, and the DDs, even in their old age, can stand up and lope great. They get better with time, too. The Eddie Haskell-ness finally starts wearing off! The owners think, 'Okay, he's 12 now, so I finally have a good five or six years of fun ahead of me!'"

The list of illustrious Dynamic Deluxe offspring includes such horses as these:

· Dynamic Duplication, 1997 AQHA

All-Around High-Point Youth Horse, holder of 11 Superiors.

· Once In A Blue Moon, 2001 Reserve World Champion Youth Showmanship, 2000 AQHA High-Point Youth Showmanship, 1996 Reserve World Champion Youth Western Horsemanship, holder of seven Superiors.

· Sweet Dynamics, 1997 AQHA High-Point Western Riding Mare, Justin Rookie of the Year 31-49 Amateur, holder of six Superiors.

· Dynamic Discovery, double-registered with AQHA and the American Paint Horse Association, 11-time APHA World Champion.

· Dynamic Fashion, earner of $26,702.05 in western pleasure monies and holder of youth, amateur and open Superiors in western pleasure.

· Deluxe Like Daddy, 2002 All American Quarter Horse Congress Champion All-Around Youth Horse.

· Dynamic In The Dark, winner of multiple 2-year-old western pleasure futurities, 1996 NSBA High-Point 2-Year-Old, 1998 Tom Powers Maturity champion.

· Dressed Up Deluxe, 2002 AQHA High-Point Trail Horse, holder of six Superiors.

On Jan. 21, 2002 — his 21st birthday — Dynamic Deluxe was euthanized due to severe and irreversible laminitis. The stallion had suffered a bout of viral-induced high fever, which in turn caused rotation of both front coffin bones. Despite the best of care, laminitis was the end result. His last crop of foals arrived later that year.

In her tribute to Dynamic Deluxe, posted at www.riversideranch.com, Cindy wrote, "His importance to me goes much further than anyone can even begin to imagine. He brought my family and me happiness, fulfillment, prosperity. DD introduced us to many of our lifetime friends. He drew people to our business so that we could enjoy our work every day. He put Riverside Ranch on the map of the horse industry."

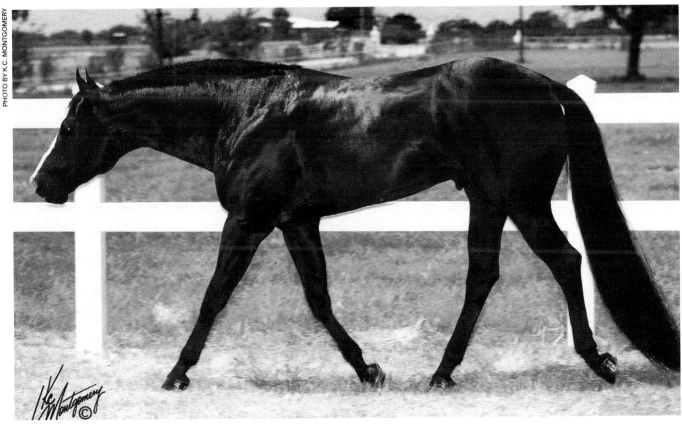

PHOTO BY K.C. MONTGOMERY

Even as an aged horse, Dynamic Deluxe maintained the unique look that set him and his offspring apart.

20

CASEYS CHARM

From humble beginnings, she went on to found a barrel racing dynasty

Bev Pechan

CASEYS CHARM WAS NEVER SHOWN, RACED OR BROKE TO RIDE.

As one of the premier barrel racing producers of all-time, however, she managed to make an indelible mark on the Quarter Horse breed. Through her own production and that of her 1st and 2nd generation offspring, the little brown mare is responsible for more than $2 million in earnings and sales.

The Caseys Charm story begins in the early 1960s, on the Egan, S.D. farm of James and Frances Loiseau (pronounced lo-i'-să_).

Pioneer Stock

"My parents were hard-working farmers with eight children," Lis Loiseau Hollmann, Hot Springs, S. D., said. "The place we all grew up on was called the Evergreen Stock Farm and it had the biggest barn in three counties. It had been homesteaded by my mother's grandparents and eventually acquired by my father."

Both James and Frances Loiseau had grown up around horses and were fond of

PHOTO BY LARRY LARSON

LARRY LARSON ©

Caseys Charm, shown here at age 23, was the cornerstone matron of one of the nation's top barrel horse lines.

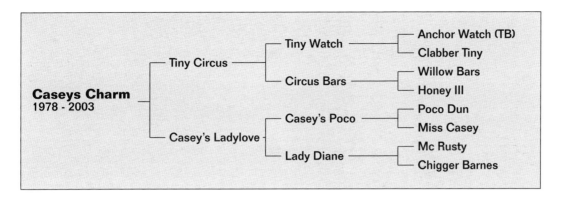

Caseys Charm
1978 - 2003

- Tiny Circus
  - Tiny Watch
    - Anchor Watch (TB)
    - Clabber Tiny
  - Circus Bars
    - Willow Bars
    - Honey III
- Casey's Ladylove
  - Casey's Poco
    - Poco Dun
    - Miss Casey
  - Lady Diane
    - Mc Rusty
    - Chigger Barnes

them. In the late 1950s, they bought their first registered Quarter Horse - Lady Sunrise - from Pat Cowan, Highmore, S.D.

In 1963, the couple attended a horse sale put on by Ted Faltinson of Westbrook, Minn. Casey's Ladylove, a 1961 buckskin filly sired by Casey's Poco and out of Lady Diane, caught Frances' eye. Although her husband was not next to her at the time, Frances bid $720 to become the filly's proud new owner.

"Good for you," was all James Loiseau said.

"She was a sweet, gentle mare," Frances recalled. "I liked her color, and she had a nice head and a big rear end, even at that age."

"Casey" became the family baby sitter and a weekend horse show entry in nearly all events. Even after she was retired to the broodmare band she was always willing and ready to run. One summer, when the Loiseau girls needed a horse to compete on, Ladylove was brought in from the pasture and taken straight to the show ring.

The mare, who was open that year, hadn't felt a saddle for 10 years. Without forgetting a thing, she re-entered the show ring with all of her old enthusiasm and effort.

The Loiseaus began breeding Casey in the late 1960s, and developed her first foals into speedy racehorses that burned up the Midwest tracks.

In 1970, Frenchmans Fox, a 1968 chestnut mare by Laughing Boy and out of Casey's Ladylove, became the first 2-year-old mare to run AAA in South Dakota. Frenchmans Luck AA - a 1969 dun full sister to "Fox" - was the dam of Frenchmans Jet AAA and 1979 South Dakota Running

Halter and Performance Record:
None.

Progeny Record:
Foals Registered: 14
Performance Point-Earners: 1
Performance Points Earned: 1

Horse of the Year; and Frenchmans Go Jet, AAA and a derby champion. (The "Frenchman" moniker that appears in many Loiseau-bred horses' names is a reflection of James' French heritage.)

The Loiseaus made every race that their horses were entered in, and James always wanted to be sure his family and friends were in the winner's circle picture celebrating the moment.

Frances Loiseau, along with husband James, was the guiding light behind the "Frenchman" line of race and arena performers.

In 1963, the Loiseaus purchased Casey's Ladylove at a Minnesota horse sale for $720.

Frenchmans Fox, a 1968 chestnut mare by Laughing Boy and out of Casey's Ladylove, was a AAA-rated racehorse. Shown with the speedy runner in this circa early 1970s shot are (from left) Jessie and Herb Ulmer, Frances and James Loiseau and trainer Pat Cowan. The jockey is unidentified.

A Charmed Life Begins

Getting back to the Caseys Charm story, James and Frances Loiseau had decided that the type of horse that suited them best was one that had a healthy dose of both speed and cow sense. As a result, they became attracted to a young stallion located in the Twin Cities area of southern Minnesota.

Tiny Circus, a 1970 brown stallion by Tiny Watch and out of Circus Bars, had been a highly-successful runner, with a 97 speed index and a Superior racehorse award to his credit. In 38 starts, he won seven races, finished second or third 10 times and earned $14,233.

At the time the Loiseaus ran across him, Tiny Circus was owned by John and Mary Hanley of Minneapolis, Minn., and was being shown in arena performance events by a promising young trainer named Tim McQuay. McQuay, of course, would go on to become a National Reining Horse Association (NRHA) Hall of Fame inductee and the association's all-time leading money-earning rider.

Tiny Circus was a horse who could do it all.

"I got the first points on 'Tiny' in calf roping," McQuay said. "I also showed him in reining, western pleasure and halter. He was a really good horse that did everything."

In time, Tiny Circus was turned over to Gary Putman, a friend of McQuay's who hailed from Kersey, Colo. Putman began team roping on the ex-racehorse and took him to the pinnacle of his show ring career as the 1979 AQHA Reserve World Champion Senior Heading Horse.

In 1977, the Loiseaus bred Casey's Ladylove to Tiny Circus. Caseys Charm, a 1978 brown mare, was the resulting foal.

When Caseys Charm was born on April Fools' Day in 1978, it was clear early on that she had definite thoughts of her own. "She was a courageous mare," Lis Hollmann said. "From the very beginning she was an independent soul. She

Caseys Charm, a 1978 brown mare by Tiny Circus and out of Casey's Ladylove, was her dam's ninth and most-renowned foal.

didn't have a lot of time for people. That's not to say she was wild or unruly. She just preferred you to treat her with a little respect."

The mare's outlook on life was no doubt predicated by the circumstances she was born into.

On Christmas Day in 1977, James Loiseau died of leukemia. While Frances continued to be deeply loyal to the horses, James' passing had taken some of the heart out of her. Several of the Loiseau broodmares were farmed out to long-time acquaintance Pat Cowan under a partnership arrangement. Casey's Charm, a member of the first foal crop to be born after James' death, was allowed to grow up relatively un-touched.

That all changed in the fall of 1983.

A Change of Venue

"My husband John and I were living in Littleton, Colo.," Lis Hollmann recalled. "We were up visiting mom and asked her what her plans were for several of the horses. There were three of Casey's Ladylove's offspring that were just out on grass. We felt something should be done with them."

Sun Frost, a 1979 palomino stallion by Docs Jack Frost and out of Prissy Cline, was the sire of seven of "Charm's" 14 foals. One of the Northern Plains' top performance sires, Sun Frost was owned by long-time family friend Pat Cowan, Highmore, S. Dakota.

The horses in question were full siblings - Caseys Charm; Frenchmans Casey, a 1979 bay gelding; and Frenchmans Favor, a 1980 dun gelding. After discussing the matter, it was agreed that the Hollmanns would take the two geldings to a trainer, Bill Meyers, St. Onge, S. D., to be made ready to sell. "Charm" would go to Colorado with the Hollmanns to become a broodmare.

"I told mom that, if she would consider selling Charm, we would be interested in buying her," Liz Hollmann said. "Her reply was, 'If you'd like to own her, I wouldn't charge you very much.'

"'How much?' I asked.

"'I'd take $700 for her,' she said.

"'That's not enough,' I replied. 'I'll give you $1,000.'

"So we bought Charm and mom and I swore an oath not to let the rest of the world know what 'softies' we were when it came to trading horses."

In time, Frances Loiseau did regain her passion for breeding good horses and seeing to it that they got into the hands of people who would use them. Caseys

Ladylove continued to be her cornerstone producer and was the dam of 15 foals, including:

- Frenchman's Bars - 1965 bay mare by Laughing Boy - S.I. 85.
- Frenchman's Fox - 1968 chestnut mare by Laughing Boy - S.I. 90.
- Frenchmans Luck - 1969 dun mare by Laughing Boy - S.I. 82.
- Frenchmans Topaz - 1981 buckskin mare by Leige Lord - S.I. 78.
- Love A Lord - 1982 buckskin gelding by Leige Lord - Superior youth barrel racing; 171 performance points.
- Caseys Lord - 1983 sorrel gelding by Leige Lord - NFR competitor; WPRA Money earner.
- PC Lady Frances - 1984 sorrel mare by Sun Frost - barrel racing winner of more than $40,000.

Motherhood

Caseys Charm entered the Hollmann broodmare band in 1984. Hauled back and forth to South Dakota to be bred, she produced Racy Casey Jay, a 1985 sorrel filly by Broadway Jay; Frenchman's Flash Frost (a.k.a. "Juarez"), a 1986 chestnut colt by Sun Frost; and French Flash Hawk (a.k.a "Bozo"), a 1987 sorrel colt by Sun Frost.

In the fall of 1987, John and Lis Hollmann were journeying from South Dakota to Colorado with Charm, Juarez and Bozo in tow.

The couple laid up for the night in Ogallala, Neb., at the home of Bud and Marla Arute. After expressing an interest in acquiring a Caseys Charm foal, the Arutes were given their choice of either Juarez or Bozo for $1,500, or $2,500 for the pair.

Bud Arute decided to take Juarez, but opted to pass on Bozo.

Both colts turned out to be high-energy and somewhat dominant geldings that were not content to just munch feed when not being ridden.

Juarez was started on barrels and worked on cattle. As a roping horse, he helped the Arutes and daughter and son-in-law Dayna and Rick Branch win

French Flash Hawk, a.k.a. "Bozo" was the most renowned of the Sun Frost – Caseys Charm offspring. Owned and ridden by Kristie Peterson, Elbert, Colo., Bozo was a five-time PRCA Barrel Racing Horse of the Year.

PHOTO BY LARRY LARSON

LARRY LARSON ©

Here's PC Frenchmanslisbet, a 1992 chestnut full sister to Bozo. While not as accomplished a performer as her famous sibling, "Lisbet" has managed to prove herself through production.

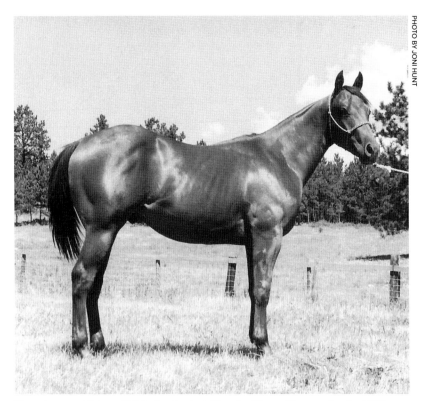

Frenchmans Irish, a 1999 chestnut stallion by Flyma Bars and out of PC Frenchmanslisbet, typifies the well-balanced, athletic-looking Quarter Horses that the Loiseau family has dedicated itself to breeding and raising.

Sold as a yearling to Terry and Julia Moore, Dierks, Ark., "Irish" has lived up to his heritage as a top barrel racer.

more than $50,000. In 1991, he placed second in the U.S. Team Roping Championship Finals.

Caseys Charm and Bozo continued on with the Hollmanns to take up residence in Littleton, Colo. Bozo proved to be a skittish colt and was subsequently traded to Mike Hatfield, Peyton, Colo., for three months' training on another horse.

Along came Kristi Peterson, Elbert, Colo., who was in the market for a barrel horse and thought Bozo had promise.

"When I got him at 2 years, he was still a stud," Peterson said. "He was very snorty; he wasn't broke and he didn't trust people. He wasn't a bronc – he was just snorty.

"My husband worked him around cattle. Then, we started him on barrels when he was a 3-year-old. He was just a natural.'

In 1992, Peterson and Bozo won the BFA World Barrel Futurity in Oklahoma City, taking both the Derby and Sweepstakes and earning $29,321. When the pair raced onto the national scene in earnest, times and records began to fall.

By the time their joint rodeo career was over, Bozo had carried Kristie to four barrel racing world championships and was five-time AQHA/WPRA barrel racing horse of the year.

"Bozo never gave less than 100 percent," Peterson remarked.

After Bozo's impressive decade-long run as a world champion open barrel racer was ended, he was turned over to the Petersons' 10-year-old daughter Jordon, for use as a youth horse.

Four years later, in 2002, the duo led the way to their first Little Britches World Championship with a total score of 634.5 points to 599.5 for the reserve horse.

A year later, they won their second Little Britches Rodeo World Championship in pole bending with 664.5 total points, far outdistancing the runner-up score of 483.5, and had an average time of 60.699, compared to the runner-up average of 63.095.

Bred to top barrel sire Fire Water Flit in 2003, "Lisbet" produced Firewater Frenchman the following spring. The well-bred palomino sold at auction as a weanling for $75,000.

A Homecoming

In 1990, John and Lis Hollmann decided to give Caseys Charm back to Frances Loiseau.

"By this time," Lis said, "Bozo was one of the best-known barrel horses in the country and Charm had a little fame as a producer. We felt it was appropriate that she should end her days with mom."

Caseys Charm was bred to Sun Frost a total of seven times. As already noted, the first two breedings resulted in "Juarez" and "Bozo."

The subsequent breedings resulted in PC Frenchmanslisbet, a 1992 chestnut mare and Bozo's only full sister. In 1993, John and Lis Hollmann also returned home and took up residence in Hot Springs, S. Dakota. Shortly thereafter - in return for having been gifted Caseys Charm - Frances Loiseau gave "Lisbet" to her daughter and son-in-law.

The remaining four Sun Frost - Caseys Charm full siblings were PC Frenchmans Chris, a 1993 palomino gelding; PC Frenchmans Mark, a 1994 palomino stallion; PC Frenchmans Hayday, a 1995 palomino stallion who sold for $65,000; and PC Frenchman, a 1996 palomino stallion who sold for $200,000.

Kissin' Cousins

At the same time that the Caseys Charm line of performers was beginning to establish itself as one of the Northern Plains' best, a close relative was doing the same.

Frenchmans Guy, a 1987 palomino stallion by Sun Frost and out of Frenchman's Lady, was bred by Frances Loiseau and sold as a 2-year-old to Bill and Deb Myers, St. Onge, South Dakota.

Just as Caseys Charm was responsible

PC Frenchman, a 1996 palomino stallion by Sun Frost and out of Caseys Charm, sold at auction for an un-precedented $200,000.

for one of the North Country's top performance lines, so was Frenchmans Guy.

In 2001, the palomino stallion was the nation's #1 barrel racing sire and, through 2003, his get have earned more than $560,000. Among his top money earners are Frenchmans Vanila, $230,000; and Frenchmans Twister, $100,000.

"Frenchmans Guy is Bozo in yellow," Kristie Peterson said. "He has the same

way of going, is the same height and weight, and has the same attitude."

Caseys Charm was bred to Frenchmans Guy three times. The crosses resulted in See You In Vegas, a 1997 palomino mare who sold for $21,000 and was subsequently re-purchased by Frances Loiseau for her broodmare band; Frenchmans Fabulous, a 1998 palomino stallion who sold twice for $30,000 and $50,000; and Frenchmans Cabaret, a 2000 palomino filly who sold for $39,000.

By the new millennium, the Caseys Charm horses were beginning to dominate the Northern Plains barrel racing scene.

Frenchmans Dox Dakota, a 1989 bay gelding by Boon Dox John and out of Caseys Charm, won the 2001 WPRA Badlands Circuit Barrel Horse Championship ridden by Cindy and Lindsey Loiseau. Boon Dox Charm, a 1990 sorrel full sister to Boon Dox John, was ridden to numerous wins in futurities and barrels by Jan Fisher.

As far as the entire Loiseau clan is concerned, all have found a way to stay involved - as horse breeders, ranchers, and rodeo and horse show competitors.

"As kids," Lis Hollmann said, "We were all involved with the horses. During the summer we rode and competed in horse shows on them. Early Saturday morning, we'd milk the cows, load up and head to a horse show. Then we'd return home and milk the cows again. On Sunday, it was the same routine."

Of the Loiseaus' eight children, Mike Loiseau remains on the home place and Jim Loiseau and Barb Loiseau Westover live within two miles. Beverly Loiseau Kennedy lives in Vermillion, S.D., and Mary Loiseau Kjerstad calls Rapid City, S.D., home. Val Loiseau lives on the Hollmann Ranch in Hot Springs, S.D., and Charles Loiseau resides in Frankfort, Kan.

Money in the Bank

The value of the Caseys Charm - Frenchman bloodlines become even more significant when they're compared to blue-

PHOTO BY LARRY LARSON

chip investments, and that's how Gary Westergren, Lincoln, Neb., chooses to look at it.

Westergren saw the Quarter Horse industry as a better substitute for the stock market in dollar return and, as he adds to his horse program, he says he has the added luxury of literally watching both his horses and his money grow.

At the 2003 Hunt Open Box Rafter Ranch Sale in Rapid City, S.D., Westergren purchased Firewater Frenchman, a 2003 palomino stallion by Firewater Flit and out of PC Frenchmans Lisbet, for $75,000.

"When I heard of the Fire Water Flit and 'Frenchman' cross and thought about the potential even before the colt was born," he said, "I knew it was going to be one-of-a-kind. I thought it would be a shame for that breeding to go somewhere else."

Previously, Westergren bought two similarly-bred prospects - Frenchmans Fancy Free and Frenchmans Belle Jet - for $28,000 and $15,000 respectively. He also co-owns Frenchmans Fire Fox, a 2002 chestnut stallion by Special Effort and out of PC Dox Fox, with John and Lis Hollmann. The young racing prospect is slated to be the first "Frenchman" horse to go to the track in 20 years.

"It doesn't pay to own anything but the best when you're looking to be in the horse business," he said. "You can tell the great athletes by the way they move; they're better than the rest."

Dr. Glenn Blodgett, DVM and breeding manager of the famed Burnett Four Sixes Ranch in Guthrie, Texas, is one of the many prominent horsemen and women who were familiar with Caseys Charm.

"Of course, I was aware of the production of Caseys Charm before I saw her in person," he said. "When I saw her, I was quite impressed with her conformation. I could see how she was producing what she was producing. She had the conformation points people want in performance - short cannon bones, low hocks and a set of hind legs lending themselves to being very athletic and for getting short, explosive speed.

"I also noted from a soundness point of

LARRY LARSON ©

Frenchmans Guy, a 1987 palomino stallion by Sun Frost and out of Frenchmans Lady, was the sire of "Charm's" last three foals. The nationally-ranked barrel horse sire was bred by James and Frances Loiseau and sold as a 2-year-old to Bill and Deb Myers, St. Onge, S.D.

view that she had a lot of bone. I liked the angle to her shoulder and pasterns and the shortness of the pasterns.

"The mare had all those things," he continued. "We have been fortunate to breed a couple of her daughters here at the Four Sixes. This mare line is very dominant. I really feel fortunate to have seen it with my own eyes."

Frenchmans Fabulous, a 1998 palomino stallion by Frenchmans Guy and out of Caseys Charm, is owned by Kenny Nichols, Waco, Tex., Glenn Nichols, Gilbert, Ariz., and Dale Barron, Axtell, Tex. A top rope and barrel racing competitor, the flashy stallion is shown here with perennial NFR qualifier Sue Miller in the saddle.

Lynn Wieshaar, the prominent Northern Plains auctioneer from Reva, S.D., is also very familiar with the Loiseau-bred mare.

"Caseys Charm was a great mare," he said. "She was bred to different stallions and produced well with anyone she was bred to.

"South Dakota has more production sales than any other state in the nation, and Caseys Charm and Bozo have done more than anyone to spark interest in the regional Quarter Horse industry."

Frances Loiseau, who retired from the family farm in 1996 and moved into a more manageable residence in the nearby town of Flandreau, is still somewhat in awe at the attention the Caseys Charm - Frenchman horses are receiving. Still, she knows her mares and their produce are worthy of the accolades. "We've been very lucky. The horses have to have the ability, but it takes the right person to bring it out," she said.

"My parents knew what good horses they had," Lis Hollmann added. "If my father was alive today, he would not be at all surprised at the prices the horses are bringing."

The End of an Era

By 2003, all of Frances Loiseau's breeding stock had been moved to the Hollmann Ranch near Hot Springs. Caseys Charm was 25 years of age, and seemed to be getting tired. She had been open for several years. Embryo transplants tried on her earlier through Dr. Blodgett and Colorado

State University showed she was still ovulating, but no conceived embryos would take past 25 days.

One snowy November day, Hollmann ranch employees Mike and Cathy Mallery noticed that Caseys Charm hadn't come up with the other mares for her grain. Since she was the "alpha mare" and usually the first one to reach the feeding station, the Mallerys alerted John and Lis Hollmann.

"Our home is 20 miles from the ranch," Lis Hollman said. "so it took a half hour or so for us to make the trip.

"Gary Westergren was at the ranch that day and he and I got in his Suburban and drove out to the pasture to search for Charm.

"We saw the mare standing alone, silhouetted against trees with white flakes swirling around her. She did not appear to be in any pain and was resting quietly. I got out and stayed with her for about an hour; until Mike and Cathy rode up on some geldings to lead her in."

Caseys Charm appeared to have had a stroke and was disoriented. It soon became apparent that nothing more could be done for her.

"I called mom and told her what the situation was," Lis Hollmann said. "Her reply was, 'Just don't let her suffer.'

"And she didn't. Charm wasn't interested in eating or drinking, but she never did seem to be in pain."

Cathy Mallery stayed with Charm, reassuring her and brushing her coat. As Cathy left the barn late that evening the aged matron softly whinnied after her.

Caseys Charm passed away before dawn. The cornerstone matron of one of barrel racing's most influential families exited the world in exactly the same manner in which she had existed in it — with quiet dignity and great import.

Caseys Charm was never shown or even broke to ride. Despite this, she remains one of the Quarter Horse breed's most-accomplished performance producers.

AUTHOR PROFILES

Patricia Campbell

Patricia Campbell is an avid equestrienne and has been riding and showing Quarter Horses her entire life. An Oklahoma State University graduate with a Bachelor of Science in Animal Science, she worked as a marketing specialist/journalist for the American Paint Horse Association from 1997 to 2002. Now a freelance professional, Campbell is editor of *Pinto Horse*, the official publication of the Pinto Horse Association of America, and *Flag's Up!*, the official publication of the United States Team Penning Association. Her freelance services include writing, photography, graphic design and advertising. Campbell currently lives in McKinney, Texas.

Sally Harrison

Sally Harrison, a former English teacher and Arabian horse owner, has been writing about and photographing horses since 1981. Her articles and photographs have appeared in numerous publications and she has written three books: *Cutting; a Guide for the Non-Pro Competitor*; *Matlock Rose, the Horseman*; and *The Cowboy Life of James L. Kenney*. She also co-authored *Pride in the Dust*. A nationally recognized equine photographer, Sally has turned her lens on countless great Quarter Horses and Thoroughbreds over the past 20 years. She also owns an equine advertising and marketing business, and lives in Arlington, Tex., with her husband, writer Alan Gold.

Frank Holmes

Frank Holmes is considered one of the foremost historians of the western horse. He has been penning horse-related feature articles and historical books for more than 35 years, and is equally-adept when it comes to recording Quarter Horse, Paint Horse and Appaloosa history. Between 1996 and 2001, he authored *The Hank Wiescamp Story* and co-authored *Legends 2-5* for *Western Horseman*. Beginning in late 2001, he authored *Wire to Wire - the Walter Merrick Story*, *More Than Color* and *Spotted Pride* under his own banner. Frank currently lives in Peyton, Colo., with his wife, Loyce.

Glory Ann Kurtz

Glory Ann Kurtz is an avid horse lover, competing in several Western disciplines, including barrel racing and cutting. She is the executive editor of *Quarter Horse News*, a semi-monthly news tabloid she helped bring from four pages to over 300 over the past 25 years. She is also editor of the *Women's Pro Rodeo Association News* and was editor during the start-up and growth of *Barrel Horse News*, the nation's largest barrel racing publication. Kurtz is the author of *Barrel Racing, Training the Wright Way*, a coffee-table book with top trainers Ed and Martha Wright. She is also the editor of the annual *Performance Horse Sale Guide*. Kurtz and her husband, Bob run a performance horse breeding operation in Boyd, Texas.

Cheryl Magoteaux

Cheryl Magoteaux is a former college horsemanship instructor, Professional Womens Rodeo Association barrel racing national champion and Womens National Finals Rodeo qualifier. She has written, edited and done photography for a wide range of publications, earning national awards and recognition. She has also done color video commentary for Waltenberry's *Reining Video Monthly*. Her company, Pro Management, provides advertising, show management, and publicity services for some of the giants in the western horse industry - including the National Reining Breeders Classic and the National Reined Cow Horse Association (NRCHA). Pro Management also produces over a dozen publications each year, including the *Stock Horse News*, NRCHA's official bi-monthly magazine.

Heidi Nyland

Heidi Nyland began riding POAs and Quarter Horses at age 5 and quickly made horses a central part of her life. A graduate of Ohio Wesleyan University's English department (B.A.) and Ohio University's Scripps School of Journalism (M.S.), Nyland is a former assistant editor for *Horse & Rider* and currently pursues a career as a professional photographer, free-lance writer and web designer. She regularly contributes to *Equestrian Retailer, John Lyon's Perfect Horse, Paint Horse Journal, The Trail Rider* and *Western Horseman*. She resides in Columbus, Ohio, where she also gives riding lessons combining Brain Gym® techniques with traditional horsemanship.

Bev Pechan

Bev Pechan grew up in Minnesota, where she began her lifelong love of horses and developed her interest in the stories of legendary horses and horsemen. While still in high school, she embarked on a successful dual career as an artist and horse show photographer. In the late 1950's, she began writing columns for national horse magazines, and is a newspaper and magazine feature writer specializing in Western history. Bev currently resides in the Black Hills of S. D. A past historian and director of Old Fort Meade Cavalry Museum near Sturgis, S. D., and a founder and director of the annual West River History Conference, she is a regular contributor to *Today's Horse* magazine.

Juli S. Thorson

Juli S. Thorson has been writing about horses and related subjects ever since she was old enough to hold a pencil. She began competing in horse shows at age 5, and continues to be a winning show competitor. Raised near Fargo, N. D., as a fourth-generation equestrienne, Juli chose a career in equine-related publishing after earning a bachelor's degree in journalism. Since then, she's served on the editorial staffs of such leading horse magazines as *Western Horseman, Horse & Rider, Performance Horse* and *Appaloosa Journal*. Her Western Horseman book, *Win With Bob Avila*, earned Equine Book of the Year honors from American Horse Publications. Juli and her husband, Edward Sala, live on a horse ranch in northern Idaho.

PHOTO INDEX

Books Published by
WESTERN HORSEMAN®

ARABIAN LEGENDS by Marian K. Carpenter
280 pages and 319 photographs. Abu Farwa, *Aladdinn, *Ansata Ibn Halima, *Bask, Bay-Abi, Bay El Bey, Bint Sahara, Fadjur, Ferzon, Indraff, Khemosabi, *Morafic, *Muscat, *Naborr, *Padron, *Raffles, *Raseyn, *Sakr, Samtyr, *Sanacht, *Serafix, Skorage, *Witez II, Xenophonn.

BACON & BEANS, by Stella Hughes
144 pages and 200-plus recipes for delicious western chow.

BARREL RACING, Completely Revised by Sharon Camarillo
128 pages, 158 photographs and 17 illustrations. Teaches foundation horsemanship and barrel racing skills for horse and rider, with additional tips on feeding, hauling and winning.

CALF ROPING by Roy Cooper
144 pages and 280 photographs. Complete coverage of roping and tying.

CHARMAYNE JAMES ON BARREL RACING by Charmayne James with Cheryl Magoteaux
192 pages and over 200 color photograps. Charmayne shares the training techniques and philosophy that made her the most successful barrel racer in history. Also included are vignettes of horses and riders that illustrate Charmayne's approach to indentifying and correcting problems in barrel racing, as well as examples and experiences from over 20 years as a world-class competitor in this exciting event.

COWBOYS & BUCKAROOS by Tim O'Byrne
176 pages and over 250 color photograps. The author, who's spent 20 years on ranches and feedyards, explains in great detail the trade secrets and working lifestyle of this North American icon. Readers can follow the cowboy crew through the four seasons of a cattle-industry year, learn their lingo and the Cowboy Code they live by, understand how they start colts, handle cattle, make long circles in rough terrain and much, much more. Many interesting sidebars, including excerpts from the author's personal journal offering firsthand accounts of the cowboy way.

CUTTING by Leon Harrel
144 pages and 200 photographs. Complete guide to this popular sport.

FIRST HORSE by Fran Devereux Smith
176 pages, 160 black-and-white photos, numerous illustrations. Step-by-step information for the first-time horse owner and/or novice rider.

HELPFUL HINTS FOR HORSEMEN
128 pages and 325 photographs and illustrations. WH readers and editors provide tips on every facet of life with horses and offer solutions to common problems horse owners share. Chapters include: Equine Health Care; Saddles; Bits and Bridles; Gear; Knots; Trailers/Hauling Horses; Trail Riding/Backcountry Camping; Barn Equipment; Watering Systems; Pasture, Corral and Arena Equipment; Fencing and Gates; Odds and Ends.

IMPRINT TRAINING by Robert M. Miller, D.V.M.
144 pages and 250 photographs. Learn to "program" newborn foals.

LEGENDS 1 by Diane Ciarloni
168 pages and 214 photographs. Barbra B, Bert, Chicaro Bill, Cowboy P-12, Depth Charge (TB), Doc Bar, Go Man Go, Hard Twist, Hollywood Gold, Joe Hancock, Joe Reed P-3, Joe Reed II, King P-234, King Fritz, Leo, Peppy, Plaudit, Poco Bueno, Poco Tivio, Queenie, Quick M Silver, Shue Fly, Star Duster, Three Bars (TB), Top Deck (TB) and Wimpy P-1.

LEGENDS 2 by Jim Goodhue, Frank Holmes, Phil Livingston, Diane Ciarloni
192 pages and 224 photographs. Clabber, Driftwood, Easy Jet, Grey Badger II, Jessie James, Jet Deck, Joe Bailey P-4 (Gonzales), Joe Bailey (Weatherford), King's Pistol, Lena's Bar, Lightning Bar, Lucky Blanton, Midnight, Midnight Jr, Moon Deck, My Texas Dandy, Oklahoma Star, Oklahoma Star Jr., Peter McCue, Rocket Bar (TB), Skipper W, Sugar Bars and Traveler.

LEGENDS 3 by Jim Goodhue, Frank Holmes, Diane Ciarloni, Kim Guenther, Larry Thornton, Betsy Lynch
208 pages and 196 photographs. Flying Bob, Hollywood Jac 86, Jackstraw (TB), Maddon's Bright Eyes, Mr Gun Smoke, Old Sorrel, Piggin String (TB), Poco Lena, Poco Pine, Poco Dell, Question Mark, Quo Vadis, Royal King, Showdown, Steel Dust and Two Eyed Jack.

LEGENDS 4 by Sally Harrison, Frank Holmes, Betsy Lynch, A. J. Mangum, Susan Scarberry, Larry Thornton
216 pages and over 230 photos. The stories of the great Quarter Horses Zantanon, Ed Echols, Zan Parr Bar, Blondy's Dude, Diamonds Sparkle, Woven Web/Miss Princess, Miss Bank, Rebel Cause, Tonto Bars Hank, Harlan, Lady Bug's Moon, Dash For Cash, Vandy, Impressive, Fillinic, Zippo Pine Bar and Doc O' Lena.

LEGENDS 5 by Frank Holmes, Ty Wyant, Alan Gold, Sally Harrison
248 pages, including about 300 photographs. The stories of Little Joe, Joe Moore, Monita, Bill Cody, Joe Cody, Topsail Cody, Pretty Buck, Pat Star Jr., Skipa Star, Hank H, Chubby, Bartender, Leo San, Custus Rastus (TB), Jaguar, Jackie Bee, Chicado V and Mr Bar None.

LEGENDS 6 by Frank Holmes, Patricia Campbell, Sally Harrison, GloryAnn Kurtz, Cheryl Magoteaux, Heidi Nyland, Bev Pechan, Juli S. Thorson
236 pages, including about 270 photographs. The stories of Paul A, Croton Oil, Okie Leo Flit Bar, Billietta, Coy's Bonanza, Major Bonanza, Doc Quixote, Doc's Prescription, Jewel's Leo Bar, Colonel Freckles, Freckles Playboy, Peppy San, Mr San Peppy, Great Pine, The Invester, Speedy Glow, Conclusive, Dynamic Deluxe and Caseys Charm

Western Horseman, established in 1936, is the world's leading horse publication. For subscription information: 800-877-5278.
To order other *Western Horseman* books: 800-874-6774 • *Western Horseman*, Box 7980, Colorado Springs, CO 80933-7980.
Web site: **www.westernhorseman.com**.

LEGENDS 7 by Frank Holmes, Glory Ann Kurtz, Cheryl Magoteaux, Bev Pechan, Honi Roberts, Heather S. Thomas, Juli Thorson

260 pages, over 300 photos. The stories of Cutter Bill, Jazabell Quixote, Rey Jay, Teresa Tivio, Big Step, War Leo, Gay Bar King, Commander King, Skip A Barb, Otoe, Quincy Dan, Doc's Dee Bar, Sonny Dee Bar, Boston Mac, Peppy San Badger, Te N' Te, Doc's Oak, Rugged Lark, Mr Conclusion and Hollywood Dun It

NATURAL HORSE-MAN-SHIP by Pat Parelli

224 pages and 275 photographs. Parelli's six keys to a natural horse-human relationship.

PROBLEM-SOLVING, Volume 1 by Marty Marten

248 pages and over 250 photos and illustrations. Develop a willing partnership between horse and human — trailer-loading, hard-to-catch, barn-sour, spooking, water-crossing, herd-bound and pull-back problems.

PROBLEM-SOLVING, Volume 2 by Marty Marten

A continuation of Volume 1. Ten chapters with illustrations and photos.

RAISE YOUR HAND IF YOU LOVE HORSES by Pat Parelli with Kathy Swan

224 pages and over 200 black and white and color photos. The autobiography of the world's foremost proponent of natural horsemanship. Chapters contain hundreds of Pat Parelli stories, from the clinician's earliest remembrances to the fabulous experiences and opportunities he has enjoyed in the last decade. As a bonus, there are anecdotes in which Pat's friends tell stories about him.

RANCH HORSEMANSHIP by Curt Pate with Fran Devereux Smith

220 pages and over 250 full color photos and illustrations. Learn how almost any rider at almost any level of expertise can adapt ranch-horse-training techniques to help his mount become a safer more enjoyable ride. Curt's ideas help prepare rider and horse for whatever they might encounter in the round pen, arena, pasture and beyond.

REINING, Completely Revised by Al Dunning

216 pages and over 300 photographs. Complete how-to training for this exciting event.

RIDE SMART, by Craig Cameron with Kathy Swan

224 pages and over 250 black and white and color photos. Under one title, Craig Cameron combines a look at horses as a species and how to develop a positive partnering relationship with them, along with good, solid horsemanship skills that suit both novice and experienced riders. Topics include ground-handling techniques, hobble-breaking methods, colt-starting, high performance maneuvers and trailer-loading. Interesting sidebars, such as trouble-shooting tips and personal anecdotes about Cameron's life, complement the main text.

RODEO LEGENDS by Gavin Ehringer

Photos and life stories fill 216 pages. Included are: Joe Alexander, Jake Barnes & Clay O'Brien Cooper, Joe Beaver, Leo Camarillo, Roy Cooper, Tom Ferguson, Bruce Ford, Marvin Garrett, Don Gay, Tuff Hedeman, Charmayne James, Bill Linderman, Larry Mahan, Ty Murray, Dean Oliver, Jim Shoulders, Casey Tibbs, Harry Tompkins and Fred Whitfield.

STARTING COLTS by Mike Kevil

168 pages and 400 photographs. Step-by-step process in starting colts.

THE HANK WIESCAMP STORY by Frank Holmes

208 pages and over 260 photographs. The biography of the legendary breeder of Quarter Horses, Appaloosas and Paints.

TEAM ROPING WITH JAKE AND CLAY by Fran Devereux Smith

224 pages and over 200 photographs and illustrations. Learn about fast times from champions Jake Barnes and Clay O'Brien Cooper. Solid information about handling a rope, roping dummies and heading and heeling for practice and in competition. Also sound advice about rope horses, roping steers, gear and horsemanship.

TRAIL RIDING by Janine M. Wilder

128 pages and over 150 color photographs. The author, who's ridden in all 48 states, Hawaii and the Yucatan over the last 20 years, has compiled a comprehensive guide that covers all the bases a trail rider needs in this fast-growing sport. She offers proven methods for developing a solid trail horse, safe ways to handle a variety of terrain, solutions for common trail problems, plus tips and resources on how to travel with horses. Interesting sidebars document her experiences on the trail.

WELL-SHOD by Don Baskins

160 pages, 300 black-and-white photos and illustrations. A horse-shoeing guide for owners and farriers. Easy-to-read, step-by-step how to trim and shoe a horse for a variety of uses. Special attention is paid to corrective shoeing for horses with various foot and leg problems.

WESTERN TRAINING by Jack Brainard

With Peter Phinny. 136 pages. Stresses the foundation for western training.

WIN WITH BOB AVILA by Juli S. Thorson

Hardbound, 128 full-color pages. Learn the traits that separate horse-world achievers from also-rans. World champion horseman Bob Avila shares his philosophies on succeeding as a competitor, breeder and trainer.

WORLD CLASS REINING by Shawn Flarida and Craig Schmersal with Kathy Swan

Shawn Flarida and Craig Schmersal have pooled their extensive expertise and collective knowledge in the pages of the book to present the complete training program that catapulted them to reining stardom.

Western Horseman, established in 1936, is the world's leading horse publication. For subscription information: 800-877-5278.

To order other *Western Horseman* books: 800-874-6774 • *Western Horseman,* Box 7980, Colorado Springs, CO 80933-7980.

Web site: **www.westernhorseman.com.**